Mobilizing Women for War

MOBILIZING WOMEN FOR WAR

German and American Propaganda,

1939-1945

Leila J. Rupp

PRINCETON UNIVERSITY PRESS
Princeton, New Jersey

Published by Princeton University Press, Princeton, New Jersey
In the United Kingdom: Princeton University Press,
Guildford, Surrey

Library of Congress Cataloging in Publication Data will be
found on the last printed page of this book

Publication of this book has been aided by a grant from the
Paul Mellon Fund of Princeton University Press.

This book has been composed in Linotype Times Roman

Printed in the United States of America by Princeton
University Press, Princeton, New Jersey

To Sidney and Walter Rupp

Contents

List of Illustrations and Graphs

Acknowledgments

This book originated as a dissertation at Bryn Mawr College. I would like to thank Bryn Mawr for its generous financial support throughout my years in graduate school; the Woodrow Wilson Foundation for a Dissertation Fellowship in Women's Studies; and the Whiting Foundation for a Whiting Fellowship in the Humanities.

The resources and staffs of the following institutions made possible the research for this book: the National Archives, the Washington National Records Center, the Library of Congress, the Hoover Institution, and Widener Library. I am especially grateful to the librarians of the Bryn Mawr College library for their indispensable aid.

I also wish to express my appreciation to Carol Orr and Judith May of Princeton University Press for their valuable editorial help.

It is a pleasure to thank Harriet Lightman and Glen Zeitzer, who read and criticized sections of my work, for providing me with stimulus and assistance throughout the process of research and writing. I am also grateful to those who read and commented on the entire manuscript: Arthur P. Dudden and Richard B. Du Boff, with special thanks to Mary Maples Dunn.

I am greatly indebted to Stephen Shapiro, who provided assistance in innumerable ways, most importantly by listening to me patiently and critically.

My greatest debt is to Barbara Miller Lane, whose constant encouragement, incisive criticism, and friendship have been invaluable.

April 1977

List of Abbreviations

BDM   Bund deutscher Mädel [League of German Girls]
DAF   Deutsche Arbeitsfront [German Labor Front]
GH   *Good Housekeeping*
KdF   Kraft durch Freude [Strength through Joy]
LHJ   *Ladies' Home Journal*
OWI   Office of War Information
RG   Record Group
SEP   *Saturday Evening Post*
SP   *Soziale Praxis*
USSBS   U.S. Strategic Bombing Survey
VB   *Völkischer Beobachter*
WHC   *Woman's Home Companion*
WMC   War Manpower Commission

Mobilizing Women for War

· 1 ·

Introduction:
Woman's Place Is in the War

The phrase "woman's place is in the war" evokes the traditional slogan concerning a woman's relationship to the home and yet suggests a very real need for the participation of women in a war economy. For this reason, the phrase suggests the themes involved in an analysis of mobilization propaganda in Nazi Germany and the wartime United States.

One might ask why such a comparison should be attempted at all, since it may seem audacious, treasonous, or at the very least in bad taste to compare Nazi Germany and the United States. I am aware of the fundamental differences in ideological foundations, methods of social control, and ultimate objectives. I do not intend to minimize the horrors of the Third Reich, although they play a minor role at most in this study. Nevertheless, despite the significant differences, the National Socialist government of Germany and the wartime government of Franklin Roosevelt in the United States had much in common.[1] A comparative study of propaganda and mobilization policies can shed light on the effects of war on the status of women in industrialized societies.

On the eve of the Second World War, both Germany and the United States were highly industrialized countries recovering from especially severe effects of the worldwide Depression. In both countries, the presence of women in the labor force led during the height of unemployment to the denunciation of "double earners," employed women whose husbands or fathers worked. In the course of mobilizing their war economies, both countries quickly solved their unem-

---

[1] For a comparison of the two governments during the Depression, see John A. Garraty, "The New Deal, National Socialism, and the Great Depression," *American Historical Review*, 78 (Oct. 1973), 907-944.

3

ployment problems and eventually developed labor short-ages. Both realized that women constituted the largest available reserve of workers. Neither country implemented a conscription system to compel women to enter the labor force, although both considered this course of action. To different extents, both utilized propaganda to urge women to take part in the war effort. For this reason, propaganda looms large in studying the mobilization of women in both countries.

That these two very different nations faced the problems of mobilizing women in similar ways speaks first for the constraints placed on a society by the existence of a highly industrialized economy, and second for the universality of sexual asymmetry in human communities. A modern industrialized society demands the participation of women in the labor force, especially in time of war. When the men leave their jobs to enter the armed forces, replacements must come from somewhere, and industry soon looks to the housekeeping women not already employed. But all societies also assign distinct roles to men and women, and these are reflected in public or popular images, defined as the descriptions or representations of people presented by the popular media for public consumption. Basic ideas about the proper roles of the sexes change extremely slowly, but public images are subject to sudden and temporary changes imposed by economic need. If the prevailing public image precludes the employment of women in fields previously defined as masculine, then the image will have to adjust to the needs of the economy in time of war.

Sex roles, in peace or war, prescribe the range of activities and modes of behavior for both sexes. Men in both German and American society were expected to support their families in peacetime and fight for their countries in wartime. Societal expectations and public images limit the full development of men and women both. But, according to feminist anthropologists, there is one crucial difference between these expectations. In all societies, they argue, achievement and status

4

are measured according to standards that rank the male above the female.[2] As Margaret Mead put it in *Male and Female*: "In every known society, the male's need for achievement can be recognized. Men may cook, or weave, or dress dolls or hunt hummingbirds, but if such activities are appropriate occupations of men, then the whole society, men and women alike, votes them as important. When the same occupations are performed by women, they are regarded as less important."[3]

Public images reflect sex roles, but the two concepts are not identical. Sex roles are based on deeply rooted beliefs about male and female nature, while public images are susceptible to rapid change in response to economic need. Neither concept necessarily corresponds to the actual experiences of men and women. Clearly each sex is a heterogeneous group, individuals varying as to class, race, religion, age, and other factors. Public images are not concerned with diversity. But one of the most important bonds women share is in fact their common public image. One cannot study the experiences of women as a group, but one can study a popular conception of women, since it treats all women alike. All German women, in the public image, were "Aryan," all American women white and middle-class.

Certain historians in the vanguard of women's history argue that the time for "prescriptive history," or the history of ideologies about women, has passed.[4] Critics call for a new kind of history that will recreate the life experiences

[2] See Michelle Zimbalist Rosaldo and Louise Lamphere, *Woman, Culture and Society* (Stanford: Stanford University Press, 1974).

[3] *Male and Female: A Study of the Sexes in a Changing World* (N.Y.: William Morrow, 1949, 1967); quoted in Rosaldo and Lamphere, *Woman, Culture and Society*.

[4] See Gerda Lerner, "Placing Women in History: A 1975 Perspective"; and Ann D. Gordon, Mari Jo Buhle, and Nancy Schrom Dye, "The Problem of Women's History"; both in *Liberating Women's History: Theoretical and Critical Essays*, ed. Berenice A. Carroll (Urbana: University of Illinois Press, 1976), pp. 357-367 and pp. 75-92.

5

of women in the past. I believe there is a tremendous need for such work, although the available sources and present historical methods may be woefully inadequate. I agree that one cannot describe the actual lives of women on the basis of what men, or women, thought about women or hoped women would be. But prescriptive history is nonetheless important because it describes one aspect of those experiences. Recent work on the methodology of women's history has emphasized the need to construct a framework of various factors for use in studying the situation of women in the past.[5] One important element in such a framework is the public image of women. I thus agree with Viola Klein that attitudes are a significant component of history: "As people generally tend to live up to what is expected of them, it seems important to expose the particular set of views held in our culture with regard to woman's social role, characteristic traits and psychological abilities."[6]

Certainly not all women live up to what is expected of them, nor do they all even try. But if they do not, they must generally be aware that their behavior does not correspond to their public image. Historians have begun to realize that popular ideologies may be at odds with reality, that the battle cry "woman's place is in the home" may have reached the peak of its popularity not only *when* women were leaving their homes in increasing numbers, but precisely *because* this was happening. But, as Klein has pointed out, this disparity is itself important: "Slowest to come are the changes in cultural attitudes and popular ideologies, and it is here that the

[5] See Lerner, "Placing Women"; Juliet Mitchell, *Woman's Estate* (N.Y.: Pantheon Books, 1971); and Sheila Ryan Johansson, "'Herstory' as History: A New Field or Another Fad?" in *Liberating Women's History*, ed. Carroll, pp. 400-430.

[6] *The Feminine Character: History of an Ideology* (1946; rpt. Urbana: University of Illinois Press, 1971), p. 1. See also Hilda Smith, "Feminism and the Methodology of Women's History," in *Liberating Women's History*, ed. Carroll, pp. 368-384.

6

causes of the typical conflict of contemporary women are to be found."[7]

This study, then, concerns public or popular images of women in prewar and wartime society. It does not attempt to analyze the actual experiences of women, black or white, rich or poor, Jewish or "Aryan," in Germany and the United States during the war. Eleanor F. Straub has examined one aspect of the wartime lives of American women through the lens of government policy in her dissertation, "Government Policy Toward Civilian Women During World War II," and provided a valuable contribution to the scanty scholarship on the American homefront.[8] There is at present no comparable work on Germany. As Straub suggested in her preface, this is a rich and open field.

Certain other aspects of mobilization and propaganda are not included in this study. I do not consider women in the armed forces. The story of the women's branches in the United States needs to be told, but that would be a book in itself.[9] Ursula von Gersdorff's introduction to her documentary history of German women in war service includes women auxiliaries employed by the armed forces;[10] the German military did not include female branches, but employed women as civilians. In the United States, the armed forces used women in noncombat roles, and eventually cooperated with the War Manpower Commission in launching joint recruitment campaigns. Even before this, military

[7] Klein, *Feminine Character,* p. 32.

[8] Ph.D. diss., Emory University, 1973.

[9] Susan Hartmann presented a paper at the National Archives 1976 Conference on Women's History in April 1976 entitled "Women in the Military Service." I am grateful to her for sending me a copy of her paper. At present, the most useful published work on women in the armed forces is the official army history, Mattie E. Treadwell, *The Women's Army Corps,* The U.S. Army in World War II, ed. Kent Roberts Greenfield (Washington: Office of Chief of Military History, Dept. of the Army, 1954).

[10] *Frauen im Kriegsdienst 1914-1945* (Stuttgart: Deutsche Verlags-Anstalt, 1969).

7

recruitment efforts closely approximated civilian mobilization propaganda.

I also do not consider in any detail the propaganda directed at housewives urging them to take up volunteer work or practice wartime housekeeping. While it is important to note that such campaigns existed in both countries, they cannot be considered "mobilization" propaganda except in a very loose sense. I have concentrated on propaganda urging women to take war jobs because it was here that the war offered the greatest challenge to the prewar public images of women.

Because I am concerned with public images, my chapters on prewar and wartime popular conceptions rely on published or public sources: books, articles, pamphlets, magazines, advertisements, photographs, posters, slide shows, radio scripts, and movies. Secondary accounts of radio and film have been consulted to support my research in the other sources, and I have concentrated on nonfictional sources directly concerned with women's "place" in society. Literature has not been considered in any detail, although fiction, especially popular magazine stories and best-selling novels, reflects and contributes to the public image of women. The exclusion of literature is justified, I believe, for a number of reasons. First, literature played a minor role at best in the creation of the Nazi ideal. I have taken note of the short stories and poems about women included in magazines and anthologies such as the *N.S. Frauenbuch* [National Socialist Women's Book], but this literature does not warrant a great deal of attention. Second, though literature is more important for the chapter on the American prewar image, the secondary sources have adequately dealt with fiction in this period.[11] Third, the war was too short a span of time to

[11] See especially William H. Chafe, *The American Woman: Her Changing Social, Economic, and Political Role, 1920-1970* (N.Y.: Oxford University Press, 1972); and Peter G. Filene, *Him/Her/Self: Sex Roles in Modern America* (N.Y.: Harcourt Brace Jovanovich, 1974).

have an immediate impact on the image of women in literature. The magazine fiction that did respond to the need for the mobilization of women was a part of mobilization propaganda, and I have taken note of it.

These are the limits of my study. I have divided it into five chapters, exclusive of the introduction and conclusion, devoting four of them to the images of women in each country before and during the war, with a middle chapter on mobilization and propaganda in both countries. The structure is determined by the nature of the material. By devoting separate chapters to public images, I hope to facilitate comparison not only between countries, but also between prewar and wartime images in each country. These comparisons revolve around the central chapter, which compares mobilization and propaganda policy in both countries.

The second chapter examines the prewar image of women in Germany as National Socialist ideology fashioned it. The Nazi ideal was a consciously new creation based on the tenets of National Socialism, but drawing heavily on traditional ideas about women. The third chapter examines the ideal American woman and suggests points of similarity with the German ideal, though Nazi ideology and American attitudes cannot be subjected to the same kind of analysis. I began my work with the assumption that there was an American "ideology," but my research in the sources convinced me that "ideology" is too rigid a term to apply to American conceptions of women.

The fourth chapter examines the mobilization of women in both countries: the statistical picture, the unenforced German conscription system, the agencies in both countries responsible for the mobilization of women, the reasons for the German decision not to conscript women, the promotional campaigns of the War Manpower Commission and the Office of War Information in the United States, and the propaganda effort in Germany. The fifth chapter looks at the image of women in wartime Germany in order to analyze the effects of mobilization propaganda on the prewar image.

9

The American wartime image is similarly analyzed in the sixth chapter. The conclusion examines the complex role of propaganda, in conjunction with other factors such as financial incentive, the availability of child care, the existence of "status barriers," and patriotism in American success and German failure to mobilize women. Next, it explores the way in which public images can adapt to the needs of the economy in wartime without challenging traditional assumptions about women's role in society. Finally, it argues that the mode of adaptation of public images to the needs of the war explains, at least in part, the lack of change in the status of women in the immediate postwar period.

· 2 ·

Mother of the Volk:
The Image of Women
in Nazi Ideology[1]

> Though our weapon . . . is only the ladle, its im-
> pact will be no less than that of other weapons.
> *Gertrud Scholtz-Klink, 1937*

During the Nazi "time of struggle" and in the early years of
the Third Reich, a complex image of women evolved from
divergent strands of National Socialist ideology. Although
Hitler and other male party leaders conceptualized a simple
and limited role for women, the debate did not end with
their pronouncements. A small group of Nazi feminists attacked the misogynist views of the top Nazi officials, arguing
that women must take an active and equal role in the
National Socialist state. The mainstream Nazi conception of
women, represented by the great bulk of Nazi literature on
women, insisted that they played a vital role in the state as
"mothers of the *Volk*."

This mainstream image evolved to some extent from interaction with more extreme views and in response to the
external reality of economic demands. But the image remained relatively stable throughout the interwar period,
while Nazi policy toward women shifted in response to the
changing economic situation, particularly the Depression.
The blend of traditional ideas and Nazi principles that
characterized the mainstream Nazi image of women gave it
the flexibility to meet altered economic circumstances and
also the potential to attract two very different groups: conservative and traditional middle-class housewives who sought

[1] A revised version of this chapter was published by the University of Chicago Press in *Signs: Journal of Women in Culture and
Society*, 3 (Winter 1977).

confirmation of their roles within the home; and their rebellious daughters who longed for an active role and rejected the bourgeois life style of their mothers. Only a thorough examination of Nazi writings on women can lead to an understanding of both the flexibility and the appeal of the Nazi picture of women.

Nazi ideology in general has been surprisingly neglected, and this is doubly true of the Nazi view of women.[2] A number of books and articles on the subject published outside the Third Reich before the outbreak of the war indicate some interest in the plight of German women.[3] During the war, Allied-sponsored pamphlets and articles discussed the role of women in Germany in an attempt to show that a propaganda campaign aimed at them might serve as a useful weapon in the war effort.[4] But once the war ended, the

[2] See Barbara Miller Lane, "Nazi Ideology: Some Unfinished Business," *Central European History*, 7 (March 1974), 3-30, on the state of scholarship on Nazi ideology.

[3] The most important work on Nazi women, upon which most later work is based, is Clifford Kirkpatrick, *Nazi Germany: Its Women and Family Life* (N.Y.: Bobbs-Merrill, 1938). Kirkpatrick, a sociologist, went to Germany in order to collect material and conduct interviews. Other books, pamphlets, and articles published before the war include: Mildred Adams, "Women Under the Dictatorships," in *Dictatorship in the Modern World*, ed. Guy Stanton Ford (Minneapolis: University of Minnesota Press, 1939), pp. 272-291; Robert A. Brady, *The Spirit and Structure of German Fascism* (N.Y.: Viking Press, 1937), pp. 199-227; *Briefe deutscher Mädel aus dem Dritten Reich* (Strasbourg: Prometheus-Verlag, 1934); Hilda Browning, *Women Under Fascism and Communism* (London: Martin Lawrence, n.d. [1934]); Commission Investigating Fascist Activities, *Women Under Hitler Fascism* (National Committee to Aid Victims of German Fascism, 1934); Theodore Deak, *Women and Children Under the Swastika: A Collection of News Items and Factual Reports of the Unbridled Terror and Oppression in the Third Reich* (N.Y.: Universum Publishers, n.d. [1936]); Alice Hamilton, "Woman's Place in Germany," *Survey Graphic*, 23 (Jan. 1934), 26-29; Doris Kirkpatrick, "Role of Woman in Germany," *The New York Times*, Sept. 26, 1937, p. 7; Ruth Frances Woodsmall, "Women in the New Germany," *Forum*, 93 (May 1935), 299-303.

[4] See, for example, Louise Dornemann, *German Women Under*

literature on Nazi Germany almost unanimously ignored women. Although once *Reader's Digest* had carried an article about Gertrud Scholtz-Klink, the leader of the Nazi women's organizations, postwar histories quickly forgot her name.[5] Not until two decades after the war did interest in women in Nazi Germany revive, notably with the publication of David Schoenbaum's chapter on women in *Hitler's Social Revolution*.[6]

Hitler Fascism: A Brief Survey of the Position of German Women up to the Present Day (London: Allies Inside Germany, 1943); Free German League of Culture in Great Britain, *Women Under the Swastika* (London: Free German League, 1942); A[rthur] Guirdham, *Revolt Against Pity: An Indictment of the Nazi Martyrdom of Women* (London: John Drowther, n.d. [1943]); Ernst Klein, "Woman in National Socialism," *Fortnightly*, 157 (April 1942), 285-292; Katherine Thomas, *Women in Nazi Germany* (London: V. Gollancz, 1943).

[5] Peter Engelman, "Lady Führer Über Alles," *Reader's Digest*, 37 (Oct. 1940), 19-22, condensed from *The Living Age*, 359 (Oct. 1940), 112-116.

[6] *Hitler's Social Revolution: Class and Status in Nazi Germany 1933-1939* (Garden City, N.Y.: Doubleday, 1966). None of the recent work on women in Nazi Germany, however, considers the image of women in Nazi ideology in any detail. Jill Stephenson, in *Women in Nazi Society* (N.Y.: Barnes and Noble, 1975), examined policy toward women in the period 1930-1940 but did not consider Nazi ideology. (See my review of Stephenson's book, *Journal of Social History*, 10 [Spring 1977], 381-383). Extending Schoenbaum's line of reasoning, Stephenson argued that economic considerations determined the status of women in the Third Reich. I agree with Schoenbaum and Stephenson that economic need determined Nazi policy toward women, but I believe that a thorough examination of Nazi ideology shows that the image of women did not have to change in response to policy shifts. Such an examination also reveals the potential double appeal of the Nazi image, one aspect of which was pointed out by Renate Bridenthal in her article, "Beyond *Kinder, Küche, Kirche*: Weimar Women at Work," *Central European History*, 6 (June 1973), 148-166; and by Claudia Koonz in "Nazi Women Before 1933: Rebels Against Emancipation," *Social Science Quarterly*, 56 (March 1976), 553-563. I would like to thank Claudia Koonz for sending me a copy of her article before

In spite of renewed interest in the subject, there is still no thorough study of women in Nazi ideology. The wealth of books, pamphlets, and articles published before and during the Third Reich testifies to the liveliness and complexity of the issues, and provides the historian with abundant source material for a reconstruction of the National Socialist image of women.

All Nazi views on the subject shared two basic principles that characterized them as National Socialist. One was the superiority of the "Aryan" race and the importance of its struggle for existence in a hostile world. The other, lauded as a guide for individual action, found expression in the

it appeared in print. See also Renate Bridenthal and Claudia Koonz, "Beyond *Kinder, Küche, Kirche*: Weimar Women in Politics and Work," in *Liberating Women's History: Theoretical and Critical Essays*, ed. Berenice A. Carroll (Urbana: University of Illinois Press, 1976), pp. 301-329. Most recently, Claudia Koonz examined shifts in Nazi policy toward women in her article "Mothers in the Fatherland: Women in Nazi Germany," in *Becoming Visible: Women in European History*, ed. Renate Bridenthal and Claudia Koonz (Boston: Houghton Mifflin, 1977), pp. 445-473.

Other books and articles on women in Nazi Germany include: Hans Peter Bleuel, *Sex and Society in Nazi Germany*, ed. Heinrich Fraenkel, trans. J. Maxwell Brownjohn (N.Y.: Lippincott, 1973); Joachim C. Fest, *The Face of the Third Reich: Portraits of the Nazi Leadership*, trans. Michael Bullock (N.Y.: Ace Books, 1970); Ursula von Gersdorff, *Frauen im Kriegsdienst 1914-1945* (Stuttgart: Deutsche Verlags-Anstalt, 1969); Richard Grunberger, *The 12-Year Reich: A Social History of Nazi Germany 1933-1945* (N.Y.: Ballantine Books, 1971); Jill McIntyre [Stephenson], "Women and the Professions in Germany, 1930-1940," in *German Democracy and the Triumph of Hitler*, ed. Anthony Nicholls and Erich Matthias (N.Y.: St. Martin's Press, 1971), pp. 175-213.

Further books and articles with information on women in Nazi Germany are: Karl Dietrich Bracher, *The German Dictatorship*, trans. Jean Steinberg (N.Y.: Praeger, 1970); Gabriele Bremme, *Die politische Rolle der Frau in Deutschland* (Göttingen: Vandenhoeck und Ruprecht, 1956); Kate Millett, *Sexual Politics* (Garden City, N.Y.: Doubleday, 1970); George L. Mosse, *Nazi Culture: Intellectual, Cultural and Social Life in the Third Reich* (N.Y.: Grosset and Dunlap, 1966).

14

slogan, *"Gemeinnutz vor Eigennutz,"* the common good before the individual good. The mainstream conception of women owed its flexibility to this second principle, for the ideal Nazi woman owed service to the state above all else. The shifting demands of economic policy, like the unchanging demands of population policy, found a common basis in the Nazi principle of sacrifice for the common good.

Using the same foundation, Nazi writers came to widely divergent views of the place of women in post-Weimar society. Too often historians have accepted the statements of Hitler as the definitive National Socialist view. Certainly Hitler's ideas cannot be dismissed, but along with the recent recognition that Hitler did not exercise dictatorial control over a monolithic party and state has come the realization that Nazi ideology evolved before 1933 in a dynamic process of exchange.[7]

Hitler's opposition to the political participation of women and his low estimation of women's abilities are well-known; women were, for Hitler, unimportant except as breeders of future generations. In a speech in April 1932, he made his famous promise: "What has the Revolution of 1918 actually done for women? All it has done is to turn fifty thousand of them into blue stockings and party officials. Under the Third Reich they might as well whistle for such things. Every woman then will get a husband for herself."[8]

Hitler, like other male party leaders, especially self-proclaimed Nazi philosopher Alfred Rosenberg, based his view of women on the concept of the polarity of the sexes. In Rosenberg's almost incomprehensible book, *Der Mythus des 20. Jahrhunderts* [*The Myth of the Twentieth Century*], the female sex represented the "lyrical" pole of humanity, the male the "architectural."[9] What Rosenberg's cosmic principle

---

[7] Lane, "Nazi Ideology."

[8] Quoted in Browning, *Women Under Fascism*, p. 3.

[9] *Der Mythus des 20. Jahrhunderts: Eine Wertung der seelisch-geistigen Gestaltenkämpfe unsere Zeit* (Munich: Hoheneichen-Verlag, 1930).

15

meant on a more concrete level was the creation of separate spheres for the two sexes. Hitler explained the idea of separate spheres in his 1934 Party Day speech to the Frauenschaft, the Nazi women's organization.[10] Man's world was the state, woman's the home, and the two worlds complemented each other. Women ought not attempt to penetrate the world of men.

According to Rosenberg, it was not only improper for women to meddle in man's sphere, it was positively dangerous. He argued that the state originated in the *Männerbund*, a group of soldiers, and maintained itself by military force. Thus the development of female influence on the state meant the beginning of decline.[11] "Emancipated" women, like male feminists, were symbols of cultural malaise. Such women had not become "architectural," only intellectual Amazons or purely erotic representatives of the sexual revolution. In either case, they had lost their own essence without attaining the masculine heights to which they aspired. *"Emancipation of woman from emancipation* is the first demand of a generation of women which would like to save people and race, the Eternal-Unconscious, the foundation of all culture, from decline."[12] Rosenberg added that women should have equal opportunity in education, physical activity, and careers, but that they should be relieved of the necessity of employment. And he stated forcefully that only men could be judges, soldiers, and rulers of the state.[13]

Joseph Goebbels agreed with Rosenberg that the in-

[10] Adolf Hitler, "Die völkische Sendung der Frau," in *N.S. Frauenbuch*, ed. Ellen Semmelroth (Munich: J. F. Lehmann, 1934), pp. 9-14.

[11] Rosenberg, *Mythus*. Rosenberg developed this argument about the *Männerbund* in an earlier article in the *Völkischer Beobachter* [*VB*]. See Alfred Rosenberg, "Der Staat, der Mann, die Frau," *VB*, April 4, 1926.

[12] Rosenberg, *Mythus*, p. 512.

[13] Although the pronouncement was generally accepted, there was some debate on the subject. See, for example, Karl Plumeyer, "Soll die Frau Richter werden?" *VB*, April 16/17, 1933.

16

fluence of women in public life represented the beginning of decline, and told a group of women leaders in 1934: "Woman's proper sphere is the family. There she is a sovereign queen. If we eliminate women from every realm of public life, we do not do it in order to dishonour her, but in order that her honour may be restored to her."[14]

Hitler urged women, within their domestic sphere, to bear numerous children in accordance with Nazi population policy, which called for a vigorously growing "Aryan" population. Just as men served the state by fighting, so women served by bearing children. The theme of childbirth as an analogue of battle was a popular one in Nazi ideology: "Every child that a woman brings into the world is a battle, a battle waged for the existence of her people."[15] Nazi leaders were aware that the exclusive childbearing role assigned to women seemed demeaning to some critics. Hitler proclaimed in his 1935 Party Day speech to the Frauenschaft: "When our opponents say: You degrade women by assigning them no other task than that of childbearing, then I answer that it is not degrading to a woman to be a mother. On the contrary, it is her greatest honor. There is nothing nobler for a woman than to be the mother of the sons and daughters of the people."[16] Gregor Strasser wrote that National Socialism intended to restore the natural order, to accord women the respect they deserved as mothers and housewives.[17]

The simple and limited role of women envisioned by the top Nazi leaders seemed demeaning not only to critics of National Socialism, but also to a small group of Nazi

[14] Quoted in Browning, *Women Under Fascism*, p. 8.

[15] Hitler, "Die völkische Sendung," p. 11. See also Gregor Strasser, "Gedanken über Aufgaben der Zukunft," *Nationalsozialistische Briefe*, June 15, 1926.

[16] Adolf Hitler, in *Das deutsche Landfrauenbuch*, ed. Anne Marie Koeppen (Berlin: Reichsnährstand Verlag, 1937).

[17] Gregor Strasser, "Die Frau und der Nationalsozialismus," *VB*, April 6, 1932.

feminists.[18] These women argued for an extension of women's role within the Nazi state, also basing their argument on National Socialist principles. The debate within the Nazi ranks over the issues raised by the feminists reveals the extent to which National Socialist doctrine could support conflicting views on women's proper role in society. It reveals as well the ideology's lack of rigidity in the early years of the party.

Emma Hadlich sparked the debate in 1926 with an article in the *Völkischer Beobachter*, the official party newspaper.[19] Hadlich attacked Elsbeth Zander, then head of the women's organization associated with the Nazi Party, and provoked a series of charges and countercharges, published in the paper from January to April 1926. Many of the issues raised surfaced again in 1933 with the publication of a book of essays, *Deutsche Frauen an Adolf Hitler* [*German Women Address Adolf Hitler*].[20] Even after the Nazi assumption of power, Nazi feminists continued to express their views. They believed that women, while different from men, were fully as capable and intelligent, and could make important contributions to the German people in many ways other than through motherhood. In a truly German society, they claimed, women would work and fight alongside their men, everyone struggling together for the community of the people. Refusing to accept current notions of women's inherent

[18] Clifford Kirkpatrick introduced the term "Nazi feminists" in 1938; see *Nazi Germany*. It is a term which may seem offensive today, but I believe that it is an accurate description of the women whose views I am about to present.

[19] Dr. E[mma] Hadlich, "Aufgaben der deutschen Frau in der Gegenwart," *VB*, Jan. 23, 1926. This article and all subsequent replies appeared in the women's supplement to the *VB*, entitled "Die deutsche Frauenbewegung." See Elsbeth Zander's reply, "Weg und Ziele des Deutschen Frauenordens," *VB*, Jan. 23, 1926.

[20] Irmgard Reichenau, *Deutsche Frauen an Adolf Hitler* (Leipzig: Adolf Klein Verlag, 1933). Another feminist work from the same press is Dorothea Klaje-Wenzel, *Die Frau in der Volksgemeinschaft* (Leipzig: Adolf Klein Verlag, 1934).

18

physical and intellectual inferiority, Nazi feminists took comfort in the popularized anthropological theory that postulated matriarchy as the earliest form of social organization.[21] But more significantly, they argued that in ancient Germanic society men and women had been equally important.

The argument between Nazi feminists and their opponents centered around the historical nature of Germanic society rather than the desirable conditions for the future, even before the Nazi assumption of power and the subsequent institution of censorship might have forced Nazi feminist views underground.[22] The feminists described an ancient

[21] See Hadlich, "Aufgaben"; and Sophie Rogge-Börner, "Denkschrift," in *Deutsche Frauen*, ed. Reichenau, pp. 7-11. The debate over matriarchy went back to J. J. Bachofen (1815-1887), a Swiss anthropologist whose controversial book, *Das Mutterrecht* (1861), argued that matriarchy was the earliest form of social organization. The publication of *Das Mutterrecht* sparked a debate that continues, somewhat abated, even today. Modern anthropologists, pointing to the fact that there are no contemporary matriarchal societies and no evidence about any in the past, dismiss matriarchy as a myth, but it continues to excite the imaginations of modern feminists. See Joan Bamberger, "The Myth of Matriarchy: Why Men Rule in Primitive Society," in Michelle Zimbalist Rosaldo and Louise Lamphere, *Woman, Culture and Society* (Stanford: Stanford University Press, 1974), pp. 263-280. Although the debate over Bachofen had died down by the start of the twentieth century, interest in matriarchal theory revived among psychologists and right-wing critics of bourgeois society in the 1920's. On this revival, see Martin Jay, *The Dialectical Imagination: A History of the Frankfurt School and the Institute of Social Research 1923-1950* (Boston: Little, Brown, 1973), pp. 94-96. The Nazi feminists, like modern feminists, saw in Bachofen the rationale for a new social order that would accord important economic and political roles to women.

[22] See Hadlich, "Aufgaben"; Rogge-Börner, "Denkschrift," in *Deutsche Frauen*, ed. Reichenau; Sophie Rogge-Börner, "Neue Erkenntnisse," *N.S. Frauen-Warte*, 1 (Jan. 15, 1933), 313-315; Richard Schultes, "Die deutsche Frau und ihre Stellung zum Mann," *VB*, Feb. 6, 1926. One woman criticized Hadlich for looking to Germanic tradition when there was no agreement about it. See Josefine v. B., "Die deutsche Frau im Kampf für Deutschlands Freiheit," *VB*, Feb. 6, 1926. Alfred Rosenberg, at this time editor of the *VB*,

Nordic utopia in which women had enjoyed full equality and opportunity to use their considerable talents for the good of their people. Women, they insisted, had functioned as priestesses, leaders, and even warriors. The Nazi feminists referred to the Edda, Icelandic sagas, and the writings of Tacitus as evidence for their view of the German past. Using the Nazi principle that pure German-ness represented the highest good, they insisted that Nazi society ought to model itself after the glorious Nordic era.

---

insisted that male leadership had been the rule among Germanic peoples. See Alfred Rosenberg, "Nachwort der Schriftleitung," *VB*, Jan. 23, 1926.

An interesting book on women in Germanic society with a feminist perspective is Lena Wellinghusen [pseud. of Lena Osswald], *Die deutsche Frau, Dienerin oder Gefährtin* (Munich: Ludendorffs Verlag, 1933). Although Wellinghusen's book closely followed the Nazi feminist line, it was a product of the Ludendorff press. Ludendorff had broken with Hitler after the failure of the Putsch. His circle, perhaps under the influence of his second wife Mathilde, did not accept the Nazi leaders' view of women. Wilhelm Hoegner, *Die Frau im Dritten Reich* (Berlin: J. H. W. Dietz, 1931), reported that even Ludendorff disapproved of the Nazi view of women (p. 9), and *Ludendorffs Volkswarte* commented on Dec. 21, 1930 that "many German women have so little pride that they run after the National Socialist Party" (quoted in SPD, *Nationalsozialismus und Frauenfrage: Material zur Information und Bekämpfung* [Berlin: Werbeabteilung der SPD, 1932], p. 62).

Works published after 1933 include: A. v. Averswald, "Die germanische Frau als Vorbild und Wegweiserin," in *Frauenbuch*, ed. Semmelroth; Gertrud Baumgart, *Die altgermanische Frau und wir* (Heidelberg: Carl Winters Universitätsbuchhandlung, 1935); Gerda Merschberger, *Die Rechtsstellung der germanischen Frau* (Leipzig: Curt Kabitzsch Verlag, 1937); Ida Naumann, *Altgermanisches Frauenleben* (Jena: E. Diederichs Verlag, 1937); Irmgard Netter, *Germanisches Frauentum* (Leipzig: Quelle und Meyer, 1936); Marie Adelhei Reuss zur Lippe, *Nordische Frau und nordischer Glaube*, Flugschriften der Nordischen Glaubensbewegung, no. 2 (Berlin: Verlag von Struppe und Winckler, n.d. [1935]); G. Vogel, *Die deutsche Frau*, vol. 1: *Die germanische Frau*, 2nd ed., Schriften zu Deutschlands Erneuerung, no. 56 (Breslau: Verlag von Heinrich Handel, n.d. [1936]).

Nazi feminists compared their Germanic paradise to the current state of affairs, and concluded that foreign, especially Jewish, influences had corrupted society.[23] They argued that Roman law and Judaism had together spread the vicious concept of women's inferiority, and only by eliminating such tainted ideas could German society purify itself. Because Jewry was largely responsible for the degeneration of the Germanic people, the woman problem could only be solved in the Germanic spirit in an anti-Semitic, National Socialist state.

The Nazi feminists played their trump card when they insisted on strict adherence to the National Socialist principle of achievement.[24] They argued that the building of a National Socialist society required the talents and efforts of every person, regardless of sex. A hierarchical leadership structure necessitated the promotion of talented women, as well as men, to the highest positions they were capable of holding. Rosenberg cleverly parried this thrust; the feminists' contention that an individual's position ought to be determined by achievement rather than sex, he insisted, confused cause and effect, since achievement was organically related to sex.[25]

The arguments based on the nature of Germanic society and the existence of a natural aristocracy were their strongest points, but the feminists also emphasized the importance of women's function as educator of children.[26] They contended

[23] Hadlich, "Aufgaben"; Hadlich, "Frauenfrage?" *VB*, April 4, 1926; Margaretha Kurlbaum-Sieber, "Nur das jüdische Gesetz nahm dem Weibe das Priestertum," in *Deutsche Frauen*, ed. Reichenau, pp. 54-58; Rogge-Börner, "Neue Erkenntnisse"; Schultes, "Die deutsche Frau."

[24] Hadlich, "Aufgaben"; Thilda Hecht, "Gedanken zur Frauenfrage," *VB*, Feb. 6, 1926; Irmgard Reichenau, "Die begabte Frau," in *Deutsche Frauen*, ed. Reichenau, pp. 13-27; Rogge-Börner, "Denkschrift," in *Deutsche Frauen*, ed. Reichenau; Margarete Rosikat, "Offener Brief an Frau Hadlich," *VB*, Feb. 6, 1926.

[25] Rosenberg, "Nachwort."

[26] Yella Erdmann, "Die Stellung der Mutter als Erziehrin ist in Gefahr!" pp. 50-53; Lenore Kühn, "Natürlicher Aristokratismus," pp. 28-39; Sophie Philipps, "Die deutsche Frau in der Politik," pp. 46-49;

21

that sons brought up to believe in the inferiority of women would have only scorn for their mothers, making it impossible for women to exert authority or fulfill their tasks as educators.

All of these arguments conformed to National Socialist principles, but at least one woman went beyond these limits and adopted lines of reasoning reminiscent of the radical bourgeois feminism of the Weimar Republic.[27] Irmgard Reichenau's essay on gifted women, a longer version of which she sent to Hitler in March 1932, argued that women had to have access to influential positions, not only for the good of the state, but also for their own personal fulfillment. She defended career women from charges of causing unemployment, preferring to remain single, and the absence of desire for children. She accused men of seeking only comfort in marriage and therefore avoiding strong and intelligent women. She insisted that talented women with careers would make better mothers than full-time mothers—heresy for a National Socialist!—and cited Maria Theresa, with her sixteen children, and Clara Schumann with her eight, as examples of accomplished women and good mothers. Reichenau warned that unused talents often broke out in other directions, as in hysteria, neurosis, or domestic tyranny.

Although few Nazi writers went as far as Reichenau, the Nazi feminist position provoked angry protests in the party press. Writers denounced the feminists as "women's righters" rather than true National Socialists.[28] They rejected appeals to the principle of achievement, calling instead for the devel-

---

Irmgard Reichenau, "Arteigenheit," pp. 40-45; all in *Deutsche Frauen*, ed. Reichenau.

[27] Reichenau, "Die begabte Frau," in *Deutsche Frauen*, ed. Reichenau. On radical feminism in the Weimar Republic, see Stephenson, *Women*, pp. 21-28. See also Richard J. Evans, *The Feminist Movement in Germany 1894-1933*, Sage Studies in Twentieth Century History, vol. 6 (London: Sage Publications, 1976).

[28] "Fest Bleiben!" *VB*, Feb. 20, 1926; Arth. Gallus, "Moderne Wahnideen," *VB*, Feb. 20, 1926; Frau Höpfner, "Streit der Geschlechter?" *VB*, Feb. 20, 1926; Rosenberg, "Nachwort."

opment of the racially pure and the "pruning" of the damaged. Or they insisted that women have at least six children in order to secure the existence of the race.

Aside from the ideological dispute itself, what is particularly interesting about this debate is the lack of doctrinal rigidity. Rosenberg noted that Hadlich's original article and Zander's reply revealed the range of ideas held by *völkisch* women, and suggested that it would be best to air these differences in public.[29] Other writers pointed out that the conflict testified to the vitality of the movement.[30] At the end of the resulting debate in the *Völkischer Beobachter*, Rosenberg left the issue to the party leadership, suggesting that all differences of opinion ought to give way before the central struggle against high finance, Marxism, and Jewry.[31] Reichenau, in raising these issues again in 1933, opened her book with two quotations from Hitler, one calling on anyone who saw danger threatening the people to work openly against the evil, the other stating that "He who loves Germany may criticize us."[32] It is impossible to gauge the extent of feminist opinion within the Nazi ranks, but Rosenberg clearly felt on the defensive. He noted in the *Völkischer Beobachter* that his comments on Hadlich's article were not meant to imply that women were inferior to men, only that their psyches differed.[33] Even after he ended the debate in the pages of the newspaper, women continued to attack him for his views.[34]

[29] Rosenberg, "Nachwort."

[30] Josefine v. B., "Die deutsche Frau"; Helene Passow, "Rechte und Pflichten," *VB*, March 19, 1926.

[31] "Antwort an Frau Dr. Hadlich," *VB*, April 4, 1926.

[32] Reichenau, *Deutsche Frauen*, p. 5.

[33] Introduction to Rosikat, "Offener Brief."

[34] In 1932, a short collection of quotations concerning women taken from Rosenberg's works appeared in the *VB* with a prefatory note indicating that the intent was to clear up the misunderstanding of his position on women and the state. See "Alfred Rosenberg und die deutsche Frau," *VB*, March 27/28/29, 1932. In another essay, Rosenberg claimed that his book had been misunderstood. See Alfred Rosenberg, "Der nationale Schicksalskampf der Frau," in *Unsere*

The publication of *Deutsche Frauen* in 1933 brought the issues raised by Nazi feminism to the attention of the newly installed Chancellor, but apparently provoked no answer, although Göring responded on March 4, 1933 that he had received the memorandum with interest.[35] The appointment of Hitler and the passage of the Enabling Act did not silence the feminists. The militant Nazi feminist journal *Die deutsche Kämpferin*, edited by Sophie Rogge-Börner, continued publication until 1937, although it ceased its criticism before that date.[36] In 1934 the journal commented on Nazi policies designed to reduce male unemployment by firing women: "For hundreds of thousands of women and girls nothing is left but suicide or prostitution."[37] When representatives of women's organizations were denied a place at Hindenburg's funeral in 1934, this further affront to the dignity of women called forth an angry protest from the journal:

This funeral was a national observance on which the attention of the whole world was concentrated, one which concerned the whole mass of the German people. That here again the mothers of the nation were publicly ex-

---

Zeit und wir: Das Buch der deutschen Frau, ed. Elsbeth Unverricht, 4th ed. (Gauting b. Munich: Verlag Heinrich A. Berg, n.d. [1935]), pp. 129-134.

Rosenberg was not the only Nazi leader forced to defend his views on women. At a meeting of Frauenschaft leaders from all the Gaue [districts] in March 1932, Gregor Strasser urged the leaders to help correct the false public impression of the position of women in National Socialism. Gottfried Feder attempted to clear up the "misunderstanding" of a statement he had made to the effect that woman's role was as maid and servant. See "Die N.S.-Frauenschaften rüsten zum Endkampf," *VB*, March 27/28/29, 1932.

[35] Reichenau, *Deutsche Frauen,* p. 11.

[36] *Die deutsche Kämpferin: Monatsschrift zur Gestaltung der wahrhaftigen Volksgemeinschaft,* published in Leipzig by Adolf Klein from 1933 to 1937. Kirkpatrick reported that Sophie Rogge-Börner was officially silenced and *Die deutsche Kämperferin* banned in 1937 (p. 297).

[37] *Die deutsche Kämpferin,* July 1934; quoted in Browning, *Women Under Fascism,* p. 9.

cluded from the community of the people, in the very hour when the last honours were being rendered the defunct head of the State, has affected all passionately German-feeling women with painful surprise and the depressing feelings of violated honour. We have not forgotten that the Reichs President, who on the 30th of January opened the doors of the German future to National Socialism, was first and foremost indebted for his victorious election to the vote of the women of all parties. Innumerable representatives of foreign Governments, each of which, if it likes, can push us over into the abyss of war to-morrow, attended the funeral of the 'father of the fatherland,' but for the mothers of the fatherland [there] was 'no room.'[38]

Nazi feminist views, after the conclusion of the debate in the *Völkischer Beobachter*, were largely, but not entirely, confined to the pages of the journal *Die deutsche Kämpferin* and the book *Deutsche Frauen an Adolf Hitler*. Occasionally an orthodox book included feminist arguments, such as the advocacy of women lawyers and judges by Ingeborg Lorentzen, which appeared in a collection of essays devoted primarily to women in "womanly" roles.[39]

Why the Nazi feminists supported National Socialism is a tantalizing question. They tended to be professional women—doctors, lawyers, academics—with a stake in a system which guaranteed women equal opportunity. It is understandable why, after 1933, they might have used Nazi principles to support a stronger position for women; but they were not simply opportunists, since they were active before 1933. What did the NSDAP offer to these women? No answer to this question is possible at this time, since little is known about the Nazi feminists as individuals.[40] Certainly

[38] Quoted in Browning, *Women Under Fascism*, p. 17.

[39] Ingeborg Lorentzen, "Die Frau in der Rechtspflege," in *Unsere Zeit*, ed. Unverricht, pp. 417-419.

[40] The only biographical information on the Nazi feminists is in Kirkpatrick, *Nazi Germany*, and this is sketchy. If enough information

25

their views were unique in the context of the conservative bourgeois women's movement. They may not have understood what Nazism would mean for women. Perhaps it was not clear that professional women would be confined to "womanly" branches of their professions.

A 1932 appeal to employed women urging them to vote National Socialist indicates how the party tried to attract working and professional women.[41] The appeal promised that all women—employed women, housewives, mothers— would be citizens of the Third Reich. No women would lose their jobs, but National Socialism would not allow women to be forced into employment. It would secure decent wages for men so that those women who wished to do so could stay at home. "But no woman who, out of personal preference, wants to take up a profession, will be prevented from doing so. . . . Germany, the great mother, embodied in National Socialism, loves and needs every one of her daughters: the one by her child's cradle and the one behind the counter, the one at the stove and the one at the lectern, the one in the factory and the one in the laboratory, every one who works honestly and selflessly for the rise of our Fatherland."

This one statement cannot fully explain the allegiance of the Nazi feminists, but it does indicate that National Socialism may have had a more complex appeal than is now understood.

The misogynist views of the top Nazi leaders, and the views of the Nazi feminists, represent opposite ends of the spectrum of Nazi ideas about women. The great majority of writers on the subject, many of them women, fall somewhere in between. This mainstream view does not actually conflict with Hitler's or Rosenberg's conceptions. It simply differs from them in that the mainstream writers were more

---

could be located, a full biographical and social analysis would be extremely interesting.

[41] "Die Frau im Beruf," *N.S. Frauen-Warte*, 1 (Nov. 1932), 194.

concerned with women's role and attributed to it a great deal of importance in Nazi society. This view permeated the literature on and for women, developing to some extent from interaction with the extreme views. From it the ideal of the Nazi woman emerges.

Basic to the mainstream view was the assumption that women played an important role in National Socialism. The very existence of the large number of books, pamphlets, articles—literature of all types—dealing with women testifies to the interest in the issue. But not all writers left the assumption unspoken, and in these cases, the implication often was that the Nazi leadership did not recognize the importance of women.

Lydia Gottschewski, a mainstream writer and early leader of women in the Third Reich who was later pushed aside, condemned the band of men that Rosenberg praised as the origin and basis of the state.[42] She argued that the *Männerbund*, which she traced to the front experience of the war and the Free Corps ethos of the postwar period, represented the opposite pole from the feminist matriarchate, and set out the National Socialist ideal of "the new unity" in opposition to both. For Gottschewski, as for the Nazi feminists, the concept of the *Männerbund* smacked of "oriental" influence. Another party member and women's leader, Guida Diehl, cautiously criticized the masculine character of the party and suggested a greater role for women.[43] Both of these women conceded that the movement had had to be essentially masculine in the time of struggle,

[42] *Männerbund und Frauenfrage: Die Frau im neuen Staat* (Munich: J. F. Lehmann, 1934). See Kirkpatrick, *Nazi Germany*, on Gottschewski.

[43] *Die deutsche Frau und der Nationalsozialismus*, 5th ed. (Eisenach: Neulandverlag, 1933). See also Baumgart, *Altgermanische Frau*; Else Frobenius, *Die Frau im Dritten Reich: Eine Schrift für das deutsche Volk* (Berlin-Wilmersdorf: Nationaler Verlag J. G. Huch, n.d. [1933]), pp. 101-110; and Charlotte Koeberle-Schönfeldt, "Matriarchat?" *N.S. Frauen-Warte*, 1 (Sept. 15, 1932), 122.

but saw no reason why the task of building a new society should not be taken up by women and men together. Gottschewski and Diehl envisioned a state in which women would play an important role, but they emphatically rejected the bourgeois women's movement as a model. This so-called "old women's movement" and the "woman question" received a great deal of attention from writers.[44] In contrast to the situation in the United States, in Germany there had always been two distinct women's movements, the socialist and the bourgeois. Nazi mainstream writers denounced both branches, in spite of the continuity in many respects between the attitudes of the predominant Protestant bourgeois women's organization, the Bund deutscher Frauen, and mainstream Nazi ideas.[45] Although the Bund deutscher Frauen upheld a very traditional conception of women's roles, its association with liberalism tainted it in Nazi eyes. "Equality of women" in the liberal sense meant masculinization. The liberal women's movement had sought special gains for women as a group, rather than working for the entire people. Worse, it spent an inordinate amount of energy pursuing reforms which would benefit only a tiny minority of educated and talented women. These women, who usually remained unmarried, had set the women's movement on a course of pacifism and internationalism. Little in this tradition could be used by those attempting to build a National

---

[44] See Gottschewski, *Männerbund*, pp. 12-32; Paula Siber von Groote, *Die Frauenfrage und ihre Lösung durch den Nationalsozialismus* (Wolfenbüttel-Berlin: G. Kallmeyer, 1933); Marie Diers, "Frauenfrage und Frauenantwort," *Kampfpause: Beilage zum Nationalem Sozialisten*, Feb. 1, 1930, reprinted in *Die nationalsozialistische Linke 1925-1930*, ed. Reinhard Kühnl (Meisenheim am Glan: Hain, 1966), p. 337.

[45] See Amy Hackett, "The German Women's Movement and Suffrage, 1890-1914: A Study of National Feminism," in *Modern European Social History*, ed. Robert J. Bezucha (Lexington, Mass.: D. C. Health, 1972), pp. 354-386; Evans, *Feminist Movement*; and Stephenson, *Women*, pp. 21-28.

Socialist women's movement.[46] Although the concept of feminism was abhorrent to the majority of Nazi women, and the term "women's movement" was often avoided because of its associations with the organization of the Weimar Republic, many writers in fact urged the creation of a women's movement consistent with Nazi principles and goals.[47]

The "new women's movement" was an "organic" outgrowth of National Socialism rather than of feminism, and was grounded in basic Nazi principles: hierarchical organization, racial purity, sacrifice for the good of the people. Women turned their backs on the selfish emphasis on "women's rights" and devoted themselves instead to women's duties. According to Gottschewski, the most essential duty of the movement was education of women in the concept of community. Paula Siber, like Gottschewski an early

[46] In spite of this consensus on the women's movement, one writer tried to reconcile National Socialism with the bourgeois women's movement. Gertrud Baumgart, *Frauenbewegung gestern und heute* (Heidelberg: Carl Winters Universitätsbuchhandlung, 1933), listed the objections each movement had to the other and attempted to show that they were groundless. She denied that National Socialism meant loss of political rights, restrictions on intellectual attainment, or loss of personality for women, and also that the women's movement was guilty of alienating women from motherhood, causing a moral decline, urging masculine occupations for women, setting unattainable goals, or adopting a Marxist orientation. She concluded that the two movements, the greatest of the century, shared a common goal: the education of women for their national and social responsibilities. See also Baumgart, *Altgermanische Frau*. Baumgart's curious views received support from Theodore Eichhoff in the pages of *Soziale Praxis* [*SP*], a forum for social planners. See "Frauenwirken am Wiederaufbau Deutschlands," *SP*, 42 (Dec. 1933), 1425-28; and "Neuere Literatur zur Frauenfrage," *SP*, 43 (Feb. 1934), 232-236.

[47] See Gottschewski, *Männerbund*, pp. 69-83; Siber, *Frauenfrage*; Gertrud Scholtz-Klink, "Weg und Aufgabe der nationalsozialistischen Frauenbewegung," in *Frauenbuch*, ed. Semmelroth, pp. 15-23. See also Lydia Gottschewski, "Weibliches Führertum: Die Eingliederung der Frau in den neuen Staat," in *Unsere Zeit*, ed. Unverricht, pp. 180-182.

29

leader of Nazi women, also defined the "woman question" not in terms of women's rights, but as the basic question of women's role in the community. She recognized that the woman question had had to be secondary while the movement was fighting to obtain power, but saw it as a vital question for the entire people in the context of a National Socialist state. German women had responded enthusiastically to the call of National Socialism, had joined together in an entirely original movement which had grown in the hearts of thousands of German women who had never belonged to the "old women's movements." For Siber, the goal was "the incorporation [*Eingliederung*] of woman in the service and the mission of the National Socialist community of the people."[48]

Gertrud Scholtz-Klink, who succeeded both Gottschewski and Siber as the leader of women and remained in this post until the end of the Third Reich, agreed that the mission of the movement was the affirmation of the value of community. Scholtz-Klink, like Gottschewski, was concerned with leadership in the women's movement.[49] The leadership principle of the party applied to the women's organizations as well, and discipline and unity were virtues expected of women. Gottschewski, sensitive to the criticism that the top leaders of the movement were men, pointed out that the lack of rivalry between male and female leaders proved the unconditional unity of the entire National Socialist movement.[50]

Nazi women discarded the tradition of the old women's movement along with the liberal concept of equality. While the Nazi feminists chose the principle of achievement from the National Socialist arsenal of ideas and used it in their battle for leadership positions, the mainstream Nazi theorists on women accepted the concept of the polarity of the sexes but insisted that women played a vital role in Nazi

[48] Siber, *Frauenfrage*, p. 32.
[49] Scholtz-Klink, "Weg und Aufgabe," in *Frauenbuch*, ed. Semmelroth.
[50] Gottschewski, "Weibliches Führertum," p. 182.

society. Like Hitler, the mainstream writers were aware of the general conviction outside of Germany that National Socialism oppressed women, and they did their best to dismiss or combat it.[51] They blamed their enemies for spreading lies about the party's hostility to women and branded the tales of National Socialism's degradation and disfranchisement of women the lies of a dying era. The efforts of both men and women were essential in the National Socialist state: "Just as the life of a plant is naturally determined by the cooperation of the male and female forces, which ultimately results in blossoms and fruit, so a political community cannot grow organically without the collaboration of the characteristic strengths of both sexes in unrestricted and versatile deployment."[52]

Since National Socialism rejected the principle of equality as the hallmark of a decadent democratic order, the main concern of writers on women was not the equality of women and men, but rather the corollary of polarity, the concept of the separate spheres and duties of the two sexes. As Hitler had proclaimed in his 1934 Party Day speech, man's world was the state, woman's primarily the home. This did not mean, for the mainstream writers, that women were restricted to the home, but that their major influence on society was exerted through the medium of the family. Rosenberg argued that the state grew out of the *Männerbund*, but far more

[51] See Hans Naujoks, *Die Wandlung der deutschen Frau* (Stuttgart: Ferdinand Enke Verlag, 1935); Sofia Rabe, *Die Frau im national-sozialistischen Staat*, Broschurenreihe der Reichs-Propaganda-Leitung der NSDAP, no. 18 (Munich: Zentralverlag der NSDAP, 1932); Gertrud Scholtz-Klink, *Einsatz der Frau in der Nation* (Berlin: Deutsches Frauenwerk, 1937); Gertrud Scholtz-Klink, "Wir alle schaffen für Deutschland," in NSDAP, Reichsfrauenführung, Presseabteilung, *Das deutsche Frauenbuch: Ein Wegweiser für die deutsche Mutter und Hausfrau* (Dortmund: Westfalen-Verlag, n.d. [1939]), pp. 4-6; Anna Zühlke, *Frauenaufgabe—Frauenarbeit im Dritten Reich: Bausteine zum neuen Staat und Volk* (Leipzig: Verlag von Quelle und Meyer, 1934).

[52] Baumgart, *Altgermanische Frau*, p. 31.

31

common was the view that the family was the basic cell of the state. Nazi ideology declared the family the "life source" of the people, according it ·a crucial role in the Nazi polity. Although Nazi policy often contradicted this ideological stance, Nazi writings on the family were important in granting significance to the woman, the key figure in, if not the head of, the family. There were obvious social and biological reasons for celebrating the family, but there were racial, cultural, and economic ones as well. Woman as mother and housewife ruled ove.· a small kingdom of her own, one to which Nazi ideology accorded a prominent place in the structure of society.[53]

National Socialism proclaimed its intention of reconstructing the family, a task which involved more than simply sending women home. Some mainstream writers lamented the fact that men spiritually abandoned the family circle and set out to return the father, as well as the mother, to the home.[54] Karl Beyer, who credited National Socialism with complet-

---

[53] This is one of the most common themes in the literature. See Baumgart, *Altgermanische Frau*; Karl Beyer, *Die Ebenbürtigkeit der Frau im nationalsozialistischen Deutschland: Ihre erzieherische Aufgabe* (Leipzig: Armanen-Verlag, 1932); Karl Beyer, *Familie und Frau im neuen Deutschland* (Langensalza: Verlag von J. Beltz, 1936); Hilde Boehm-Stoltz, "Die Nationalsozialistin und die Familie," *VB*, Jan. 20, 1932; Diehl, *Deutsche Frau*; Wilhelm Frick, *Die deutsche Frau im nationalsozialistischen Staate*, Fr. Manns Päd. Magazin, no. 1400 (Langensalza: Hermann Beyer und Söhne [Beyer und Mann], 1934); Frobenius, *Frau*; Gottschewski, *Männerbund*; Lydia Gottschewski, "Von nordischem Frauentum," in *Frauenbuch*, ed. Semmelroth, pp. 42-48; Henrich Hansen, *Das Antlitz der deutschen Frau* (Dortmund: Westfalen-Verlag, n.d. [1934]); Rabe, *Frau*; Gertrud Scholtz-Klink, *Verpflichtung und Aufgabe der Frau im nationalsozialistischen Staat* (Berlin: Junker und Dünnhaupt, 1936); Ellen Semmelroth and Renate von Stieda, "Zum Geleit," in *Frauenbuch*, ed. Semmelroth, p. 5; Siber, *Frauenfrage*; L. Thimm, "Die oberste Aufgabe der nationalsozialistischen Frauenbewegung," *VB*, Sept. 4, 1926; Zühlke, *Frauenaufgabe*.

[54] Beyer, *Familie und Frau*. See also Elisabeth Bosch, *Vom Kämpfertum der Frau* (Stuttgart: Alemannen-Verlag, 1938); Frick, *Deutsche Frau*; Frobenius, *Frau*; Gottschewski, *Männerbund*.

ing the reconstruction of the family, pointed out that a woman's place was in the home, but in a real home, one complete with a father. Other writers felt that this goal was yet to be reached.

It is not at all clear what Beyer and the others meant by "returning the father to the home," but it is a rather odd suggestion in any case. What specific role the man could play in a home where the woman took full responsibility for raising and educating the children, as well as carrying out all of the domestic and cultural tasks, is not obvious. Perhaps this call for real fathers reflected uneasiness over the demands made on men by the military and civilian organizations of a party which glorified male comradeship, courage, and the "front experience." Or perhaps it was an expression of cultural despair, the longing for a preindustrial society in which the family worked as a unit in the home or on the farm.

If the man's role in the family was unclear, the woman's was not. A woman's first and foremost duty was, not surprisingly, to be a mother. A great number of books and pamphlets praised and glorified the German mother, often in an overly sentimental fashion, in an apparent attempt to create a Nazi mother cult or appeal to traditional sentiments on motherhood.[55] Woman's biological role took on heightened importance for the Nazis because of the declining German birthrate. The number of live births per 1,000 women of childbearing age had dropped from 128 in 1910 to 90 in

[55] See Ludwig Frühauf, *Deutsche Frauentum, deutsche Mütter* (Hamburg: Hanseatische Verlag, 1935); Magda Goebbels, *Die deutsche Mutter: Rede zum Muttertag, gehalten im Rundfunk am 14. Mai 1933* (Heilbronn: Eugen Salzer Verlag, 1933); Magda Goebbels, "Mutter sein . . . ," in *Unsere Zeit*, ed. Unverricht, pp. 155-159; *Mutter: Ein Buch der Liebe und der Heimat für Alle* (Berlin: Mutter und Volk Verlagsgesellschaft, 1934); NSDAP, Amt Schriftumspflege, *Ausstellung "Frau und Mutter—Lebensquell des Volkes"* (Berlin: Wilhelm Limpert Druck- und Verlagshaus, n.d. [193-]); Ingeborg Wessel, *Mütter von Morgen* (Munich: F. Bruckmann, 1936). Magazines and collections of essays (especially the *N.S. Frauenbuch*) are full of poems and stories about mothers.

33

1922 to 53 in 1932.[56] Concern for population growth was not unique to the Nazis, nor were their solutions original.[57] But the Nazi goal of an empire peopled by "Aryans" dictated the encouragement of childbearing and, necessarily, great concern for motherhood. Although the Nazis simultaneously raised the alarm over the declining birth rate and cried out for territory to feed Germany's overcrowded population, there was no logical inconsistency in these positions. For the Nazis, Germany's strength depended on a booming birth rate and enough land to support the increasing population.

The Nazis attributed the dangerous decline in the birth rate to the poisonous atmosphere of the liberal era. Feminism had convinced women that motherhood was beneath their dignity, so women had begun to use birth control and have abortions. Nazi writers sometimes blamed women for this dangerous state of affairs, and sometimes defended women against these charges.[58] An exchange in the *Völkischer Beobachter* illustrates this minor controversy. Frau Dr. Thimm accused women of lacking the desire for children, and an anonymous article sprang to the defense of women by claiming that they longed for children but were forced by the economic situation to prevent their births. This article pointed out that the problem was a social one that could only be solved by the creation of a National Socialist state in which unemployment and the housing shortage could be eliminated. Other writers felt that both women and men had lost their desire for offspring as a result of liberal and Marxist teachings, and that only a spiritual renewal could purge them of these poisonous influences and reawaken the desire for children.[59]

[56] *Statistisches Jahrbuch für das deutsche Reich*, 1934, p. 32.

[57] See Stephenson, *Women*, pp. 37-40.

[58] See the exchange in the *VB*: Frau Dr. L. Thimm, "Die oberste Aufgabe"; and "Nationalsozialistische Frauenarbeit," *VB*, Oct. 2, 1926. Other writers who dealt with this issue include: Baumgart, *Altgermanische Frau*; Frick, *Deutsche Frau*; Siber, *Frauenfrage*; and Zühlke, *Frauenaufgabe*.

[59] Frick, *Deutsche Frau*; Siber, *Frauenfrage*, pp. 19-21.

Nazi policy called on women to bear numerous children, but ideology granted women importance not only as the bearers, but also as the educators, of children. The mainstream writers realized that in order for the mother to exert her beneficial influence, her status would have to be upgraded. That National Socialism respected and valued a woman's work as mother and housewife was a frequent theme in the literature.[60] The celebration of Mother's Day, a holiday imported from the United States in 1923 and appropriated by the Nazis, the creation of the Medal of Honor for prolific German mothers, and the Frauenschaft-sponsored schools for teaching the skills of child care—all of this showed concern for honoring German mothers and recognizing motherhood as a skilled and valuable occupation.

Although a woman's role as mother was her most important one, Nazi ideology created new responsibilities for women within the home. Lydia Gottschewski, head of the Frauenschaft before Scholtz-Klink, wrote that a woman's work in protecting her family could not be confined to the house because her children went into the streets and brought outside influences into the home.[61] In accordance with her primary duties, a woman would have to concern herself with the world outside her home. But this was not a call to community service so much as a recognition of the wider

[60] See Beyer, *Ebenbürtigkeit*, pp. 9, 14; Else Boger-Eichler, *Von tapferen, heiteren und gelehrten Hausfrauen* (Munich: J. F. Lehmann, 1937); Frobenius, *Frau*, p. 53; Gottschewski, *Männerbund*, p. 57; Hansen, *Antlitz*; Rabe, *Frau*, pp. 7-8; Annemarie v. Scheele, "Von der Treue im Kleinen," in NSDAP, *Das deutsche Frauenbuch*, pp. 7-9. Hansen included in his text a letter from a Hamburg woman to Hitler expressing her joy over her four children and telling him how she had realized that motherhood was better than political success. These thoughts had come to the woman, she wrote, " . . . as you, my Führer, drove proudly by me, and I was a little envious because fate had not made me a man, had not made me an Adolf Hitler."

[61] "Die Nationalsozialistin in Volk und Staat," *N.S. Frauen-Warte*, 1, Sonderaufgabe (n.d. [1932?]), 2-4.

implications of a woman's duties within the family. Through these duties a woman could support racial, cultural, and economic policy on the national level.

Racial policy demanded the preservation of the purity of the "Aryan" race, and women served as the main targets of the propaganda in this area.[62] "Aryan" women had not only to marry and bear numerous children, they had to choose their partners carefully in order to keep the race pure. This involved understanding the importance of health, recognizing secondary racial characteristics, and inquiring into the ancestry of one's intended spouse. Women's racial consciousness would have to be raised in order for them to meet their racial responsibilities. Although the Nuremberg Laws of 1935 took care of the danger of intermarriage, Nazi ideology placed great importance on the woman as the major bulwark against racial degeneration. In spite of the emphasis on racial purity in the literature on and for women, there is little reflection of the kind of pornographic anti-Semitism so prevalent in *Mein Kampf* and Julius Streicher's newspaper, *Der Stürmer*. Although Hitler and Streicher were apparently obsessed with the image of the Jew as seducer of "Aryan" women, the women's organizations expressed little concern with the supposed threat of Jewish lust.[63]

[62] Woman's racial responsibility was a common theme. For examples, see Frobenius, *Frau*, pp. 38-52; Gottschewski, "Von nordischem Frauentum," in *Frauenbuch*, ed. Semmelroth, pp. 42-48; Prof. M. Staemmler, "Die Frauen und die Rassenpflege," in *Frauenbuch*, ed. Semmelroth, pp. 122-128; "Zehn Gebote für die Gattenwahl," *N.S. Frauen-Warte*, 3 (Nov. 1934), 295. Women were warned not only to be racially conscious in choosing a husband, but also in such mundane matters as purchasing clothes. The *VB* carried several articles on the danger of Jewish fashion. See Walter Bohe, "Die Aufgaben der Frauenwelt in der NSDAP," *VB*, June 18, 1927; Edith Gräfin Salburg, "Die Entsittlichung der Frau durch die jüdische Mode," *VB*, June 18, 1927; Johanna Schulze-Langendorff, "Mode und Zeitgeist," *VB*, March 11/12, 1928; Frau L. Schünemann, "Deutsche Kleidung für die deutsche Frau!" *VB*, July 9, 1927.

[63] An unsigned article in the *VB* in 1927 complained that the wom-

Cultural policy called on women to guard German culture against foreign influence and to transmit it lovingly to their children.[64] The Nazis hoped to transform the home as a means of restoring German life to its pristine state. There is an echo in this hope of the convictions of modern architects in the Weimar Republic who believed that the house as "living machine" could transform the lives of its inhabitants.[65] In the Nazi case, the woman was supposed to cook German meals, supply the house with German furnishings, sing German songs, wear German clothes, decorate with German art—and thus instill in her children a love for German culture, customs, and morality.

In the area of economic policy, the housewife carried responsibility for supporting the national striving for self-sufficiency.[66] Nazi economic policy favored an autarchic

---

en's organizations were oblivious to the danger of Jewish sexuality. See "Wo bleiben die Frauenvereine?" *VB*, Feb. 27/28, 1927.

[64] See, for example, Beyer, *Ebenbürtigkeit*, pp. 4-7; Wera Bockemühl, "Die Gestalterin des Hauses," in *Frauenbuch*, ed. Semmelroth, pp. 242-249; Frobenius, *Frau*, pp. 67-86; Agnes Gerlach, "Wie kleide ich mich deutsch, geschmackvoll und zweckmässig?" in *Frauenbuch*, ed. Semmelroth, pp. 230-235; Hans Hickmann, "Die deutsche Hausmusik," in *Frauenbuch*, ed. Semmelroth, pp. 194-200; Martha Unger, "Deutsche Frauen in der Welt," in *Frauenbuch*, ed. Semmelroth, pp. 37-40; Josef Magnus Wehner, "Die kulturelle Sendung der deutschen Frau," in *Frauenbuch*, ed. Semmelroth, pp. 166-171.

[65] See Barbara Miller Lane, *Architecture and Politics in Germany, 1918-1945* (Cambridge: Harvard University Press, 1968).

[66] See Ruth Graf, "Neuorientierung in der Wirtschaftsfürsorge," *SP*, 45 (April 1936), 402-408; F. Hamm, "Augen auf, deutsche Frau!" *VB*, Dec. 28, 1931; Dr. Schlick, "Hauswirtschaftliche Schulung—ein Gebot der Stunde," *SP*, 45 (Jan. 1936), 17-20; Scholtz-Klink, *Einsatz*; Scholtz-Klink, *Verpflichtung*; Sofia Rabe, "Die Frau als Käuferin," in *Unsere Zeit*, ed. Unverricht, pp. 429-437; Else Vorwerck, *Die Hausfrau im Dienst der Volkswirtschaft*, Grundlagen, Aufbau und Wirtschaftsordnung des nationalsozialistischen Staates, vol. 3 (Berlin: Industrieverlag Spaeth und Linde, n.d. [1937]); Else Vorwerck, "Hausfrau und Nation," in *Unsere Zeit*, ed. Unverricht, pp. 451-459; Else Vorwerck, "Wirtschaftliche Alltagspflichten der deutschen Frau

state as the answer to the problems of foreign exchange shortage, unfavorable balance of trade, and possible blockade in case of war. Germany had to buy from abroad only what was absolutely essential and not available in Germany, and German science had to search for substitutes for even these materials. The housewife, as the major consumer, played an important part in this economic plan. Women could serve the nation by purchasing only goods produced in Germany, boycotting Jewish stores, supporting the *Mittelstand* by shopping in small stores rather than department stores, and buying carefully in order to raise the standard of living. As a side result of the new tasks of the German housewife, she would win respect because of the intelligence and ability required of her. Gertrud Scholtz-Klink remarked in a speech in 1937: "Though our weapon in this area [the battle for self-sufficiency] is only the ladle, its impact will be no less than that of other weapons."[67]

Nazi ideology proclaimed the reconstruction of the family and the significance of a woman's role as mother, housewife, guardian of racial purity, transmitter of German culture, and supporter of national economic policy. But in practice, Nazi policy tended to pull the family apart and minimize the importance of the woman. The demands of population policy eventually proved detrimental to the family, since they led to a liberalization of the divorce law and the acceptance or encouragement of illegitimate children.[68] The regimentation of men, women, and children into separate organizations that demanded a large expenditure of time also militated

---

beim Einkauf und Verbrauch," in *Frauenbuch*, ed. Semmelroth, pp. 89-97.

[67] Scholtz-Klink, *Einsatz*, p. 7.

[68] *Soziale Praxis*, a journal of social policy, cautiously supported the encouragement of childbearing by single women. See Hans Bernsee, "Das Problem der ledigen Mutter und die deutsche Volksgemeinschaft," *SP*, 46 (May 1937), 579-582; and an untitled anonymous article in *SP*, 46 (June 1937), 753-754. See Bleuel, *Sex and Society*, pp. 154-156; and Stephenson, *Women*, 41-44, 63-71.

against family life. The glorification of the *Männerbund* and male comradeship conflicted with the stated desire to make men into good fathers. The idea of returning the father to the home had no place in a society which taught its boys, as the Labor Service did, to "die laughing." In fact, the father had little role to play in a family where the educational, cultural, and economic tasks fell to the woman. He remained, in theory, the patriarch, but this position of authority conflicted with the importance granted to the woman. The authoritarian state took from the family many of its functions and challenged its integrity by encouraging children to report any treasonous sentiments expressed by their parents. In spite of the regime's expressed desire to strengthen the family, the requirements of an authoritarian state led to an attack on the family.[69]

Although Nazi policy tended to threaten the position of the family as the "basic cell" of the state, the ideology proclaimed the reconstruction of the family and the reinstatement of the woman as housewife and mother. But the employed woman was by no means forgotten or rejected. Too often the Nazi emphasis on the woman as wife and mother has been mistaken for a blanket condemnation of the employed woman. Nazi policy varied with the economic situation, but even during the Depression the Nazis did not intend to remove all women from employment. Even in the

[69] See Lewis A. Coser, "The Case of the Soviet Family," in *The Family: Its Structure and Functions*, ed. Rose Laub Coser (N.Y.: St. Martin's Press, 1964), pp. 526-545; Alfred Meusel, "National Socialism and the Family," *Sociological Review*, 28 (Apr., Oct. 1936), 166-186, 389-411; and Philip E. Slater, "Social Change and the Democratic Family," in *The Temporary Society*, ed. Warren G. Bennis and Philip E. Slater (N.Y.: Harper and Row, 1968), pp. 20-52. Slater argued that any authority intervening between parent and child has a democratizing impact on the family, regardless of intent. The paradox of an authoritarian regime attempting to transform society is that the regime must teach the child to reject parental auhority in order to bring about change, but if it does this it has destroyed the basis of political authoritarianism.

worst times, Nazi writers argued that some women were forced to work by economic necessity and that some jobs were best handled by women. As a writer in a social policy journal put it, "the employed woman cannot be ignored in the economic life of the great industrial countries."[70]

The principle of sacrifice for the state justified discrimination against employed women in the first years of the Nazi regime as well as the encouragement of employment after 1936. "*Gemeinnutz vor Eigennutz*" meant that women would leave or enter the labor force as the economy demanded. As Paula Siber stated in an address in 1933: "If ever the right of woman to employment will be recognized, National Socialism will recognize it. Only because of the present severe emergency has that right in many cases been taken from her. For if the rights of the people come before the rights of the individual, then the question of providing for the fathers of families must be urgently considered. In recognition of this law of the life of our people, the present generation of women must make sacrifices."[71]

The question of the employment of women received a great deal of attention in Nazi literature.[72] Some writers

[70] *SP*, 44 (Jan. 1935), 49.

[71] *SP*, 42 (Dec. 1933), 1516. See also Kurt Ammon, "Zur Frage des Doppelverdienertums," *SP*, 42 (Sept. 1933), 1139-41; *SP*, 46 (Aug. 1937), 1021-30; and " 'Ersatz' von Männerarbeit durch Frauenarbeit?" *SP*, 47 (Sept. 1938), 1094-95.

[72] See Baumgart, *Altgermanische Frau*; Edith Benz, *Frauenarbeit, Bildung und Nation: Schriftenreihe zur nationalpolitischen Erziehung*, no. 10 (Leipzig: Eichblatt-Verlag [Max Zedler], 1934); Deutsche Arbeitsfront, Frauenamt, *Tagewerk und Feierabend der schaffenden deutschen Frau* (Leipzig/Berlin: Verlag Otto Beyer, 1936); Gertrud Ehrle, *Leben spricht zu Leben: Wirklichkeitsbilder aus dem Alltag der Frau*, 3rd ed. (Freiburg i. B.: Herder, 1941); Hedwig Förster, "Die Aufgaben der Frau im Dritten Reich," in *Unsere Zeit*, ed. Unverricht, pp. 147-155; Frick, *Deutsche Frau*; Hilde Fries, "Aussichten der Frau in den akademischen Berufen," in *Unsere Zeit*, ed. Unverricht, pp. 403-404; Frobenius, *Frau*, pp. 87-100; Gottschewski, *Männerbund*, pp. 55-69; F. Hamm, "Frauenberuf und Nationalsozialismus," *VB*, Feb. 24, 1932; Suse Harms, *Die deutschen Frauenberufe* (Berlin:

espoused the view that no women would work outside the home in an ideal society, but this extreme view was rare.[73] The vast majority of the mainstream Nazi authors believed that the best situation for women was as full-time housewife and mother, but they recognized that economic necessity and the surplus of women over men made this an impossible dream for many women. Furthermore, there were certain jobs that were best performed by women. The Nazi concept of separate spheres for men and women meant that girls should be taught by women teachers, sick women treated by women doctors, and family legal problems handled by women lawyers.[74] Aside from the professions, there were many other areas in which women's special talents were needed. Thus, while the employment of married women was generally considered harmful to the family and national population policy, Nazi writers recognized that there were many women who could never marry and would have to

Junker und Dünnhaupt Verlag 1939); Johann von Leers, "Die berufstätige Frau," *Das Deutsche Mädel*, n.d. [Feb. 1935?], pp. 8-9; "Mädel am Werk," *Das Deutsche Mädel*, n.d. [June 1936?], pp. 14-15; *N.S. Frauen-Warte*, 3 (Jan. 1935), 4 (Nov. 1935), 5 (March 1937); Naujoks, *Wandlung*; Richard Peikow, *Die soziale und wirtschaftliche Stellung der deutschen Frau in der Gegenwart*, Ph. D. diss., Berlin, 1937 (Berlin-Charlottenburg: K. v. R. Hoffmann, 1937); Rabe, *Frau*; Alice Rilke, "Die erwerbstätige Frau im Dritten Reich," in *Frauenbuch*, ed. Semmelroth, pp. 64-69; Toni Saring, "Berufsbilder der weiblichen Jugend," in *Unsere Zeit*, ed. Unverricht, pp. 390-400; Siber, *Frauenfrage*; Aenne Sprengel, "Die Bauersfrau als Berufstätige in der Landwirtschaft," in *Frauenbuch*, ed. Semmelroth, pp. 98-105; Hildegard Villnov, "Die Frau in der sozialen Arbeit," in *Frauenbuch*, ed. Semmelroth, pp. 70-73.

[73] See Benz, *Frauenarbeit*, p. 10; and Rabe, *Frau*, pp. 9-12. According to Rabe, "The employment of women means urbanization, urbanization means the degeneration of woman, and therefore the decline of the people" (p. 11).

[74] See McIntyre, "Women and the Professions"; and Stephenson, *Women*, pp. 147-184. McIntyre/Stephenson argued that the concept of separate spheres was so important that, on balance, women professionals profited from Nazi policies.

support themselves. For these women, and temporarily for married women whose husbands earned too little to support their families, work consistent with woman's nature provided suitable employment.

"Womanly work," the official term for employment considered to accord with woman's nature or essence, included agricultural labor, social work, domestic service, nursing, education, and any profession concerned with women or children. In such jobs, unmarried women could employ their "spiritual maternity" and all women could be mothers, metaphorically at least.[75] The concept of "womanly work," accepted in the earliest Nazi writings, did not change in response to economic conditions as policy did. As the need for women in areas outside the realm of "womanly work" increased, Nazi ideology labelled such employment a woman's sacrifice for her people.

The ideal might be as Wilhelm Frick, Nazi Minister of the Interior, stated in his book on women in the National Socialist state: "The mother must be able to devote herself entirely to her children and family, the wife to her husband, and the unmarried girl must be assigned to those occupations which correspond to her feminine essence."[76] But as the economy developed ever greater needs for labor, the ideology adapted without changing the concept of "womanly work."

National Socialist ideology denounced individualism and the concept of employment for reasons of personal fulfillment for both women and men, but at least one Nazi writer defended women who practiced professions because of an inner "calling."[77] Alice Rilke argued, in the official "women's book" of the Frauenschaft, that these women had the right

[75] This phrase, according to Baumgart, originated with Henrietta Schrader-Breymann in the mid-nineteenth century and was picked up by Siber. It appears also in Gottschewski, *Männerbund*; and Naujoks, *Wandlung*.

[76] Frick, *Deutsche Frau*, p. 10.

[77] Rilke, "Erwerbstätige Frau," in *Frauenbuch*, ed. Semmelroth.

to use their God-given talents for the good of the nation. This argument came dangerously close to feminist reasoning, and in fact Rilke, in a manner reminiscent of the Nazi feminists, justified her argument in terms of the National Socialist achievement principle. An official publication of the Women's Office of the German Labor Front, while insisting that most women would gladly exchange their jobs for husbands if they could, recognized that some women entered a profession because of natural talent and inclination:

> In contrast to those women who are willing to retire from their work or profession to assume the new duties of marriage, these do not consider their profession as something temporary but as the highest purpose of their lives. It would be a complete misunderstanding of the national socialist philosophy of life to fear that an arbitrary limit would be imposed upon those women who extend their influence beyond the sphere of house and family. . . . They utilize the feminine and maternal forces within them in the interest of the whole of their nation. Through them the 'feminine principle' operates and the will to serve their people is as unalterably rooted in their consciousness as in that of the German mothers.[78]

By simplifying Nazi attitudes toward women's role in the family and employment, most historians and contemporary critics of the regime have failed to understand women's support of the party. But these historians have overlooked the complexity of Nazi ideology and failed to distinguish the prominent misogynist view from the mainstream view. They have failed to recognize that perhaps the Nazi concept appealed to a great number of women because it accorded

[78] DAF, Frauenamt, *Tagewerk*, p. 14. This somewhat unusual recognition of a woman's commitment to her profession may be due to the fact that this publication was intended as propaganda in foreign countries, since it appeared with text in German, English, French, and Italian. This quotation is from the English text.

them a prominent place in society by virtue of the roles which they themselves considered their primary ones.[79]

Contemporary critics of National Socialism sometimes recognized this aspect of Nazi appeal.[80] As Ruth Woodsmall reported in 1935: "For the great majority [of German women] the present doctrine and practice of narrowing woman's sphere of action means little change and certainly no sacrifice, but rather the glorification of the role to which they have always been committed."[81] Of course, this was only true for upper or middle-class housewives. Working class women may have detested their jobs, but they could not quit, and the Nazi glorification of woman as mother and housewife could do little for them. Even so, Gertrud Scholtz-Klink recognized this problem and told women, in her 1935 Party Day speech, that "the decisive thing is that the woman at the machine will be made to feel that she, in her position, has also to represent her nation, like all other women."[82] Likewise, professional women who enjoyed their careers suffered if they lost their jobs in the early years of the Third Reich. But there is nothing surprising about the much remarked upon level of support for National Socialism from middle-class conservative women.

Although Nazi ideology on women may have appealed to those who yearned for a mythical past in which women de-

[79] Schoenbaum, *Hitler's Social Revolution*, argued that the labor shortage created a new status of relative if unconventional equality for women, but he did not deal with women's status as mother and housewife. Renate Bridenthal, "Beyond *Kinder, Küche, Kirche*," suggested that modernization was a retrogressive, constricting force for women during the Weimar Republic, leading many to respond to the appeal of a romanticized past of children, kitchen, church. Koonz, "Nazi Women," developed this theme fully.

[80] See Hamilton, "Woman's Place," p. 28; Hoegner, *Frau*, pp. 11-12; Thomas, *Women*, p. 68; Woodsmall, "Women," p. 301.

[81] Woodsmall, "Women," p. 301.

[82] Gertrud Scholtz-Klink, "To the Women of Germany," address delivered to the Women's Congress, Reich Party Congress, Nuremberg, 1935, mimeographed copy in the Hoover Institution Library, pp. 6-7.

voted themselves wholeheartedly to their children and their homes, the Nazi image of the ideal woman was not a simple reconstruction of the Victorian ideal. In a manner reminiscent of the youth movement of the 1920's, the ideal Nazi woman was not frail and helpless, but strong, vigorous, athletic, able to do hard physical work if her labor were needed by the state. The numerous collections of photographs of women, many used as propaganda for the Labor Service, show women working in the fields, doing calisthenics, and practicing trades, as well as caring for children, cooking, and working at other more typical "womanly" tasks.[83] One such book commented: "The modern girl is an athlete. If there were no other difference from the girls of earlier eras, this would certainly be noticeable. The girls of our era are healthy and limber, tanned in the sun and wind."[84] Another work on women pointed out that young women were taller

[83] See Clementine zu Castell-Rüdenhausen, *Glaube und Schönheit: Ein Bildbuch von dem 17-21 jährigen Mädeln* (Munich: Zentralverlag der NSDAP, n.d. [1940]); DAF, Frauenamt, *Tagewerk*; Gustav von Estorff, *Dass die Arbeit Freude werde! Ein Bildbericht von den Arbeitsmaiden* (Berlin: Zeitgeschichte-Verlag Wilhelm Andermann, 1938); Hansen, *Antlitz*; Seraphine Jaeger, *BDM in Bamberg* (Bayreuth: Bauverlag Bayerische Ostmark, 1936); Freya Overweg, *Erzählung und Bilder aus dem Leben im Reichsarbeitsdienst für die weibliche Jugend* (Wolfenbüttel: G. Kallmeyer, 1938); Gertrud Zypries, *Das Gesicht des Arbeitsdienst für die weibliche Jugend* (Munich: Zentralverlag der NSDAP, n.d.). The image of women as strong and athletic is most apparent in publications of the Labor Service and the BDM. The contrast between the *N.S. Frauen-Warte*, the magazine of the Frauenschaft, and *Das Deutsche Mädel*, the journal of the BDM, especially in the early years, is striking. Although the *Frauen-Warte* carried political propaganda, it was to a large extent a "women's magazine" on the American model, with patterns for sewing, recipes, fashion, and excerpts from novels. *Das Deutsche Mädel*, on the other hand, projected an image of the strong, healthy, capable, active German woman. It emphasized health, sports, service, and education. A series on famous women included biographies of a doctor, a champion discus thrower, a pilot, and a poet.

[84] Castell-Rüdenhausen, *Glaube*, p. 38.

than their mothers, "hardened by sport, muscular and weathered," and commented that this made laughable the reproach that National Socialism made women into "baby machines."[85] Ruth Woodsmall commented on this image of women on the occasion of a visit to a Women's Labor Service camp: "If you follow the girls through their day's program, beginning at five A.M. with a brisk half hour of calisthenics and continuing through a steady routine of hard manual farm labor of all kinds, you will carry away an impression that this is no Mid-Victorian ideal of a woman's sheltered life in the home and that a generation of young Amazons is being trained for the physically fit future motherhood of Germany."[86]

Certainly one reason for the emphasis on health and exercise was concern for childbearing, and the new standards of physical beauty prized broad-hipped women, unencumbered by corsets, who could easily bear children. But the concept of individual sacrifice for the good of the people entailed the possibility of hard work, even "unwomanly" work. And of course, not all "womanly work" was clean and light. The Nazi glorification of the peasantry and the soil, best represented by Minister of Agriculture R. Walther Darré's "blood and soil" ideology, meant that the peasant woman who labored in the fields, cared for the garden and poultry, cooked the meals, cleaned the house, and bore numerous strong healthy children, was a prime example of the Nazi ideal.[87]

[85] Frobenius, *Frau*, p. 57.

[86] Woodsmall, "Women," p. 301.

[87] Works on the peasant woman include: Brigitte von Arnim, "Die Aufgaben der deutschen Landfrau," in *Unsere Zeit*, ed. Unverricht, pp. 425-428; Marie Berta Freiin von Brand, et al., *Die Frau in der deutschen Landwirtschaft, Deutsche Agrarpolitik*, ed. M. Sering and C. von Dietze, vol. 3 (Berlin: Verlag Franz Vahlen, 1939); R. Walther Darré, *Das Bauerntum als Lebensquell der nordischen Rasse*, 2nd ed. (Munich: J. F. Lehmann, 1933); R. Walther Darré, *Neuadel aus Blut und Boden* (Munich: J. F. Lehmann, 1930); Anne Marie Koeppen, "Die bäuerliche Frau in ihrer kulturellen Aufgabe," in *Frauenbuch*, ed. Semmelroth, pp. 106-112; Koeppen, *Landfrauen-*

The glorification of the peasant woman in an industrialized economy attests to the conflicts of a modernizing society, conflicts which Nazi ideology successfully exploited. The idealization of the peasant woman was grounded in the past, while the emphasis on the modern athletic woman looked to the future. The confusion between physical strength and high status is typical of the Nazis, yet the emphasis on physical prowess is important in understanding the double appeal of Nazi ideology.

The Bund deutscher Mädel [League of German Girls], the female section of the Hitler Youth, was especially concerned with creating a new image of the German woman. Rejecting the images of the school girl, the flapper, the dutiful daughter, and the career woman, one writer turned to the heroic woman in wartime, the German mother who could take on a man's work in an emergency, who could write a courageous letter to her husband at the front without knowing from where her next meal would come.[88]

The Women's Labor Service and the BDM propagated an image which held out the promise of a vigorous and exciting life to enthusiastic and idealistic young women committed to National Socialism. But the ideal embraced much that was traditional. The young athlete or agricultural worker was, after all, primarily a future mother. This basic fact united the image of the youthful German woman with that of the older married woman.

Nazi ideology on women was, like Nazi ideology in general, a strange mixture of traditional conservative ideas, vague longings for a mythical past, and acceptance of the needs of a modern economy. The result of the blending of

---

buch; Sprengel, "Bauersfrau," in *Frauenbuch*, ed. Semmelroth, pp. 98-105.

[88] Erna Bohlmann, "Ziele und Weg des BDM," in *Frauenbuch*, ed. Semmelroth, pp. 30-36. Margarete Mallmann, "Für die politische Erziehung," *Das Deutsche Mädel*, n.d. [Jan. 1935?], pp. 2-3 also pointed to the women of the First World War as a model for German women.

1. The ideal Nazi woman. From *Deutsches Frauenschaffen: Jahrbuch der Reichsfrauenführung*, 1937

ideas and the controversy among Nazi theorists was the creation of an ideal that reflected the conflicts and confusion confronting a society in the process of modernization.

The young woman in the BDM or Labor Service contributed her energies to the betterment of the community, while her mother served the nation as the cornerstone of the family, the "mother of the *Volk*." Either way, the ideal Nazi woman would serve her people and her country, making whatever sacrifices were demanded of her.

What Nazi ideology proclaimed was not necessarily so. But public images of women can exert a powerful appeal, and the mainstream Nazi view had the potential to attract two very different groups: conservative and traditional women who sought confirmation of their worth as wives and mothers in a world in which feminism challenged traditional sex roles, and younger restless women, also from conservative and nationalist backgrounds, who longed for an active role and rejected the staid bourgeois life of the "older generation."[89] It is not difficult to understand how Nazism might

[89] Some insight into the appeal of Nazism for women can be gained from a reading of the autobiographies of women party members who had joined or been sympathetic to the movement before 1933. Theodore Abel, a political scientist, organized an essay contest in Germany in 1934, offering prize money for the most detailed and trustworthy accounts of the personal lives of people who had joined the NSDAP, or were sympathetic to it, before January 1, 1933. Of 683 manuscripts collected, 48 were by women. Over a hundred manuscripts have been lost, but the remainder are housed in the Hoover Institution Archives. Abel wrote a book based on the collection, *Why Hitler Came Into Power* (N.Y.: Prentice-Hall, 1938), but he excluded the women's contributions, noting that he would consider them in a separate article, which he never wrote. Peter Merkl, *Political Violence Under the Swastika: 581 Early Nazis* (Princeton: Princeton University Press, 1975), examined all of the autobiographies, including those of the women, using quantitative methods. He concluded generally that the women's motives in joining the party were often personal or derived from social predicaments. Claudia Koonz made use of the Abel collection in her article, concluding that Nazi women were generally from conservative and religious backgrounds and longed for a society in which traditional female roles would be accorded higher status. My reading of the autobiographies confirmed this, and suggested that women played a fairly active role in the early party.

An extremely interesting memoir, which attempted to explain the appeal of Nazism for a young woman, is Melita Maschmann, *Account Rendered: A Dossier on my Former Self*, trans. Geoffrey Strachan (London: Abelard-Schuman, 1964). Maschmann was a

have appealed to such women. Whether it delivered or not, Nazi ideology promised women security and meaning in what was, from a conservative and nationalist point of view, a world gone mad.

---

high-level BDM official and head of a Labor Service camp in the East. She recounted how she, as the child of a nationalist and anti-Semitic family, rejected her parents' bourgeois life style and found meaning in her every act through her work with the party.

· 3 ·

"Occupation: Housewife": The Image of Women in the United States

I've been a home woman and I've been a career woman. And I tell you quite frankly I was never so worth while in my life as when I was washing diapers for three children all at the same time and cursing my fate.

Elizabeth Cook, 1931

At a meeting of magazine editors and writers in the post-Second World War United States, Betty Friedan heard a group of men discuss the limited nature of women's interests and commented in *The Feminine Mystique*: "As I listened to them, a German phrase echoed in my mind—'*Kinder, Kuche* [sic], *Kirche*,' the slogan by which the Nazis decreed that women must once again be confined to their biological role. But this was not Nazi Germany. This was America."[1]

Friedan was not the first, nor the last, to draw attention to the parallels between the emphasis in Nazi ideology on women's childbearing role and the traditional American emphasis on woman as wife and mother. As an examination of the image of women in Nazi ideology shows, Nazi women were not wholly confined to their biological role. Ironically, the public image of women in the United States in the period before the outbreak of the Second World War was actually more limited than the Nazi image. Reflecting the mood of peace and unconcern for world affairs that characterized the United States in this period, the New Woman who emerged from popular commentary was a traditional wife and mother. Like the mainstream Nazi image of women, the American

[1] Betty Friedan, *The Feminine Mystique* (N.Y.: Dell, 1963), p. 32.

51

image was characterized by a high degree of continuity throughout the interwar period. In spite of the excitement over the New Woman who embodied a revolution in manners and morals in the decade of prosperity, and despite the fear of unemployment that accompanied the Depression, the literature relentlessly propagated an image of the American woman as wife and mother.

A systematic comparison between Nazi ideology and American conceptions of women is not possible. First of all, although the Nazi image built on traditional German views, Nazi ideology represented a particular political and social viewpoint. German views as a whole would be more directly comparable to American ones, but the subject here is the use of Nazi and American images of women in mobilization propaganda during the war. Second, the Nazi literature on women is a body of official material, written and published by the Nazis, and no equivalent body of material exists to give an "official" American view of women. Finally, Nazi writers assumed that the coming to power of a National Socialist government would mean or meant that an entirely new society could be created. They designed blueprints for this new society, including suggestions for the role of women. No such opportunity existed in the United States.

Nevertheless, it is possible to draw some parallels between the Nazi and the American images of women. American writers, like the Nazis, shared a common cultural tradition despite their diversity of opinions. It is possible to eliminate the extremes and concentrate on the dominant views of American women as expressed publicly to wide audiences. Few books concerned with the role of women appeared in the interwar period, so the most important forum for discussion of the issues was the periodical literature. This chapter is based primarily on a sample of articles, listed in the *Reader's Guide to Periodical Literature* for the years 1918 to 1941, from a variety of large circulation periodicals.[2]

[2] My conclusions, based on this sample, are supported by William

The emerging images of women are primarily white, middle-class views, expressions of the group that largely determines the values of American society. For, as Robert Smuts pointed out in his *Women and Work in America*, "America has long been known as a nation where most families consider themselves middle class, and pattern their behavior accordingly, as far as their resources permit."[3] Margaret Mead expressed the same sentiment in a more picturesque way: "People in America of course live in all sorts of fashions, because they are foreigners, or unlucky, or depraved, or without ambition; people live like that, but *Americans* live in white detached houses with green shutters. Rigidly, blindly, the dream takes precedence."[4]

The 1920's saw the advent of the so-called New Woman in the United States. Lauded or condemned, she has come down in history as a young woman who bobbed her hair, displayed her knees, smoked, drank, danced, and petted. The flapper was the essence of the revolution in manners and morals. According to the standard textbook account, the

---

H. Chafe's book, *The American Woman: Her Changing Social, Economic, and Political Role, 1920-1970* (N.Y.: Oxford University Press, 1972). Although I did not make use of the fiction of the period, I found that two unpublished studies of fiction support my conclusions on American images of women. See Donald R. Makosky, "The Portrayal of Women in Wide-Circulation Magazine Short Stories, 1905-1955," Ph.D. diss., University of Pennsylvania, 1966; and B. June West, "Attitudes Toward American Women as Reflected in American Literature Between the Two World Wars," Ph.D. diss., University of Denver, 1954. Historians writing about women in the interwar period have made good use of literature. See Chafe, *American Woman*, and Peter G. Filene, *Him/Her/Self: Sex Roles in Modern America* (N.Y.: Harcourt Brace Jovanovich, 1974). For pictorial support of my thesis that continuity is the major characteristic of the public image of women, see Carol Wald, *Myth America: Picturing Women 1865-1945*, text by Judith Papachristou (N.Y.: Random House, 1975).

[3] (1959; reprint ed., N.Y.: Schocken Books, 1971), p. 32.

[4] *Male and Female: A Study of the Sexes in a Changing World* (N.Y.: William Morrow, 1949, 1967), p. 258.

American woman won the vote and then turned to the pursuit of pleasure. The flapper, though obviously a simplistic image, is one of the most astonishingly tenacious in American history.[5]

In the standard image, the New Woman's demand for freedom in manners and morals seemed shocking, but even more basic was her new economic independence. Although F. Scott Fitzgerald's flappers seemed never to stop dancing, the standard account portrayed them working a full work week as typists or salesgirls. Women's new employment opportunities, and the supposed dramatic increase in the number of employed women, were thought to be responsible for the new morals.

In reality, the New Woman was not such a new phenome-

[5] Arthur Link's characterization of the New Woman is typical of the textbook image, and worth quoting at length: "The outward signs of the so-called emancipation were even more frightening to persons who believed in the old way of life. As the barriers fell on all sides women began smoking cigarettes and, what seemed worse to traditionalists, demanded and asserted the right to drink with men. As women went to work in larger numbers they began to discard historic badges of femininity and, ironically, sought to make themselves over in the image of man. The first casualty of feminine independence was the traditional dress that covered the neck and arms and assiduously hid the ankles from masculine view. The average skirt was about six inches from the ground in 1919. From this time on the ascent was spectacular, until the skirt had reached the knees or even above by 1927. At the same time women discarded their corsets and de-emphasized the upper reaches of their anatomy, usually with fearful results. Finally, to complete the defeminization, women sheared their tresses and wore their hair straight and short. But there was one curious exception to this trend. The shorter skirts and hair became the more women used cosmetics—lipstick, rouge, and mascara. It seemed as if the face had became the last refuge of femininity." (*American Epoch: A History of the United States Since the 1890's*, vol. 2 [N.Y.: Alfred Knopf, 1967], pp. 274-275).

For an excellent review of the historiography of the New Woman from the 1920's to the present, see Estelle B. Freedman, "The New Woman: Changing Views of Women in the 1920's," *Journal of American History*, 61 (Sept. 1974), 372-393.

non. William Chafe has argued that the conception of the 1920's as a period of economic emancipation for women is a myth.[6] He has shown that the upsurge in the employment of women came in the first decade of the twentieth century and that there was little change in the 1920's, although there was a shift into clerical work and an increase in the proportion of older and married women in the labor force. Changes in employment patterns of women during the First World War fed the myth but did not affect the long-term trend.

Interestingly, this myth of the economic emancipation of women in the twenties had its counterpart in Germany. Contemporary commentators and historians believed that with the end of the war and the granting of suffrage, women in the Weimar Republic were entering a golden age of equality. Renate Bridenthal has destroyed this myth for Germany, as Chafe did for the United States, in her article on women in the labor force in the Weimar Republic.[7] In both countries women had been entering the labor force at a steady rate, but the public eye only focused on them in the 1920's, proclaiming that a revolution had occurred.

The war had something to do with this myth in both countries. German and American women in wartime had taken over many jobs that previously had been reserved for men, and although this was a brief and temporary phenomenon, it opened the eyes of the public to the growing group of women who worked outside the home. As with the Second World War, there seemed to be a general feeling at the time that the war had changed the status of American women, primarily because so many were employed.[8]

[6] Chafe, *American Woman*, pp. 48-65.

[7] Renate Bridenthal, "Beyond *Kinder, Küche, Kirche*: Weimar Women at Work," *Central European History*, 6 (June 1973), 148-166. See also Renate Bridenthal and Claudia Koonz, "Beyond *Kinder, Küche, Kirche*: Weimar Women in Politics and Work," in *Liberating Women's History*, ed. Berenice A. Carroll (Urbana: University of Illinois Press, 1976), pp. 301-329.

[8] See, for example, Emily Newell Blair, "Where Are We Women Going?" *Ladies' Home Journal (LHJ)*, 36 (March 1919), 37; W. L.

But women had not, except briefly during the war, made breakthroughs into new areas of employment, and their public image, cigarettes notwithstanding, continued to present them as wives and mothers. The New Woman was widely discussed in the periodical literature.[9] Women had just won the right to vote, but the New Woman was not political. She was supposed to be economically independent, yet she seemed not to work. Although a great many writers com-

George, "Women in the New World: Her New Job: Earning Her Own Living," *Good Housekeeping (GH)*, 76 (Jan. 1923), 14-15; William Howard Taft, "As I See the Future of Women," *LHJ*, 36 (March 1919), 27. Blair, while pointing out that the war was affecting women's status, recognized that only five percent of the women war workers had never worked before the war, adding that most had shifted from domestic work or work in textile factories to the higher paying munitions factory jobs.

[9] See "And We Learned About Women From Them," *Woman's Home Companion (WHC)*, 47 (March 1920), 9; Chester T. Crowell, "Sisters Under Their Skins?" *Independent*, 104 (Dec. 1920), 390-391; Will Durant, "Modern Woman: Philosophers Grow Dizzy as She Passes By," *Century*, 113 (Feb. 1927), 418-429; W. L. George, "Is There a Change in Morals?" *GH*, 76 (Feb. 1923), 78; Charlotte Perkins Gilman, "The New Generation of Women," *Current History*, 18 (Aug. 1923), 731-737; "Hopeless Wails Against the 'New Woman,'" *Literary Digest*, 84 (Jan. 17, 1925), 49-50; Leta S. Hollingsworth, "The New Woman in the Making," *Current History*, 27 (Oct. 1927), 15-20; Downing Jacobs, "A New Type of Beauty: American," *Delineator*, 96 (Feb. 1920), 16-17; Edward S. Martin, "New Freedom and the Girls," *Harper's*, 153 (Aug. 1926), 389-392; "A Mere Man Asks, 'How Should I Like to Be a Woman?'" *Literary Digest*, 73 (May 20, 1922), 59-62; "Middle-Class Women," *Nation*, 127 (July 1928), 55; George Jean Nathan, "Once There Was a Princess," *American Mercury*, 19 (Feb. 1930), 242; William Lyon Phelps, "Women," *LHJ*, 42 (Nov. 1925), 16; Berta Ruck, "Why I Should Like My Boy to Marry an American Girl—and Why I Shouldn't," *LHJ*, 37 (April 1920), 41; Helen Welshimer, "Does Miss Modern Surpass Her Sister of Long Ago?" *Independent Woman*, 13 (Jan. 1934), 6-7; Albert Edward Wiggam, "New Styles in American Beauty: Brains and Pulchritude Now Go Together," *World's Work*, 56 (Oct. 1928), 648-658; W. E. Woodward, "Why I Would Like to be a Woman," *Pictorial Review*, 31 (June 1930), 19.

mented on her new habit of smoking and drinking in public, and on her bobbed hair and short dresses, the New Woman who emerged from the contemporary reports was not simply the flapper of literary and historical fame. She was an ideal woman, beautiful, well-dressed, intelligent, educated, informed, fun-loving, progressive, independent, competent, dominating, and bold. To non-Americans, she seemed extraordinarily independent and assured, often superior to the American man because she had the leisure to keep informed while he slaved away at an office to support her. In fact, many Americans, as well as Europeans, felt that American women dominated their husbands.[10] The image of the New Woman is typified by a Norman Rockwell *Saturday Evening Post* cover from 1925 showing a woman, her hair bobbed, lounging in an easy chair, reading a newspaper and eating candy.[11]

This image is clearly of the middle or upper-class woman. In fact, the New Woman seems suspiciously like an updated version of the Victorian lady, simply more educated, open, and freer in her manners. Her education and intelligence were used in social conversation, her competence assured a well-run household, her dominance over her husband was only in minor matters, and her boldness led to smoking in public. She was hardly what Charlotte Perkins Gilman, feminist author of *Women and Economics*, would have called an independent woman. Some commentators did not envy

[10] See Dorothy Sabin Butler, "Men Against Women," *Forum*, 94 (Aug. 1935), 79-84; John Foster Fraser, "Is the American Woman Superior to the American Man?" *LHJ*, 36 (Sept. 1919), 51; W. L. George, "Hail Columbia! The American Woman," *Harper's*, 142 (March 1921), 457-469; Philip Gibbs, "Some People I Met in America," *Harper's*, 139 (Sept. 1919), 457-471; E. W. Howe, "These Women!" *Forum*, 83 (April 1930), 244-246; Ellsworth Huntington, "Why the American Woman is Unique," *Nation*, 125 (Aug. 1927), 105-107; "Our American Matriarchs," *Literary Digest*, 96 (Jan. 21, 1928), 13; "Our Petticoat Government Through German Eyes," *Literary Digest*, 109 (June 27, 1931), 15.

[11] *Saturday Evening Post (SEP)*, June 27, 1925.

2. Norman Rockwell portrays the "New Woman." Reprinted with permission from *The Saturday Evening Post* © 1925 The Curtis Publishing Company

women their leisure. One anonymous man commented that he might enjoy economic dependence, but what he could not stand would be "the intolerable invasion of my private ownership of my own body, mind, and soul involved in the universal assumption that I must devote them all to the purposes of seduction—must powder and primp and corset, and mince and glance and smile and smile and be a vampire still."[12]

Not all observers of the New Woman saw only this image of the middle-class lady of leisure. Dorothy Bromley, in 1927, pictured a "Feminist-New Style" distinct from the old feminist, the veteran of the suffrage struggle.[13] Her version of the New Woman was someone in her twenties or thirties who desired both a career and marriage, but who rejected the image of the angry feminists who ranted about equality and absurdities such as the right to retain one's maiden name. Bromley's Feminist-New Style believed that men and women were fundamentally different, even in mental qualities. She wanted a career, but not at the expense of a personal life. She frankly liked men and enjoyed working with them more than with other women. She felt no loyalty to women as a group, since most were petty, narrow, and trivial, and their leaders strident and ambitious. She was well-dressed, attractive, and proud of her feminine charms. She rejected feminist slogans and campaigns to liberate women from household work. She thought free love impractical rather than immoral. She conceded that most women needed a husband and children for their fullest development. She demanded more freedom and honesty within marriage. The Feminist-New Style lived consciously in the vanguard of change and was well on her way to becoming the equal of men, according to Bromley.

Bromley felt that the New Woman combined whatever was best in the traditional woman and in the feminist, but there is no evidence that hers was a widespread view. In his book on sex roles in the United States, Peter Filene called the idea

[12] "A Mere Man," p. 61.
[13] Dorothy Dunbar Bromley, "Feminist-New Style," *Harper's*, 155 (Oct. 1927), 552-560.

"revised feminism," arguing that the 1920's were a brief interlude of belief in the possibility of combining marriage and a career, before the onset of the Depression and the ensuing return to domesticity.[14] He cited Sinclair Lewis's novel *Main Street*, the story of Carol Kennicott, as a parable of revised feminism.[15] In spite of Carol Kennicott and Bromley's Feminist-New Style, however, revised feminism had no discernible impact on the popular image of American women. Women could vote and many women worked, but the ideal woman (who was never identified with feminism) still sought her fulfillment primarily in her role as wife and mother.

Filene saw the Depression as ringing the death knell on revised feminism. Certainly it was an overwhelming experience and a decisive factor in fostering social change, but it seems that, as Chafe has persuasively argued, the ideology of domesticity was firmly in force before the Great Crash. In fact, the Depression seems to have had little effect on the American image of women, perhaps simply strengthening existing convictions.

It did arouse spirited attacks on employed women who snatched jobs from unemployed men, and raised the specter of an unemployed man supported by his wife's wages. But even before the unemployment crisis added urgency to the question, American writers had speculated on the appropriateness of women working.[16] The nature of the discussion

[14] Filene, *Him/Her/Self*, pp. 131-168.

[15] Ibid., pp. 153-156.

[16] On the question of employment for women, see: Grace Adams, "American Women Are Coming Along," *Harper's*, 178 (March 1939), 365-372; "American Women of Today and Yesterday," *LHJ*, 40 (April 1923), 34; V. F. Calverton, "Careers for Women—A Survey of Results," *Current History*, 29 (Jan. 1929), 633-638; "Can a Woman Run a Home and a Job, Too?" *Literary Digest*, 75 (Nov. 11, 1922), 40-63; Poppy Cannon, "Pin-Money Slaves," *Forum*, 84 (Aug. 1930), 98-102; Claire-Howe [Ruth Howe and Claire Sifton], "Return of the Lady," *New Outlook*, 164 (Oct. 1934), 34-38; Robert L. Duffus, "Should Young Women Go to Work?" *Collier's*, 72 (Dec. 1, 1923), 32; Grace Nies Fletcher, "He Wants My Job!" *Independent Woman*, 14 (May 1935), 154; Rita S. Halle, "Do You

confirms the impression that the popular image of women generally confined them to wifehood and motherhood.

The "woman question" in the United States was, much more than in Nazi Germany, the question of whether a woman could successfully combine marriage and a professional career. Although some writers recognized the existence of women who worked at unrewarding jobs in order to support their families, these were not the women in the public eye. In the public image, employed women were "pin-money workers," women who worked in order to buy themselves unnecessary luxuries, or feminists selfishly seeking fulfillment in their careers.[17] The question of work for single women was not an issue; it was generally assumed that women would work at "suitable" work until they married. As a report on a meeting sponsored by the Department of Labor concerning women in industry stated: "Practically every speaker at that meeting recognized that women's interest in industry was at best only temporary, a stop-gap between whatever girlhood lay behind her and marriage."[18]

Yet that same report admitted that the problem of combining marriage and a career had not been solved, although the author clearly preferred women to stay at home. The report stated: "There is no social problem of today that arouses so much bitterness of discussion and conflict of opinion as the question of whether a wife can satisfactorily combine a business career with the profession or function or whatever you may wish to call it of being a wife."[19]

A few writers saw the problem in terms of the relationship between women and men.[20] As Maud Ballington Booth, who

---

Need Your Job?" *GH*, 95 (Sept. 1932), 24-25; Genevieve Parkhurst, "Is Feminism Dead?" *Harper's*, 170 (May 1935), 735-745; Genevieve Parkhurst, "Women Beware!" *Pictorial Review*, 35 (July 1934), 4; David Snedden, "Probable Economic Future of American Women," *American Journal of Sociology*, 24 (March 1919), 528-565.

[17] See Chafe, *American Woman*, p. 64.

[18] "American Women of Today," p. 34.   [19] Ibid.

[20] See "Can a Woman"; Mabel Barbee Lee, "The Dilemma of the

with her husband headed Volunteers of America, put it: "For a woman to be successful in home and career her husband must cooperate. Sometimes he must take her place."[21] Dorothy Thompson, in a more general way, felt that the United States was no paradise for women because they did not live in a vital, creative relationship with men.[22]

"Can a woman run a home and a job, too?" This was the question *Literary Digest* asked 250 "prominent" women, defined in this case as married women listed in *Who's Who*, a definition that included a number of women prominent only because married to prominent men.[23] Four-fifths of those questioned felt that women could do both "if they had brains." An even larger majority, however, felt that a woman's first concern should be her home and family. This emphasis on the home aspect of women's experiences was echoed in most of the periodical literature. As in Nazi ideology, motherhood was the central role for women; motherhood had in fact received special recognition in 1914 when Congress passed the act establishing Mother's Day. With this gesture, motherhood was enshrined as a sentimental and patriotic institution.

Glorification of motherhood, as the results of the *Literary Digest* survey showed, was not confined to those who believed women could not handle jobs. One woman who felt women could work and run a home as well was Anne Rogers Minor, President-General of the National Society of the Daughters of the American Revolution. But she insisted that a woman's first concern was her family: "The main thing is that the biggest and most sacred work in life is being a good

---

Educated Woman," *Atlantic*, 146 (Nov. 1930), 590-595; Sinclair Lewis and Dorothy Thompson, "Is America a Paradise for Women?" *Pictorial Review*, 30 (June 1929), 14-15; Florence Guy Woolston, "The Delicatessen Husband," *New Republic*, 34 (April 25, 1923), 235-238.

[21] "Can a Woman," p. 52.
[22] Lewis and Thompson, "Is America," p. 15.
[23] "Can a Woman."

mother, having a large family of children and bringing them up to be good citizens and good men and women."[24] Most articles extolling the virtues of motherhood featured the theme of motherhood as service to society; it was in the American tradition that a woman should be an educated mother of citizen sons. As David Snedden, a sociologist, put it: "The mother of children is the logical primary custodian of children's well-being; and in their rearing will be found, inevitably, the best vocation for many women—best for the individual herself and best for the society which she serves."[25]

Even a feminist like Charlotte Perkins Gilman saw motherhood as the primary function of women: "Women are first, last and always mothers, and will so continue. But while motherhood in the past was grievously warped and hindered by various kinds of oppression and injustice, the motherhood of the future will be wiser, stronger, more effective in improving humanity."[26]

Mothers could serve society in various ways. One was bearing and raising sons of genius. Arthur Brisbane, writing in *Pictorial Review*, lauded the mothers of 1934 as the most important women of the year, giving first place to a mother of quintuplets. Although he seemed by this gesture to honor quantity rather than quality, he wrote: "It is better to be the mother of a Michelangelo than a second-rate 'lady painter'; the mother of a Shakespeare, a Dante, or Homer, than a 'very pleasing lady poet.' "[27]

[24] Ibid., p. 47.

[25] Snedden, "Probable Economic Future," p. 528.

[26] Gilman, "New Generation," p. 737.

[27] Arthur Brisbane, "As I See Them: Women of 1934," *Pictorial Review*, 36 (Jan. 1935), 18-19. Other articles emphasizing women's role as mother include: Harriet Abbott, "What the Newest New Woman Is," *LHJ*, 37 (Aug. 1920), 154; "American Women of Today"; Cannon, "Pin-Money Slaves"; Elizabeth Cook, "The Kitchen-Sink Complex," *LHJ*, 48 (Sept. 1931), 12; Rose Wilder Lane, "Woman's Place Is in the Home," *LHJ*, 53 (Oct. 1936), 18; Lee, "Dilemma"; Dorothy Thompson, "If I Had a Daughter," *LHJ*, 56 (Sept. 1939), 4.

concern for the preservation of the race.[28] This was, of course, a major theme in Nazi ideology on women. Racial science and race consciousness were nowhere near as popular in the United States, although sporadic racial violence and severe discrimination made the United States at least as dangerous and unpleasant for blacks as Germany was for Jews before the war. But race consciousness in the United States enjoyed an upsurge of popularity in the 1920's, marked by a general concern with "race suicide," an issue tied up with immigration restriction and nativism.[29] White, Anglo-Saxon, Protestant, middle-class women owed it to their "race" to bear enough children to offset the hordes of illiterate foreigners threatening to destroy American values.

Mothers also contributed to the welfare of society by extending their maternal instincts beyond the family circle. Gilman wrote that great changes could result "from a new sense of the duty of women to the world as mothers—mothers not merely of their own physical children, but world mothers in the sense in which we speak of city fathers, only with their duties more nobly apprehended and more practically fulfilled."[30]

The concept of women as "world mothers," the counterpart of Nazi "spiritual maternity," was not new to American society. Jane Addams had publicized the notion that women's duties as wife and mother, in an urban environment, led her to an interest in improving municipal, state, and even

[28] See Mary Austin, "Woman Looks at her World: A Review of Feminine Progress for the Past Twenty-Five Years," *Pictorial Review*, 26 (Nov. 1924), 8-9; Mrs. O. H. P. Belmont, "Women as Dictators," *LHJ*, 39 (Sept. 1922), 7; John Corbin, "The Forgotten Woman," *North American Review*, 216 (Oct. 1922), 455-466; Gilman, "New Generation"; Huntington, "Why the American Woman"; Wiggam, "New Styles."

[29] See John Higham, *Strangers in the Land: Patterns of American Nativism 1860-1925* (1963; reprint ed., N.Y.: Atheneum, 1973).

[30] Gilman, "New Generation," p. 734.

national government.[31] The call to "enlarged housekeeping" urged women with free time to become concerned citizens, a "mother class" which could exert its influence in support of cleaner streets, better playgrounds, and more extensive community services.[32]

Motherhood and housekeeping, women were told, were professions one could practice with pride.[33] One article proclaimed: "Maternity must no longer be regarded as a function, but as a profession. The family is preserved primarily by the wife."[34] David Snedden called for vocational training in homemaking, and women's colleges began to institute curricular changes aimed at preparing women for marriage and the home.[35] Women, Poppy Cannon lamented, were being persuaded that they were worthless unless they had jobs, while the standardization and mechanization of households meant that "the adventure of cooking with raw materials is going out of housework along with the excitement of periodic cleaning."[36] Elizabeth Cook pleaded for the upgrading of the status of the housewife, arguing that women should be proud

---

[31] See Jane Addams, *Newer Ideals of Peace* (Chatauqua, N.Y.: The Chatauqua Press, 1907), pp. 180-207.

[32] See Emily Newell Blair, "What Are We Women Going To Do?" *LHJ*, 36 (May 1919), 47; Eugene Davenport, "You Can Change the World," *LHJ*, 29 (Jan. 1922), 23; Catharine Oglesby, "It's Up to the Women," *LHJ*, 50 (March, April, May, June 1933), 46, 44, 108, 51; Anna Steese Richardson, "The Modern Woman and Her Problems," *WHC*, 57 (June 1930), 25-26.

[33] See "American Women of Today"; Benjamin R. Andrews, "The Home Woman as Buyer and Controller of Consumption," *Annals*, 143 (May 1929), 41-48; Cannon, "Pin-Money Slaves"; Cook, "Kitchen-Sink Complex"; Hildegard Kneeland, "Woman's Economic Contribution in the Home," *Annals*, 143 (May 1929), 33-40; Snedden, "Probable Economic Future." See also Chafe, *American Woman*, pp. 102-107.

[34] "American Women of Today," p. 34.

[35] Snedden, "Probable Economic Future," p. 529. See Chafe, *American Woman*, p. 103.

[36] Cannon, "Pin-Money Slaves," p. 101.

of their accomplishments, should rid themselves of the "kitchen-sink complex" that made them feel guilty because they were not Susan Anthony or Amelia Earhart. Cook warned that "if women wish the home and the family to continue they must be advertisements for it."[37] With a rhetorical flourish reminiscent of the organic metaphor so dear to Nazi writers, Cook exclaimed: "Just as a rose comes to its fullest beauty in its own appropriate soil, so does a home woman come to her fairest blooming when her roots are struck deep in the daily and hourly affairs of her own most dearly beloved."[38]

Life magazine paid tribute to the American housewife just before Pearl Harbor with an eight-page spread entitled, "Occupation: Housewife."[39] The article described the duties and joys of Jane Amberg, thirty-two years old, resident of Kankakee, Illinois, and mother of three. Photographs showed her cooking, cleaning, chauffeuring, decorating the house, watching the children, sewing, laundering, shopping, and entertaining. *Life* concluded: "In the movies, in fiction and advertising in women's magazines, the modern U.S. housewife is portrayed as the sort of woman who keeps her figure, her husband, her makeup and her humor no matter how tough the going. One effect of this constant propaganda is that millions of U.S. women are doing just that."[40]

Much of this kind of glorification of women's role as mother and housewife appeared in women's magazines, catering to an audience of housewives who did not need to be persuaded to forego careers; but, as Chafe has argued, "the magazines provided reinforcement for existing attitudes and helped to justify their perpetuation."[41] Two writers at the time denounced the women's magazines for this narrow concentration on the home. Silas Bent, anticipating Betty

[37] Cook, "Kitchen-Sink Complex," p. 12.
[38] Ibid.
[39] *Life*, Sept. 22, 1941, pp. 78-85.
[40] Ibid., p. 84.
[41] Chafe, *American Woman*, p. 107.

Friedan by thirty-five years, pointed out that advertisers subsidize women's magazines because it is in their interest to keep women at home buying new products: "There is thus a conspiracy to regiment the opinion and the thought of the women of this country, or at least of those women who read women's magazines. It is a tacit conspiracy, I think, an unspoken bargain. It is not necessary for the advertiser to say to the editor: There is no sense putting notions into your readers' heads that they can combine Home-making with a Career or that there is any other Career than Home-making, or that there is anything of the least interest which does not begin or end beside the steam-radiator."[42]

Elizabeth Schlesinger was less radical in her denunciation.[43] She believed that the existence of twelve million subscribers to the five most popular ten-cent magazines for women indicated that women were not dissatisfied with the inane fiction and total lack of discussion of public affairs. But, she argued, the editors should take responsibility for training women as citizens and broadening their horizons. She noted optimistically that the *Woman's Home Companion*, which had the largest circulation of the five magazines, had the least limited intellectual scope, indicating perhaps that women were more interested in public affairs than the editors assumed.

Others raised their voices in protest against the confinement of women to their traditional roles. Mrs. O. H. P. Belmont, president of the National Woman's Party, wrote a now famous article for the *Ladies' Home Journal* entitled "Women as Dictators."[44] W. L. George predicted in *Good Housekeeping* that in the future there would be no housewives and no homes, provoking the editorial comment, "We

[42] Silas Bent, "Woman's Place Is In the Home," *Century*, 116 (June 1928), p. 208.
[43] Elizabeth Bancroft Schlesinger, "They Say Women Are Emancipated," *New Republic*, 77 (Dec. 1933), 125-127.
[44] Mrs. O. H. P. Belmont, "Women as Dictators," *LHJ*, 39 (Sept. 1922), 7.

Don't Believe It; Do You?"[45] V. F. Calverton, in an optimistic article, asked: "Is a woman's proper place in the home, as Mr. Green [William F. Green, president of the AFL] maintains? Is her real job that of motherhood, as many others contend? Should society exercise every means to force her to stick to that job? Is woman intended for nothing more than her fundamental biological function? The answer to these questions have [sic] already been made by the women themselves. To assign the home as the one fundamental place for woman was to cripple her character."[46]

But these voices were in the minority. There were feminists in the interwar period, although the organized women's movement had split over the issue of the Equal Rights Amendment of the National Woman's Party. But they were not shapers of public opinion nor creators of the public image of women. Many people at the time apparently believed, as did Ruth Howe and Claire Sifton, that feminism was dead.[47] The women's magazines betrayed a lingering suspicion of feminists, and throughout the period carried articles by ex-feminists or prominent women urging women to find their true fulfillment in the home. The development of this genre suggests that the public image of women was on the defensive, perhaps challenged by feminism and the trend of increasing female employment.

Harriet Abbott condemned as self-centered women who wanted wifehood and motherhood as well as the newer freedoms of the business world, and applauded women for re-learning the "world-old values" for women. Sincere and honest women, she argued, agreed with the old truth that there is no job more demanding than child-rearing. "Every girl

[45] W. L. George, "No Housewives, No Homes," *GH*, 76 (May 1923), 90; see also W. L. George, "What is a Home?" *GH*, 76 (April 1923), 79.

[46] Calverton, "Careers for Women," p. 636. See also Duffus, "Should Young Women."

[47] Claire-Howe, "Return of the Lady." See Filene, *Him/Her/Self*, p. 141; and Chafe, *American Woman*, pp. 112-132.

who shirks marriage because its homely duties are irksome,"
she warned, "every woman who refuses to have children,
every mother who needlessly delivers her home and her children into the care of a servant is using her saw-toothed ax on
progress. And in selfishly seeking her own comfort or satis-
fying her personal ambitions, she smothers her womanhood."[48]

Abbott's "Credo of the newest new woman" is worth
quoting in full:

> I believe in woman's rights; but I believe in woman's
> sacrifices also.
> I believe in woman's freedom; but I believe it should
> be within the restrictions of the Ten Commandments.
> I believe in woman suffrage; but I believe many other
> things are vastly more important.
> I believe in woman's brains; but I believe still more
> in her emotions.
> I believe in woman's assertion of self; but I believe
> also in her obligation of service to her family, her neigh-
> bors, her nation and her God.
> Following that faith we have the most modern expres-
> sion of feminism. The newest new woman deifies not
> herself, but through her new freedom elects to serve
> others.[49]

Good Housekeeping carried an article by an anonymous
woman, a famous woman who, according to the editorial
comment, would be admired for centuries. Her story of dis-
appointment at having been denied the prizes of a woman's
life, a home, husband, and children, was offered to all the
young women who were thinking of careers. The author
wrote that she was not unhappy, that she had succeeded in
her career beyond her wildest dreams. She was not bitter or
regretful. But, she added, "I count my gains small beside my

[48] Abbott, "What the Newest," p. 154.
[49] Ibid.

69

losses. I have no mate, no child, no home—only substitutes for them."[50]

Elizabeth Cook, who had tried both lives, commented: "I've been a home woman and I've been a career woman. And I tell you quite frankly I was never so worth while in my life as when I was washing diapers for three children all at the same time and cursing my fate."[51]

Rose Wilder Lane told of her career as a radical feminist and businesswoman and concluded that she had failed because she had tried to be a human instead of a woman. She advised girls to forget about careers and become wives and mothers. She wrote:

> Your business is to be a woman. Your career is to make a good marriage, to spend the days and the years of your life and all the resources of your mind and spirit in deepening and enriching and making fruitful in life values the union of feminine and masculine that is marriage.
>
> Use whatever talents you may have as adornments or as food for your femininity. Be deeply, fundamentally, wholly feminine. Be proud that you are the bearer of life, the giver of life values. Recognize and foster in your whole self the feminine life element, the deep unconscious wisdom of creation, with its power to reject and to choose, to which masculinity is always submissive, and accept the responsibility of that power.[52]

In the same vein, Dorothy Thompson, foreign correspondent and radio commentator, told women that they would only be happy if happily and securely married, with several healthy and loving children. She argued that it was better to devote one's talents to one's husband, thus making him a better man and a greater success, than to exercise them in

[50] "I Wish I Had Married and Found Life," *GH*, 77 (Nov. 1923), p. 141.
[51] Cook, "Kitchen-Sink Complex," p. 148.
[52] Lane, "Woman's Place," p. 96.

one's own behalf. She cited approvingly the case of a talented woman writer who gave up everything for her husband, a famous writer. She could have been a talented poet, but became instead the wife of a genius.[53]

Thompson herself was a fascinating and enigmatic woman whose life was perhaps representative of the prominent anti-feminist career woman. She believed that happy marriage and devotion to a man were most important to a woman, yet she herself could not live without the career which her second husband, Sinclair Lewis, resented so bitterly. While writing glowingly of housewifery and motherhood, she spent long periods away from home and neglected her own son. Whether as a result of these contradictions or for other reasons, Thompson's personal life was unhappy.[54]

Women writers like Abbott, Cook, Lane, and Thompson urged women to devote themselves fully to their husbands and children, and thus reinforced the public image of the American woman as an intelligent and educated middle-class person who renounced a career in order to use her talents and training as a good mother and skilled housewife.

Betty Friedan saw little difference between the Nazi sentence to a life of *Kinder, Küche, Kirche*, and the American image that limited women to "one passion, one role, one occupation."[55] The ideal woman in both countries was a mother and housewife, responsible for maintaining the race and the family. Just as Nazi ideology denounced or ignored non-"Aryan" women or opponents of the regime in describing the ideal woman, so the American image excluded non-white, non-Americanized, and poor or working-class women. The Nazi principle of exclusion was deliberate, the American

[53] Thompson, "If I Had," p. 4. Another article of this type is Corra Harris, "The Happy Woman," *LHJ*, 40 (Nov. 1923), 33.

[54] Thompson also glorified heterosexual relations in spite of her attraction to women. See Marion K. Sanders, *Dorothy Thompson: A Legend in Her Time* (N.Y.: Avon, 1973); and Vincent Sheean, *Dorothy and Red* (Boston: Houghton Mifflin, 1963).

[55] Friedan, *Feminine Mystique*, p. 32.

not, but the end result was the same: the ideal could only be attained by a fraction of the female population.

Nazi ideology would no doubt have welcomed a society in which all women could have stayed at home, but it recognized right from the start that this was an impossible dream, and so made a place for women engaged in suitable work in order to support their families. The dominant American image of women ignored the existence of women who worked for reasons of economic necessity. The debate in the United States over the employment of women centered on the question of whether a married woman could choose to have a home and a career too. In Germany, the important problem was the definition of suitable or "womanly" occupations for those who had to work. This basic difference may be simply a reflection of the economic situations in the two countries. Although the Depression struck both heavily in the 1930's, it had been preceded by a period of prosperity in the United States, while defeated Germany had recovered from the war only after ruinous inflation. More German families may have needed the woman's wages in order to survive economically, thus keeping working women in the public eye. Traditionally, women comprised a greater proportion of the labor force in Germany than in the United States. The issue there was jobs for women, not careers for married women.

Whatever the reason for the difference, the American image was a solidly middle-class one that assumed that the American man was successful in business and able to support his wife in a comfortable home. She, in turn, devoted herself to the housework she could not any longer find a servant to do, and to her children. Although once the sturdy yeoman farmer had seemed a desirable model representing independence and simplicity, there was no hint of the Nazi peasant ideal in American images of women.[56] The yeoman farmer

[56] See Richard Hofstadter, *The Age of Reform: From Bryan to F.D.R.* (N.Y.: Vintage Books, 1955), pp. 23-36, on the ideal of the yeoman.

72

had been replaced by the businessman, and a devoted wife and mother seemed a necessary part of the equipment for his business career.

Nazi ideology demanded sacrifice for the good of the state of both men and women. On the basis of this cardinal duty, women were expected to do whatever was necessary for the defense and preservation of the people. This element of readiness to sacrifice set up the justification for the use of women in "unwomanly" tasks in case of war. No such trapdoor existed for American women. They were expected to use their leisure time for public service, but this did not involve stepping out of their roles as mothers and housewives. Nazi ideology consciously concerned itself with the possibility of war, as war seemed the only means of achieving certain foreign policy goals. American society turned with revulsion from the thought of war, even as the government shirked responsibility for maintaining peace, and no public ideal of women's role in wartime developed.

On the eve of the Second World War, the ideal woman in both countries was above all a mother with duties and functions radiating from this central role. How the images would change in the course of the war, and how they would affect responses to the emergency, was an open question.

Mobilization and Propaganda Policies in Germany and the United States

Although, at the beginning, I myself, and probably the majority of the leading personalities of the party and of the womanhood with me, believed that for certain reasons an obligatory service for women should be decreed, I am of the opinion that all responsible men and women in party, state and economy should accept with the greatest veneration and gratitude the judgment of our Fuehrer Adolf Hitler, whose greatest concern has always been the health of the German women and girls; in other words, the present and future mothers of our nation.

Fritz Sauckel, 1942

Eventually the neighbors are going to think it very strange if you are not working. They'll be working too. In fact, any strong, able-bodied woman who is not *completely occupied* with a job and a home —is going to be considered a 'slacker' just as much as the man who avoids the draft.

suggested copy, OWI campaign

The outbreak of war came as a surprise to German society in 1939, and American society in 1941, despite all the previous indications that war was imminent. War altered the conditions and assumptions behind the public image of women in both societies, calling on women to meet new demands and take on new responsibilities. Many of these changes could be reconciled with the primary role of woman as wife and mother. The need for women to take up the work of men, releasing them for service in the armed forces, could not. Yet both societies took steps, sometimes hesitantly,

74

sometimes boldly, to mobilize women for the war effort. Lacking clear-cut policy on the mobilization of women, the German government passed but did not enforce the registration of women for civilian labor, and urged women to take jobs, but did not make use of intensive propaganda campaigns to aid in this task. In contrast, the United States never instituted civilian conscription, choosing instead to launch comprehensive propaganda campaigns designed to sell war work to women.

The United States succeeded in mobilizing its women, while Germany did not. Germany's female labor force increased by only 1 percent from 1939 to 1944, while the American female labor force increased by 32 percent from 1941 to 1945.[1] Graph I illustrates the increase of the American female labor force and the stagnation of the German. That the German female labor force was approximately the same size as the American in 1940, although the German female population was only about 60 percent of the American, is explained by the existence of a large agricultural sector in the German female labor force. Approximately 40 percent of female workers in Germany were engaged in agriculture, while the comparable American figure was less than 10 percent.[2] This difference reflects the vastly different agricultural conditions in the two countries. In Germany, there were still many small family farms where women helped their husbands or fathers. About 75 percent of the women engaged in agriculture in Germany were unpaid family members.[3] The high participation rate of German women, then, does not represent an advanced stage of mobilization but rather the large agricultural sector.

[1] See the appendix for statistics and explanation of sources. See also Clarence D. Long, *The Labor Force in War and Transition: Four Countries*, Occasional Paper, no. 36 (N.Y.: National Bureau of Economic Research, 1952).

[2] Statistisches Reichsamt, *Statistik des deutschen Reichs*, 556/1, p. 2; *Historical Statistics*, p. 74.

[3] *Statistik des deutschen Reichs*, 556/1, p. 2.

GRAPH I

The Female Labor Force, Germany and the United States,
1939-1945

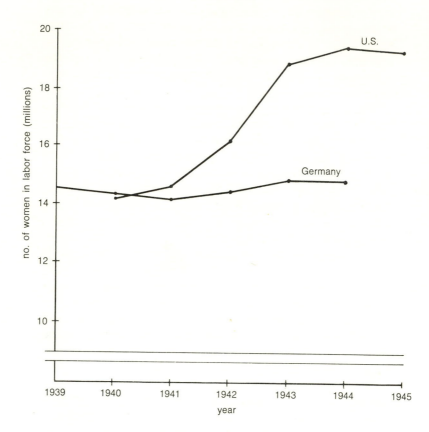

Taking all sectors together, German women made up approximately half of the native German civilian labor force. But this large percentage simply reflects the fact that the removal of German men from the labor force to serve in the armed forces was compensated by the importation of foreign workers. German women's share of the total civilian labor force, including foreign workers, increased slightly throughout the war, but the total civilian labor force dropped by 8 percent from 1939 to 1944. Even the influx of foreign workers could not counteract the loss of men to the armed forces. Graph II represents the composition of the German labor force, showing the steady decrease in male civilian employment that was not offset by additions to the foreign

GRAPH II

The Composition of the German Labor Force,
1939-1944

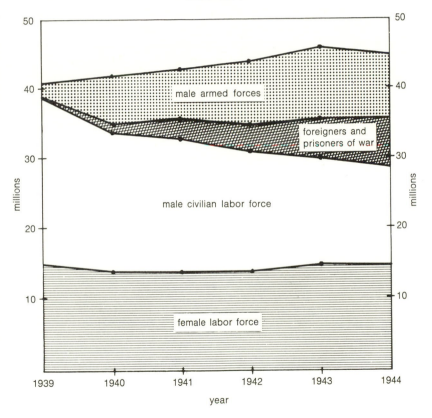

or female labor forces. There were no German women in military service, but 470,500 women were employed by the armed forces in 1943-44.[4]

No outside labor supply, comparable to the foreign workers and prisoners of war used in Germany, was available to the United States. Instead women filled the need for civilian labor created by men entering the armed forces. Women's share of the total labor force increased during the war, from 29 percent in 1941 to 37 percent in 1944. Graph III represents the composition of the American labor force. The overall success of the United States in mobilizing labor is indicated by the small drop in the male civilian sector, relative to the German, and by the increase in women working. The figures for the female labor force include women in the various women's branches of the armed forces. At the peak in 1945, women in the military numbered only 240,000, a mere 1.2 percent of the total female labor force.[5]

Germany failed to mobilize women for the war effort, despite a conscription system, gradually enacted into law by the government, that led early observers of German labor policy to conclude that Germany possessed "a system of regimentation of labor, in scope and intensity such as the world has never seen. . . ."[6] Reversing the Depression policy of urging women to relinquish their jobs to unemployed men, the German government passed a series of measures designed to bring more women into the labor force even before the outbreak of war.[7] These included the introduction of the

[4] Ursula von Gersdorff, *Frauen im Kriegsdienst 1914-1945* (Stuttgart: Deutsche Verlags-Anstalt, 1969), p. 74.

[5] See the appendix.

[6] L[udwig] Hamburger, *How Nazi Germany Has Mobilized and Controlled Labor* (Washington: The Brookings Institution, 1940), pp. 57-58. See also "The Employment of Women in Germany Under the National Socialist Regime," *International Labour Review*, 44 (Dec. 1941), 617-659; and Judith Grünfeld, "Mobilization of Women in Germany," *Social Research*, 9 (Nov. 1942), 476-494.

[7] The Nazi government took two basic approaches to the problem of reducing the number of women in the labor force during the

GRAPH III

The Composition of the American Labor Force, 1940-1945

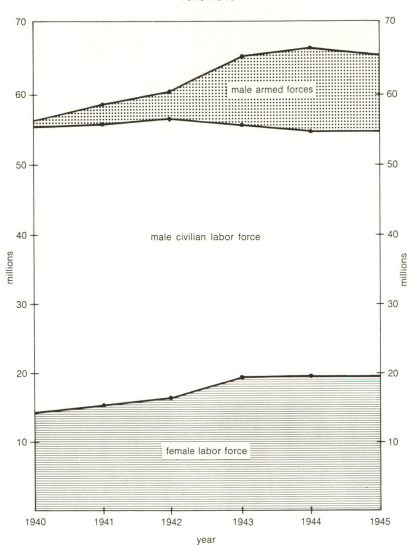

male armed forces

male civilian labor force

female labor force

millions

millions

year

Labor Book, a tool with the potential for controlling and mobilizing the entire labor force; the creation of a compulsory term in the Labor Service; the introduction of the Duty Year; and the issuance of a decree providing for the conscription of women and men for specific tasks.

Introduced by a law of 1935, the Labor Book contained information on an individual's training, employment history, and personal characteristics, and wage earners and employees were required to submit it to their employers.[8] The introduction of the Labor Book anticipated the need for investigating and controlling labor; German economic periodicals envisaged it as a tool useful for identifying and mobilizing housewives with industrial experience.[9]

A few months after the introduction of the Labor Book,

Depression. One was negative, a campaign against "double earners," employed women whose husbands or fathers worked. A June 1933 act called for the dismissal of married women officials who were not dependent on their earnings and could be supported by close relatives (*Reichsgesetzblatt*, 1933, I, p. 433). For an excellent account of Nazi policy toward professional women, see Jill McIntyre, "Women and the Professions in Germany, 1930-1940," in *German Democracy and the Triumph of Hitler*, ed. Anthony Nichols and Erich Matthias (N.Y.: St. Martin's Press, 1971), pp. 175-213. The second approach was positive, and included the marriage loan program, instituted in June 1933 (*Reichsgesetzblatt*, 1933, I, p. 323). In order to reduce unemployment as well as encourage marriage and motherhood, the government offered loans without interest of up to one thousand marks to racially fit couples about to marry if the woman had worked at least six months within the preceding two years and promised not to work until the loan was repaid. On both of these approaches, see Jill Stephenson, *Women in Nazi Society* (N.Y.: Barnes and Noble, 1975).

[8] *Reichsgesetzblatt*, 1935, I, p. 311; *Reichsgesetzblatt*, 1935, I, p. 602. A law of 1939 extended the coverage of the Labor Book; see *Reichsgesetzblatt*, 1939, I, p. 824.

[9] H. W. Singer, "The German War Economy in the Light of German Economic Periodicals," *Economic Journal*, 50 (Dec. 1940), 534-546. Singer based his series of reports, which appeared from 1940 to 1944, on articles from *Der deutsche Volkswirt* and *Der Vierjahresplan*.

legislation made a term in the Labor Service compulsory.[10] Originally the Labor Service had served as an emergency device to meet the unemployment crisis, but it was transformed, in the course of the developing labor shortage, into a means of introducing young women and men into the labor force. Its educational role was always as important as its economic one; ideological indoctrination in National Socialism was paramount. But the Nazi leadership also hoped to win women over to the joys of working the land. Women in the Labor Service, uniformed and housed in camps, divided their days among work outside the camp, usually in agriculture, ideological training, physical exercise, and cultural activities. The Labor Service Law of 1935 obligated all German youth of both sexes to serve their people in the Labor Service, but not until 1939 did this become binding on women.[11] Despite the theoretically compulsory nature of the female Labor Service, its numbers never increased beyond 150,000.[12] The conflicts among Nazi officials on the question of mobilizing women, as will be discussed later, resulted in the nonenforcement of such measures.

Another tack taken by the government in order to increase the female labor force in agriculture was the introduction of the Duty Year, a compulsory year of labor decreed by Hermann Göring as Commissioner of the Four Year Plan in 1938.[13] This decree forbade the hiring of single women under twenty-five unless their Labor Books showed that they had worked for a year in agriculture or domestic service. A woman could fulfill her Duty Year requirement by serving a term in the Labor Service, by an apprenticeship in agriculture or housework, as a regular wage earner in agricul-

---

[10] *Reichsgesetzblatt*, 1935, I, p. 769.

[11] *Reichsgesetzblatt*, 1939, I, p. 1693.

[12] See Frieda Wunderlich, *Farm Labor in Germany 1810-1945* (Princeton: Princeton University Press, 1961), p. 322.

[13] *Reichsarbeitsblatt*, 1938, I, p. 46; *Reichsarbeitsblatt*, 1938, I, p. 48. Both decrees are reprinted in Ilse Arnold, *So schaffen wir! Mädeleinsatz im Pflichtjahr* (Stuttgart: Union Deutsche Verlagsgesellschaft, 1941), pp. 14, 106.

ture, or by serving two years as a nurses' aid, kindergarten teacher, or welfare worker. Although intended primarily to bring women into agriculture, this measure reflected the Nazi conviction that certain jobs corresponded to the "essence" of women.

Both the Duty Year and the Labor Service were indirect methods of mobilizing women. A decree issued in 1938 provided for the conscription of women and men for a limited period of time for specific tasks.[14] On the basis of this decree, men went to work on the Siegfried Line, but no women were mobilized.[15]

Germany's attack on Poland in September 1939 and the resulting declarations of war precipitated legislation making a term in the Labor Service compulsory for young single women not otherwise occupied, but a decisive attempt at mobilization came only in January 1943. Although a defense law, passed in 1935, had called in vague terms for the service of all German women and men in case of war, this theoretical universal conscription had not, in practice, affected women.[16] The first direct mobilization measure, the Law for the Defense of the Reich, provided for the registration of women seventeen to forty-five and men sixteen to forty-five.[17] Those who worked at least forty-eight hours a week, those who employed five or more persons, those employed in agriculture or health services, students, pregnant women, and women with one child under six or two children under fourteen received exemptions. Goebbels, named Plenipotentiary for Total War in July 1944, raised the age limit on the registration of women from forty-five to fifty.[18]

No agency ever acquired complete control over labor

[14] *Reichsgesetzblatt*, 1938, I, p. 652; *Reichsgesetzblatt*, 1939, I, p. 206.

[15] Hamburger, *How Nazi Germany*, p. 43.

[16] *Reichsgesetzblatt*, 1935, I, p. 609.

[17] *Reichsgesetzblatt*, 1943, I, p. 67.

[18] See the United States Strategic Bombing Survey (USSBS), *The Effects of Strategic Bombing on the German War Economy*, Overall Economic Effects Division, October 31, 1945, pp. 38-39.

mobilization. The proliferation of agencies and the system of organized chaos so characteristic of the Nazi state extended to the area of labor supply. In the early years of the war, the Ministry of Labor competed with the Office of the Four Year Plan, as well as with the procurement offices of the armed forces. After Albert Speer became Minister of Armaments Production in February 1942, he agitated for the consolidation of labor control. Hitler responded to the chaotic situation by creating a new office without eliminating any of the old ones. Fritz Sauckel took office as Plenipotentiary General for Labor Supply in March 1942, but labor mobilization remained a bone of contention until the end of the war.

Because there was no clear allocation of responsibility, a decision to enforce the conscription of women could be blocked by any one of several officials. Hitler and some other top officials, notably Göring, opposed the drafting of women, fearing that great moral and physical harm would result. When Sauckel took office as Plenipotentiary General for Labor Supply, he drew up a program calling for a levée en masse of German women and youth, but Hitler rejected it, ostensibly because there was no time to wait for the training of German women.[19] He ordered Sauckel to use foreign labor instead. Not satisfied with sparing German women from conscription, Hitler actually ordered Sauckel to procure women from the East to help German housewives in their domestic tasks.[20]

In a program drawn up in April 1942, a month after he took office, Sauckel rejected the idea of obligatory service for all German women: "Although, at the beginning, I myself, and probably the majority of the leading personalities

[19] Interrogation of Sauckel, International Military Tribunal, *Trial of the Major War Criminals Before the International Military Tribunal*, XIV, pp. 621-622.

[20] "The Labor-Mobilization Program, April 20, 1942," U.S. Chief of Counsel for the Prosecution of Axis Criminality, *Nazi Conspiracy and Aggression*, III, p. 52.

of the party and of the womanhood[21] with me, believed that for certain reasons an obligatory service for women should be decreed, I am of the opinion that all responsible men and women in party, state and economy should accept with the greatest veneration and gratitude the judgment of our Fuehrer Adolf Hitler, whose greatest concern has always been the health of the German women and girls; in other words, the present and future mothers of our nation."[22]

Sauckel stated that he could not enumerate all the reasons for this decision, but asked for confidence as an "old fanatical" Gauleiter [district leader]. He admitted that the decision might seem unfair to women already employed in defense and essential civilian industries, but commented that "an evil cannot be remedied by spreading it to the utmost." The only way to eliminate the injustice was to win the war and remove all women from unsuitable jobs that endangered their health, the birth rate, and family and national life. Hitler wished to protect women from moral and mental harm, and this aim would be endangered by mass conscription and employment of women: "It is impossible to compare the German Woman with the German Soldier in this case, because of the existing fundamental natural and racial differences between men and women."[23]

After learning of Hitler's opposition to the conscription of women, Sauckel adopted this position and defended it vigorously against the advocates of total mobilization, especially Speer. Speer repeatedly urged the complete mobilization of the German population.[24] Although two and a half

[21] Presumably the German here reads "Frauenschaft" and refers to the women's organization. The documents in *Nazi Conspiracy and Aggression* have been translated into English.

[22] *Nazi Conspiracy and Aggression*, III, p. 53.

[23] Ibid.

[24] *Trial of the Major War Criminals Before the International Military Tribunal*, XLI, pp. 460, 468, 486, 487. See Albert Speer, *Inside the Third Reich*, trans. Richard and Clara Winston (N.Y.: Avon, 1970), pp. 294-295. On the conflict between Sauckel and

million women registered at the employment offices by the end of March 1943, as ordered in the January registration law, the results in terms of additions to the labor force were negligible.[25] When Sauckel did finally call for total mobilization in April 1943, he gave the responsibility for implementing the mobilization measures to the Gauleiters, who did not enforce conscription because they did not believe in the need for total war and felt that total war measures would weaken the population's will to resist.[26] Even after the January 1943 registration law and Sauckel's April 1943 proclamation, Speer continued to complain of the lack of mobilization. At a meeting of Gauleiters in October 1943, Speer stressed the seriousness of the situation and demanded the total mobilization of labor reserves, including German women, among other measures.[27] After this meeting, Speer went to talk to Hitler about his program, and Hitler rejected the idea of mobilizing women.[28]

Goebbels' appointment as Plenipotentiary for Total War in July 1944 and his desperate attempt to shut down all inessential activities came too late. German retreat and defeat, combined with Allied bombing, created such chaos that evaluation of this last period of the war is difficult.[29] Nothing like total mobilization was possible in the confusion. In spite of Speer's warnings, Germany went down to defeat with a partially mobilized female labor force.

Hitler's concern for protecting German women from labor that might harm them as childbearers certainly played a role in the failure to mobilize women, but it is difficult to believe that he would have protected women to the extent

---

Speer, see also Edward L. Homze, *Foreign Labor in Nazi Germany* (Princeton: Prniceton University Press, 1957), pp. 204-229.

[25] Gersdorff, *Frauen im Kriegsdienst*, pp. 383, 384; from Bundesarchiv Koblenz 43 II/654b.

[26] *Trial of the Major War Criminals*, XLI, pp. 486, 488-489.

[27] Ibid., p. 487.   [28] Ibid., p. 488.

[29] USSBS, *Effects*, pp. 38-39.

of hindering Germany's chances of victory. If Hitler had been truly and unalterably opposed to the conscription of women, why would he have approved the various registration and conscription measures that provided the Nazi state with a thorough system of mobilization on paper? The seeming paradox of a full mobilization plan only partially implemented makes sense if one accepts the conclusion first offered by the United States Strategic Bombing Survey report on the German war economy, a conclusion confirmed by the research of Burton Klein, Clarence Long, and Alan Milward.[30] As Long stated: "The real reason for Germany's manpower shortcomings may well be its conviction during the crucial years that it need not mobilize completely in order to win."[31] The Strategic Bombing Survey characterized as a "Blitzkrieg strategy" Hitler's belief that the war could be won without an all-out effort, without demanding inordinate sacrifices in terms of rationing of consumer goods, or labor conscription. Germany's early victories lulled Hitler into a false sense of confidence. This reluctance to mobilize the country as a whole, along with the conflicting views of top Nazi leaders on the propriety of mobilizing women, contributed to the failure to mobilize women for the war effort.

Germany had an unimplemented labor conscription system, competing bureaucratic structures interested in labor supply, and a leadership resistant to the idea of conscripting women. The United States lacked a labor conscription program on paper, but shared with Germany the latter two characteristics. Throughout the war various United States agencies fought for complete control over labor recruitment and allocation. But, despite some support for a national system of registration and conscription, and a continuing debate

[30] See Burton H. Klein, *Germany's Economic Preparations for War* (Cambridge: Harvard University Press, 1959); Long, *Labor Force in War*; Alan S. Milward, *The German Economy at War* (London: Athlone Press, 1965); USSBS, *Effects*.

[31] Long, *Labor Force in War*, p. 44.

on the merits of such a system, the government ultimately relied on a voluntary system of labor recruitment.

The attack on Pearl Harbor brought to an abrupt halt the lingering concern with reducing the number of women in the labor force, the heritage of the Depression in the United States just as in Germany.[32] But the outbreak of war did not mean the immediate end of unemployment, nor did it motivate the government to create an agency with sole responsibility for labor mobilization. In deference to public opinion, Roosevelt's administration had done little planning for labor mobilization in case of war. Not until April 1942, four months after Pearl Harbor, was a separate agency concerned with labor supply established. The War Manpower Commission, headed by Paul V. McNutt, was a policy forum, rather than an operating agency, and could not enforce compliance with its directives. Throughout 1942 the WMC, faced with the indifference of employers, labor, and members of Congress who saw no need for labor controls in a situation still devoid of serious labor shortages, could not exert control. Other agencies concerned with labor competed with the WMC and refused to bow to its authority. In spite of a major reorganization in December 1942, the WMC remained essentially an advisory body without the power to allocate labor among war production, civilian production, and the armed forces.[33] It operated primarily through the

[32] The United States, too, witnessed a campaign against "double earners." Article 213 of the National Economy Act of 1932 permitted discrimination in hiring and firing against a married federal employee whose spouse was also a government employee (*U.S. Statutes At Large*, 47, part 1, p. 406). Although directed at eliminating nepotism, it proved to be a useful tool for dismissing women. State legislatures introduced discriminatory legislation, and local school systems practiced discrimination against married women. See William H. Chafe, *The American Woman: Her Changing Social, Economic, and Political Role, 1920-1970* (N.Y.: Oxford University Press, 1972), pp. 102, 283.

[33] The most important source on the development of the WMC is the official government history: U.S. Bureau of the Budget, *The*

United States Employment Service, taken over from the states by the federal government in 1942. The official government history of the wartime administration evaluated the labor agencies and concluded: "The Employment Service remained throughout the war the most important civilian agency concerned with labor supply. The War Manpower Commission in its final form was basically a reconstituted employment service under new top management and with the addition of certain training functions transferred from other agencies."[34]

The WMC, aware that the largest reserve of available labor consisted of women, created a Women's Advisory Committee to the WMC in August 1942. This move pleased few of the women who had been agitating for a greater role for women in policy-making. The Women's Advisory Committee, as these women suspected, turned out to have no power, no means of implementing decisions, and no influence with the War Manpower Commission. Other agencies too, especially the Women's Bureau, sought a role in the recruitment of women, but none found the means of affecting policy.[35]

United States at War, Historical Reports on War Administration, no. 1 (Washington: U.S. Government Printing Office, 1946), pp. 182-189. Also useful are Chester W. Gregory, *Women in Defense Work during World War II: An Analysis of the Labor Problem and Women's Rights* (Jericho, N.Y.: Exposition Press, 1974), pp. 18-20; Thomas M. Hills, "The War Manpower Commission and its Problem, April 18, 1942-February 1, 1943," MBA thesis, Wharton School, University of Pennsylvania, 1943; Paul A. C. Koistinen, "Mobilizing the World War II Economy: Labor and the Industrial-Military Alliance," *Pacific Historical Review*, 42 (Nov. 1973), 443-478; Eleanor F. Straub, "Government Policy Toward Civilian Women During World War II," Ph.D. diss., Emory University, 1973, pp. 30-34.

[34] U.S. Budget Bureau, *U.S. at War*, p. 178.

[35] See Straub, "Government Policy," pp. 48-62. Straub published an article based on the dissertation, but focusing on the Women's Advisory Committee: "United States Government Policy Toward Civilian Women During World War II," *Prologue*, 5 (Winter 1973),

In spite of the weaknesses of the labor recruitment and allocation system, labor shortages did not act as a restraint on production until 1943. At this time, in response to the critical labor shortages on the West Coast, the agencies responsible for labor supply agreed to cooperate in the matter of labor allocation. The West Coast Plan, as worked out by the agencies involved, might have led to a national system of labor distribution but the war was over before the plan could be generally adopted.[36]

Because of the improvised nature of labor recruitment and the conflicts among competing labor agencies, many people both in and outside of government supported the idea of compulsory labor registration for women. Women's organizations were especially vocal in their support. Although Roosevelt announced in May 1942, at the time of the creation of the WMC, that registration was unnecessary, support for the plan did not die. Citizen action eventually culminated in the introduction of a bill in Congress in 1943 calling for a universal obligation for men eighteen to sixty-five and women eighteen to fifty. Despite continual debate of the bill and the issue, and Roosevelt's support after 1944, the bill never passed.[37]

Although the government feared that the imposition of labor conscription measures would seem to represent the adoption of methods characteristic of the Fascist enemy, it would no doubt have resorted to such controls, in spite of ideological objections, had this been necessary. Arthur J. Altmeyer, executive director of the War Manpower Commis-

---

240-254. See also Mary Anderson, *Woman at Work: The Autobiography of Mary Anderson as Told to Mary N. Winslow* (Minneapolis: University of Minnesota Press, 1951), especially pp. 249-250.

[36] U.S. Budget Bureau, *U.S. at War*, pp. 429-444.

[37] On the debate over national service legislation and the Austin-Wadsworth bill, see Koistinen, "Mobilization," pp. 457-460; Richard Polenberg, *War and Society: The United States, 1941-1945* (Philadelphia: Lippincott, 1972), pp. 176-182; Straub, "Government Policy," pp. 150-154; U.S. Budget Bureau, *U.S. at War*, pp. 187-188, 450-455.

sion, tried to reconcile the possibility of such measures with democratic theory: "If legal controls should be forced upon us, we will not be abandoning democratic methods and ideals. . . . If we have such controls, it will be because it has been decided that in an all-out struggle for survival, we cannot leave to chance or caprice the rationalization of our labor market and the fullest possible utilization of the manpower and womanpower of the country."[38]

The War Manpower Commission, left without the means to enforce its decisions and without a system of registration and conscription, worked to maximize the effectiveness of voluntary recruitment. Local communities enthusiastically launched enrollment drives, in which women filled out questionnaires describing their work experience, their willingness to accept employment, and their child care responsibilities. After a few such drives, the WMC rejected this method, deciding that the results in terms of women actually added to the labor force were meager.[39] At this point, the WMC turned to the policy of promotion. After a trial test of a massive, multimedia educational campaign in the Baltimore area, the WMC called for intensive recruitment efforts backed up by national publicity campaigns in 1943. The policy of selling the war became the government's major strategy in the task of labor mobilization.

The policy of promotion led the WMC into close cooperation with the Office of War Information, the government propaganda agency. "Propaganda" was a word assiduously avoided by government officials, smacking as it did of totalitarian mind control. For reasons that will be discussed below in conjunction with the German propaganda effort, the United States government refused to admit that it engaged in propaganda on the home front. "Information" was the official word for the material disseminated by the

[38] Arthur J. Altmeyer, "If Legal Controls Should Come," *Employment Security Review*, 9 (Sept. 1942), 20.
[39] On enrollment drives, see Straub, "Government Policy," pp. 105-112.

OWI, the "strategy of truth" the official term for its method. Yet even those who insist that the Office of War Information did follow a strategy of truth admit that it did not always tell the whole truth, that its truth was selective, and that military considerations sometimes necessitated slanting the truth.[40] Using a functional definition of propaganda as the ideas or information a government (or other organization) releases, sponsors, and promotes, truthfulness is irrelevant. In the early days of the war, the United States concealed military losses from the public, just as Germany did in the last years of the war.[41] In both countries, when the news was good, the government followed a strategy of truth. Propaganda in the United States concerning the course of the war was more truthful than similar German propaganda in part because, for most of the war, the news was better.

Roosevelt set up the Office of War Information in June 1942 as an agency to explain government policy and release information to the public.[42] It consisted of an overseas branch and a domestic branch, and the domestic branch soon ran into trouble. A conflict developed between the writers, formerly employed by the Office of Facts and Figures and incorporated into the OWI at its creation, and the advertising executives in charge of the promotional campaigns.[43] The writers wanted simply to inform the people and disapproved of the Madison Avenue approach employed by the advertising personnel. The quarrel ended with a mass resignation by the writers and researchers in April 1943. In a statement

[40] See Allan M. Winkler, "Politics and Propaganda: The Office of War Information, 1942-1945," Ph.D. diss., Yale University, 1974. Winkler's thesis provides a good account of the development of the OWI, although he accepted the OWI's conception of its work and did not treat the issue of what propaganda is.

[41] See ibid., pp. 52-61.

[42] On the OWI, see U.S. Budget Bureau, *U.S. at War*, pp. 203-233; Sydney Weinberg, "What to Tell America: The Writers Quarrel in the Office of War Information," *Journal of American History*, 55 (June 1968), 73-89; Winkler, "Politics and Propaganda."

[43] See Weinberg, "What to Tell America."

issued to the press, they complained that the domestic branch of the OWI was controlled by "high-pressure promoters who prefer slick salesmanship to honest information."[44]

The writers' walkout was only the beginning of the trouble. Congress expressed displeasure over what it considered the partisan bias of the agency, and also disapproved of certain Office of War Information publications, particularly one entitled "Negroes and the War," which some members of Congress complained favored racial equality. The result was an attack on the appropriation of the domestic branch in the summer of 1943. With its budget cut to the point of ineffectiveness, the domestic branch ceased to generate materials for home use and became a coordinating agency which worked through other government agencies.

Despite the budget cut, the Office of War Information continued to sponsor material published by other agencies, publish limited circulation pamphlets for the use of the media and advertisers, and coordinate promotional campaigns.[45] The office sent out monthly guides to magazine writers and editors, newspaper editors, and radio commentators, suggesting approaches to war topics and allocating time and space so that the various media might emphasize the same themes at the same time.[46] The OWI also supervised and

[44] Quoted in ibid., p. 87, from *The New York Times* and the *Washington News*, April 14-16, 1943.

[45] The Records of the Office of War Information (RG 208) are housed in the Washington National Records Center, Suitland, Maryland. These records are invaluable for a study of wartime propaganda activities.

[46] The OWI published the *Magazine War Guide*, with supplements for the editors of, and writers for, specialized magazines; *The Women's Page, Fortnightly Budget*, and *Fortnightly News Letter* for the editors of women's pages in newspapers; and the *Women's Radio War Program Guide* for radio commentators and program directors. Copies of *Magazine War Guide* and a list of supplements can be found in RG 208, Box 1700; copies of the *Women's Radio War Program Guide* are located in RG 208, Box 748.

distributed films on current war topics.[47] Perhaps most importantly, it maintained a close relationship with the world of advertising.[48] The War Advertising Council loyally supported government campaigns, urging advertisers to keep up war-related advertising. As one pamphlet prepared by the War Advertising Council in cooperation with the Office of War Information and the War Manpower Commission put it: "Advertising is a medium peculiarly fitted to present facts in ways that carry conviction."[49] So a barrage of advertising descended on advertisers themselves, urging them to devote all or half of each ad to government themes, or to work war themes into advertising copy. The War Advertising Council assured advertisers that war-related advertising was the best way to sell products or win good will during the war.

In order effectively to sell the war to women, the WMC and the OWI organized promotional campaigns designed to convince women to take war jobs. The War Manpower Commission clearly stated its belief in the need for persuasion in the first campaign plan, drawn up in 1942.[50] It also in-

[47] See RG 208, Box 161, File "Publications: OWI Misc." and RG 208, Box 1548. On the OWI's relationship with Hollywood, see Gregory Black and Clayton Koppes, "OWI Goes to the Movies: The Bureau of Intelligence's Criticism of Hollywood, 1942-43," *Prologue*, 6 (Spring 1974), 44-59.

[48] See, for example, the letter from Paul McNutt to Chester J. LaRoche, Chairman of the War Advertising Council, Oct. 6, 1943, RG 208, Box 168; "Advertising's Part in Civilian Mobilization," RG 208, Box 170; "Quarterly Readership Survey of Magazine Advertising," RG 208, Box 170; "Are People Reading Institutional Ads?" RG 208, Box 171; "The Blue Book: Case Histories of Wartime Advertising Successes," RG 208, Box 171; "Advertising Goes to War," RG 208, Box 171; "Put Your Advertising to Work for More Women at War," RG 208, Box 167; "Women in the War . . . For the Final Push to Victory," RG 208, Box 168; "How Industry Can Help the Government's Information Program on Womanpower," RG 208, Box 167.

[49] "Put Your Advertising to Work for More Women at War," RG 208, Box 167.

[50] "U.S. Government Campaign on Manpower," revised as of Dec. 5, 1942, RG 208, Box 166.

dicated what the government thought of the population: "Simplicity is all important because of the limited receptivity and limited understanding of the great majority of the people whom we must reach." Government campaigns would "condition" the minds of women, men, and children to the changes and sacrifices which the war entailed.

All of the government promotional efforts designed to recruit women for war work included both a national campaign to acquaint the public with the problem, and intensive local campaigns in areas short of labor actually to recruit women. This pattern prevailed because labor shortages were local and the WMC wanted them met by local labor, since areas of labor shortage invariably had housing shortages as well.

The WMC launched the first campaign, addressed to both women and men, in December 1942. The plan called for the trial run of a massive multimedia local campaign in Baltimore. Another major campaign began in March 1943, followed by the largest effort yet in September 1943. The September campaign sought to recruit women for jobs in essential civilian services, such as stores, restaurants, hospitals, day nurseries, and laundries, rather than in war industries. Recognizing that such jobs were often underpaid, boring, unglamorous, and low in status, the campaign set out to "sell" them to women and their husbands: "It is almost impossible under present conditions to make many of these jobs more attractive. A laundry, even with the most modern plant and equipment is still a pretty unpleasant place to work. These jobs will have to be glorified as a patriotic war service if American women are to be persuaded to take them and stick to them. Their importance to a nation engaged in total war must be convincingly presented."[51]

The last campaign began in March 1944. Sponsored by the Office of War Information, the War Manpower Commission, and the armed forces, this represented the first joint

[51] "Basic Program Plan for Womanpower," Aug. 1943, RG 208, Box 168.

effort among recruiters of civilian and military womanpower. The campaign reflected the government's belief that women knew of the need for their participation but were reluctant to take war jobs.[52] Advertising rose to the challenge of recruiting the women "who are hardest to 'sell.' "[53]

All of these campaigns used similar media techniques. Under allocation plans worked out by the Office of War Information, radio stations devoted entire shows, spot announcements, and special features to the campaign. The OWI distributed professionally prepared announcements and recordings made by famous radio personalities.[54] Special womanpower short films, including *Glamour Girls of 1943*, appeared in theaters across the country.[55] The OWI urged magazines to picture women workers on their front covers in September 1943, and arranged a competition for the best cover, with prizes awarded at a special exhibition at the Museum of Modern Art in New York.[56] The Retailers War Campaign Committee published a calendar for retailers with suggested advertising techniques, including displays of work clothes, and a schedule to coordinate war advertising.[57] The War Advertising Council encouraged the advertisers of all kinds of products to tie in the war themes with their ads.[58] Posters and billboards urged women to take up employment. The War Manpower Commission issued a special pamphlet

[52] "OWI Women in the War Campaign," RG 208, Box 591.

[53] "Put Your Advertising to Work for More Women at War," RG 208, Box 167; "Women in the War . . . For the Final Push to Victory," RG 208, Box 168; "How Industry Can Help the Government's Information Program on Womanpower," RG 208, Box 167.

[54] "Womanpower Spots," RG 208, Box 587; "America at War Needs Women at Work," RG 208, Box 168.

[55] "Basic Program Plan for Womanpower," RG 208, Box 168. See also Richard R. Lingeman, *Don't You Know There's a War On?* (N.Y.: G. P. Putnam's Sons, 1970), pp. 227-228.

[56] *Magazine War Guide*, July/Aug. 1943, RG 208, Box 1700; letter from Dorothy Ducas to Mary Brewster White, July 29, 1943, RG 208, Box 156, File "Womanpower."

[57] "Retailers War Program, Official Calendar," RG 208, Box 171.

[58] "Basic Program Plan for Womanpower," RG 208, Box 168.

for the use of government officials in areas of labor shortage.[59] Besides offering a package of advertising copy, recordings for radio, films, posters, speeches, and slogan stencils for use by the Boy Scouts in painting sidewalks, the WMC proposed that officials set up a roster of women war workers in the city hall and inscribe the names of new workers with great ceremony.

The government suggested that the media use a number of tactics in trying to convince women to take war jobs. The first plan called for an appeal on the basis of good wages, equal to men's, and suggested that women be told that war work was "pleasant and as easy as running a sewing machine, or using a vacuum cleaner."[60] Subsequent campaign plans recommended these themes regularly, in spite of cautions to the effect that wages must not be emphasized to the point of increasing consumer spending and inflation, and that the war must not be made to seem a picnic.[61]

The March 1943 campaign, under the slogan "The More Women at Work, the Sooner We'll Win," introduced the idea that women could save lives by taking a job and thus helping to end the war sooner. This turned into a threat at times: "Every idle machine may mean a dead soldier."[62] The War Manpower Commission counselled caution in the use of this appeal as well, noting that war messages should not imply that a woman taking a job would save some particular soldier's life, since some men were bound to die in any case.[63]

The plan for the big campaign in September 1943 suggested the standard appeal to patriotism and the lure of money, but also added some new themes. Suggested copy still threatened women without jobs with responsibility for

[59] "America at War Needs Women at Work," RG 208, Box 168.
[60] "U.S. Government Campaign on Manpower," revised as of Dec. 5, 1942, RG 208, Box 166.
[61] Ibid. See also "Preliminary Supplement (A) to the U.S. Government Campaign on Manpower," RG 208, Box 166.
[62] "Preliminary Supplement (A)," RG 208, Box 166.
[63] Ibid.

prolonging the war, but now also accused them of being slackers. In response to the worry that the neighbors might look askance at a respectable woman working in a factory, women were to be told: "Eventually the neighbors are going to think it very strange if you are not working. They'll be working too. In fact, any strong, able-bodied woman who is not *completely occupied* with a job and a home—is going to be considered a 'slacker' just as much as the man who avoids the draft."[64]

The campaign plan also recommended special appeals to husbands, telling them it would be no reflection on their ability to support their families for their wives to take war jobs. Suggested copy addressed men boldly: "It may be a bit of a shock, but YOU are going to have to help!"[65] The government even argued that it was entirely natural for women to work: "Women can stand a lot, and actually they are workers by tradition. It is only in recent years, and mostly in the United States, that women have been allowed to fall into habits of extraordinary leisure."[66] Even more radical was the copy recommended for singling out the reluctant potential worker: "Are you so blinded by 'woman's rights' that you have forgotten that nothing but WORK ever earned them? Are you being old-fashioned and getting by just by being a 'good wife and mother?' "[67]

Many of these same approaches were used to encourage women to join the armed forces, but military recruitment faced the more difficult task of presenting the military, traditionally the quintessential male preserve, as a suitable and desirable place for women. Without going into military

[64] "U.S. Government OWI Womanpower Campaigns," RG 208, Box 156, File "Womanpower."

[65] Ibid. See also "Womanpower Spots," RG 208, Box 587, 1-minute spot no. 2. The March 1943 campaign also appealed to husbands to understand that their wives must work in order to win the war. See "Preliminary Supplement (A)," RG 208, Box 166.

[66] "U.S. Government OWI Womanpower Campaigns," RG 208, Box 156.

[67] Ibid.

recruitment in any detail, it is interesting to note that the Office of War Information believed that appeals to patriotism would not suffice for recruiting women for military service. The reason, the OWI claimed, was that women feared that such service would destroy their femininity and remold them into half-male, half-female hybrids.[68] Therefore the OWI recommended the following type of appeal to women's femininity: "Many service women say they receive more masculine attention—have more dates, a better time—than they ever had in civilian life. Their uniforms have been styled by some of the world's greatest designers to flatter face and figure—their poise and carriage are improved—they are recognized everywhere as representative of American womanhood at its best."[69]

Military, like civilian recruitment, cajoled and threatened women in an attempt to fill quotas. The implicit assumption behind the appeals and threats—that women joined the war effort only reluctantly—angered the Women's Advisory Committee to the War Manpower Commission. The committee, along with some government officials, objected to the campaign booklet for the 1944 campaign. These critics believed that the government unjustly accused women of refusing to take war jobs, when in reality external factors prevented women from working.[70] Such criticism echoed the earlier objections of Mary Brewster White, an OWI official, to the "passionate meaningless hysteria" of the campaigns. She commented: "As I see it, our job is to *explain* and *reassure*—not just to recruit, appeal, urge, exhort, declaim, and announce."[71]

[68] "Women in the War . . . For the Final Push to Victory," RG 208, Box 168.

[69] "Put Your Advertising to Work for More Women at War," RG 208, Box 588.

[70] See the letter from Verda Barnes to Sophie Nack, Clearance Officer, Feb. 15, 1944; letter from Rhea Radin and Glenn Miller, Bureau of Manpower Utilization, to Sophie Nack, Feb. 16, 1944; RG 208, Box 587, File "Womanpower."

[71] Memorandum from Mary Brewster White to Robert L. Ferry, Aug. 13, 1943, RG 208, Box 156, File "Womanpower."

Despite objections, the government continued to recruit, appeal, urge, exhort, declaim, and announce until the need for labor slackened and the layoffs began. Left without the power to conscript women for war work, the War Manpower Commission had great success with its policy of selling the war to women, though certainly the opening up of high-paying factory jobs to women meant that many took advantage of the situation even without special encouragement. Government propaganda ignored working women and poor women, perhaps assuming that they needed no coaxing. Black and other minority women still faced obstacles, for employers would not change their hiring practices until forced by the lack of white male labor. But the government campaigns addressed exclusively the women new to the labor force between 1941 and 1945, and assumed that all of these women were housewives reluctant to take jobs. The government set out to sell the war to them, and, whether they needed persuading or not, it fashioned elaborate campaigns to do the job.

The propaganda effort in Germany was much less forceful, if more forthright. Although the Nazi government had the means to organize the same kind of intensive campaigns utilized by the American government, it did not do so in order to mobilize women. The Nazi government had no qualms about its propaganda activities, and felt no need to disguise its propaganda agencies with other names. Hitler had emphasized the importance of propaganda in *Mein Kampf*, and the party had used propaganda techniques throughout the "time of struggle." In contrast to American officials, Nazis saw nothing wrong with this. One propagandist explained the attitude of "the democracies" toward propaganda as a consequence of selfish individualism. In an article in the official party newspaper for propagandists, Gerhard Baumann argued that the democracies used propaganda as a political tool in the power struggle among classes, religions, and other groups.[72] Each group used it as

[72] "Nationalsozialistische und 'demokratische' Propagandagrundsätze," *Unser Wille und Weg*, Nov. 1940, pp. 124-125.

a means of attaining its own ends, which had nothing to do with the general interest. Since it was clear to everyone that the propaganda of any group worked only for that group's self-interest, the term "propaganda" took on a pejorative meaning. In contrast, National Socialist propaganda served the party's goal: the unity of the German people. Since the goal was honorable, so was the tool. Goebbels made explicit this Machiavellian approach: "Propaganda in itself has no basic method. It has only a goal, and this goal is always called, in politics: conquest of the masses. Every means that helps to attain this goal is good. And every means irrelevant to this goal is bad."[73]

It is interesting to speculate on the actual reasons for the negative associations of the term "propaganda" in the United States. The Nazis considered it a legitimate political tool because they accepted right from the start the premise that people could easily be swayed. Hitler revealed his low opinion of the intelligence of the masses in *Mein Kampf* when he emphasized the need for simplicity in propaganda.[74] The American government, committed in theory to the belief that every citizen was competent to exercise his or her reason in making choices, hesitated to admit publicly that it used its enormous power to influence people. In private, government officials emphasized the limited understanding of the public, but to broadcast such opinions would not win votes.[75] As a result of the use of the term "propaganda" by Nazi Germany and its avoidance by the United States, the term became even more definitely associated in the American public mind with complete untruth.

The Nazi Party recognized the importance of propaganda very early, and made extensive use of propagandistic tech-

[73] Quoted in NSDAP, Gau Oberdonau, *Propagandisten-Fibel* (Wels: Leitner, n.d. [193-]).

[74] Adolf Hitler, *Mein Kampf*, trans. Ralph Manheim (Boston: Houghton Mifflin, 1943), pp. 176-186.

[75] See "U.S. Government Campaign on Manpower," revised as of Dec. 5, 1942, RG 208, Box 166.

niques in "the time of struggle." Goebbels became propaganda chief of the party in 1929, and created an organization that later coexisted with the state propaganda ministry. The party agency [the Reichspropagandaleitung] consisted of five functional divisions, dealing with "active propaganda," culture, radio, film, and "liaison with offices of the state." This functional division existed on each territorial level of the agency, from the national to the cell level. Shortly after Hitler's appointment, he created the first national propaganda ministry in Germany, the Ministry of Popular Enlightenment and Propaganda, and appointed Goebbels to head it. Goebbels modelled the structure of this state ministry after that of the party organization, adding divisions for press, theater, creative arts, music, writing, propaganda abroad, foreign press, and tourism. The Propaganda Ministry, like the party agency, developed a territorial structure based on the hierarchical leadership principle. The party and state organizations existed side by side, with many corresponding offices, including the top one, held by the same person. Although Goebbels headed both organizations, his control of propaganda was never total. Jurisdictional rivalries abounded, particularly over control of the press, culture, and foreign propaganda.[76]

Soon after German troops had marched into Poland, Goebbels set down some basic guidelines on party prop-

[76] See Z. A. B. Zeman, *Nazi Propaganda* (London: Oxford University Press, 1964), pp. 38-53; and Edward N. Peterson, *The Limits of Hitler's Power* (Princeton: Princeton University Press, 1969), pp. 55-59. Other works on Goebbels and the Propaganda Ministry include: Jay W. Baird, *The Mythical World of Nazi War Propaganda, 1939-1945* (Minneapolis: University of Minnesota Press, 1974); Willi A. Boelcke, *The Secret Conferences of Dr. Goebbels: The Nazi Propaganda War 1939-1943*, trans. Ewald Osers (N.Y.: E. P. Dutton, 1970); Ernest K. Bramsted, *Goebbels and National Socialist Propaganda, 1925-1945* (East Lansing: Michigan State University Press, 1965); Helmut Heiber, *Goebbels*, trans. John K. Dickinson (N.Y.: Hawthorn Books, 1972). None of these works, however, covers wartime propaganda concerning homefront activities.

aganda and distributed them to each Gauleiter and to the head of the party propaganda office in each Gau.[77] He gave as a unifying theme for all party propaganda the slogan, "The Fighting and Sacrificing Homefront." Wartime, he stated, demanded the utilization of all means in the task of shaping the attitude of the homefront. This attitude was crucial, as the experiences of the war of 1914-1918 had shown. To assure the strength of the homefront, Goebbels called on the political leaders of the party [*Politische Leiter*] to organize the people for the war effort.

Goebbels distinguished three major areas of propaganda: political propaganda, propaganda aimed at control of consumption, and propaganda encouraging active participation in the war effort. The main task of political propaganda was to explain to the people the nature of the enemy and the goals of the war. The media available included meetings, slide lectures, films, posters, pamphlets, badges, and word of mouth. Local officials could obtain the necessary materials from the national party propaganda office. Goebbels noted that posters placed at all busy intersections, at all transportation stops, on all trains and buses, in marketplaces, in shop windows, in government offices, and in all other public places would assure that propaganda reached everyone in Germany.

The second area of propaganda, on the control of consumption, primarily addressed housewives. Pamphlets, radio lectures, slogans in shop windows, and messages spread by word of mouth would urge women to use goods in plentiful supply, thus preventing serious shortages.

Propaganda designed to encourage active participation called on those at home to send newspapers to soldiers at

[77] Joseph Goebbels, "Richtlinien für die Durchführung der Propaganda der NSDAP," Sept. 23, 1939, Records of the NSDAP (T-81), Roll 84, Frame 95624-95633. The Records of the NSDAP are part of the captured German documents collection microfilmed under the supervision of the American Committee for the Study of War Documents. Indices for the entire series appear in *Guides to German Records Microfilmed at Alexandria, Virginia* (Washington, 1958-). Guides 3, 20, and 35 cover the Records of the NSDAP.

3. "Victory at any price!" A Nazi war poster. Courtesy of the Library of Congress

the front, provide entertainment and companionship for soldiers in hospitals, collect scrap materials, help in agricultural work, contribute time to the National Socialist welfare organization, organize kindergartens and day nurseries for the children of soldier fathers and working mothers, and provide hospitality for those who had left home in order to work in another section of the Reich. In general, the homefront would act to show its support of the soldiers at the front.

Goebbels expressed concern above all for uniformity. A weekly radio program called "The Party's Hour: The Party Speaks—The People Listen," would provide a forum for leading party members to speak to the people and emphasize national concerns. Those who lacked radios would gather in public places to hear the broadcast. As a general measure, all posters, pamphlets, and other materials had to be submitted to the national office for approval.

The hierarchical structure of both the party and state organizations provided the means for assuring that propaganda was uniform throughout the Reich. The national offices, after deciding on policy, issued directives to the regional offices.[78] The party propaganda office published a newspaper which carried information on speakers, films, posters, and exhibitions.[79] Although it ceased publication in June 1941, its function was taken over by a monthly publication which provided information for speakers on various

[78] Folder of propaganda directives from the Propaganda Ministry to the Gaupropagandaamt Hessen-Nassau, 1942-1944, Records of the NSDAP (T-81), Roll 24, Frame 21743-22084; Folder of propaganda directives from the Reichspropagandaleitung to the Gaupropagandaamt Hessen-Nassau, 1941-1944, Records of the NSDAP (T-81), Roll 117, Frame 137407-137979. Because a large part of the records of the Propaganda Ministry was destroyed at the end of the war, leaving mostly material on internal administration, the Records of the NSDAP are the best source of propaganda directives.

[79] *Unser Wille und Weg: Monatsblätter der Reichspropagandaleitung der NSDAP*, April 1931-June 1941.

topics according to the official propaganda line.[80] The party office issued a "slogan of the week" that appeared on posters throughout the Reich. Films, slide shows, and exhibitions distributed by the national offices provided entertainment and political indoctrination in the most isolated corners of Germany.[81] The party maintained bulletin boards or showcases in every community where posters and other materials were displayed. And the Propaganda Ministry supervised the press and published its own pamphlets.

For the dissemination of propaganda addressed to women, the propaganda organizations depended to a large extent on the Frauenschaft, the women's organization.[82] This fact itself probably indicates the low priority attached to such propaganda, for the Frauenschaft was not an important or powerful organization in the Nazi hierarchy. Gertrud Scholtz-Klink, head of all women's organizations, told a meeting of women officials in 1940 that the Frauenschaft had responsibility for explaining to women their role in the war effort and recruiting them for war service in industry.[83] The

[80] *Aufklärungs- und Redner-Informationsmaterial der Reichspropagandaleitung der NSDAP und des Reichspropagandaamtes der Deutschen Arbeitsfront.*

[81] See "Die Arbeit der Lichtbild-Propaganda im Kriege," *Unser Wille und Weg*, Jan. 1940, pp. 4-5; "Die 'Parole der Woche,'" *Unser Wille und Weg*, Jan. 1940, pp. 6-8.

[82] Throughout this section I refer to the women's organizations as the Frauenschaft, in order to minimize confusion, although the operating organization was actually called the Deutsches Frauenwerk. The relationship between the two organizations is very confusing. The Frauenschaft, headed by the Reichsfrauenführerin [Reich Women's Leader] Scholtz-Klink, served as an elite or executive organization, admitting members only by invitation after January 1936. The Frauenwerk accepted individual members or entire groups and served as the operating agency. In some Nazi literature, the entire organization is referred to as the NSF/DFW (NS-Frauenschaft/Deutsches Frauenwerk).

[83] Gertrud Scholtz-Klink, "Kriegseinsatz der werktätigen Frau," *Sonderdruck zum Nachrichtendienst der Reichsfrauenführung*, Aug. 1940, p. 3.

Frauenschaft, organized territorially to correspond to the political division of the Reich, sent its directives down the hierarchy to the local women's officials.[84]

The Press and Propaganda Division of the Frauenschaft became the most important section for the task of explaining to women their work in the war.[85] It took responsibility for the periodicals of the women's organization as well as other publications.[86] An official information service supplied articles for the rest of the press.[87] The Press and Propaganda Division also produced radio programs for women, distributed films and slides, maintained public displays of posters, developed a photographic archive, and sponsored exhibits.

The journal of the Frauenschaft, the *N.S. Frauen-Warte*, urged women to join the war effort from the beginning of the war. In October 1939, an article called on women to report to the employment offices if they could work full time, or to volunteer with the Frauenschaft if they could not.[88] A 1941 article, reporting on a speech Hitler gave before the Reichstag, told of the millions of women already working in factories, on farms, and in offices, and urged hundreds of thousands of women to take these millions as a model.[89]

[84] File of the Kreisfrauenschaftsleiterin Kochem, Records of the NSDAP (T-81), Roll 75, Frame 86320-86358; File of the Kreisfrauenschaftsleiterin Strassburg, Records of the NSDAP (T-81), Roll 75, Frame 86359-86488. See also folder of miscellaneous items concerning the Frauenschaft, 1937-1945, Records of the NSDAP (T-81), Roll 75, Frame 86489-86522. The papers of the Reichsfrauenführung did not survive the war.

[85] See *Deutsches Frauenschaffen im Kriege: Jahrbuch des Reichsfrauenführung*, 1941.

[86] The Reichsfrauenführung published three periodicals: *N.S. Frauen-Warte, Die deutsche Hauswirtschaft*, and *Frauenkultur im Deutschen Frauenwerk*.

[87] *Nachrichtendienst der Reichsfrauenführung.*

[88] "Wo melden sich Frauen zur Mitarbeit?" *N.S. Frauen-Warte*, 8 (Oct. 1939).

[89] "Und wo warst Du im Kriege?" *N.S. Frauen-Warte*, 9 (June? 1941), 386. For Hitler's speech, see *Hitler: Reden und Proklama-*

Scholtz-Klink spoke frankly to the leaders of the Frauen-schaft in 1940, explaining the failure of voluntary registra-tion.[90] She reported that women who knew the meaning of work and the so-called upper ten thousand responded to the nation's need, but that the middle layer of women sat tight in their middle-class happiness and resisted the call. She believed that the Frauenschaft could reach the hearts of the poor and the minds of the educated rich, but had failed to reach the middle sections of society. She stressed the im-portance of appealing to all women without exception.

In an attempt to reach women of all stations, Scholtz-Klink addressed the problem of combining housework and war work. Carefully affirming the importance of housework, she told women who spent their days scouring their houses, ironing, fulfilling their husbands' every wish, and serving meals punctually, that these activities were fine in peacetime: "But now there is a war on, and at the moment there are women so overburdened that they work eight, ten, and twelve hours, and have their housework in addition. Then the hus-band must wait a moment for his soup, or a neighbor must warm it up for him."[91]

In another speech on the same topic, Scholtz-Klink sug-gested that men could warm up their food themselves with-out losing a shred of their dignity. She reminded the men who objected that cooking was not man's work that thousands of soldiers did it every day without anyone im-pugning their maculinity.[92]

Neither Scholtz-Klink nor the Frauenschaft determined policy, but they did help to implement it. Much of the

---

tionen 1932-1945, ed. Max Domarus (Würzburg: Max Domarus, 1963), II, p. 1708.

[90] Scholtz-Klink, "Kriegseinsatz," pp. 3, 4.

[91] Ibid., p. 3.

[92] "Rede der Reichsfrauenführerin Frau Gertrud Scholtz-Klink im Sportspalast in Berlin am 13. Juni 1940," *N.S. Frauen-Warte,* 9 (July 1940), 24-25. See also "Und wo warst Du im Kriege?" and "Wenn die Frau doppelten Dienst tut . . . ," *VB,* Jan. 28, 1940.

material distributed by the Frauenschaft addressed women in their roles as housewives and mothers, and had little to do with mobilization for the war effort. Most of the films and slide shows, for example, concerned children, motherhood, and housework rather than employment in war industries. [93] Propaganda aimed at women did not ignore the war, but it did reflect Hitler's policy of not enforcing the conscription of women, of not mobilizing women. After the outbreak of the war, Rudolf Hess opened an exhibition honoring the German woman as wife and mother, an exhibition that toured the Reich.[94] As late as 1944, local sections of the party held elaborate celebrations to honor Germany's mothers on Mother's Day.[95]

The party did sponsor slide shows on women's contributions to the war effort.[96] But there seems to have been only one major campaign, similar to the American ones, aimed at recruiting women for work directly related to the war. Under the slogan, "Frauen helfen siegen" [Women help win the war], the government attempted in 1941 to encourage the voluntary enlistment of women for war work.[97] Rudolf Hess

[93] See *Deutsches Frauenschaffen im Kriege*, 1941. See also "Filme helfen uns!" *N.S. Frauen-Warte*, 8 (Feb. 1940), 341.

[94] "Frau und Mutter—Lebensquell des Volkes," *N.S. Frauen-Warte*, 8 (Feb. 1940), 326-327; for the catalog of the exhibition, see Hans Hagemeyer, *Frau und Matter, Lebensquell des Volkes*, 2nd ed. (Munich: Hoheneichen-Verlag, 1943).

[95] Folder of material on Muttertag 1944, Records of the NSDAP (T-81), Roll 173, Frame 314486-314534; see also Directive on Muttertag 1942, Records of the NSDAP (T-81), Roll 117, Frame 137659-137661.

[96] NSDAP, Amt Lichtbild der Reichspropagandaleitung der NSDAP, *Der Einsatz der deutschen Frau im Kriege: Einziges parteiamtliches Lichtbildvortragsmaterial der NSDAP* (Dresden: Dr. Güntz-Druck, n.d. [1941?]). The Reichsfrauenführung also produced a slide show entitled *Fraueneinsatz im Kriege*.

[97] Directive to speakers on the special campaign "Deutsche Frauen helfen siegen," March 18, 1941, Records of the NSDAP (T-81), Roll 117, Frame 137924-137925. See also the collection of photographs, *Frauen helfen siegen: Bilddokumente vom Kriegseinsatz unserer Frauen und Mütter* (Berlin: Zeitgeschichte-Verlag, 1941).

launched the campaign with a radio speech. The party propaganda office instructed the press to prepare the public with
stories of women in war jobs, and sent out a directive to
speakers instructing them to take up the points set out by
Hess. These points included the expression of gratitude to
women already involved in war work, an appeal to women
to contribute to the war effort, and a special appeal to the
upper classes to demonstrate their National Socialist convictions, their love of Germany, and their commitment to the
community of the people. The directive suggested that the
speakers appeal to the women's sense of honor and that they
warn women of the shame and embarrassment that awaited
those who had not contributed to the war effort at the end
of the war.

The "Frauen helfen siegen" campaign was not followed up
by a series of similar campaigns.[98] The Propaganda Ministry
sent out a directive to all Gau propaganda chiefs in 1943
ordering more propaganda about married women with children who had taken up war jobs, but this was not part of an
intensive campaign.[99] Collections of Nazi wartime posters include few picturing women, and these generally do not
treat the mobilization of women for war work.[100] This does

[98] It is always difficult to prove negative statements such as this one,
but an examination of the propaganda directives from the Propaganda
Ministry and the Reichspropagandaleitung included in the Records
of the NSDAP (T-81), Roll 24, Frame 21743-22084, and Roll 117,
Frame 137407-137979, provides no indications of other campaigns.
None of the books, articles, pamphlets, photographic collections,
newspapers, or magazines that I have surveyed makes any mention
of such a campaign. In fact, the evidence on the "Frauen helfen
siegen" campaign indicates that it was probably not on as large a scale
as the American campaigns, although this is difficult to measure.
The *VB* made no mention of Hess's radio speech or the launching
of the campaign.

[99] Directive from the Propaganda Ministry to all Gaupropaganda-
leiters, Feb. 12, 1943, Records of the NSDAP (T-81), Roll 24,
Frame 21944-21945.

[100] See the poster collection at the Library of Congress; the Mueller
and Graeff Poster Collection, Box 4, in the Hoover Institution

not mean that German propaganda ignored women or over-looked the contribution they could make to the war effort. The German government, like the American, utilized various media in an effort to influence the population. The Nazi Party relied on propaganda long before the outbreak of the war. Although it did not launch comprehensive campaigns, and did not make use of commercial advertising to support government policies, the German government did try to instill in German women and men the idea that they must sacrifice their own personal interests for the good of Germany. This general theme provided the keynote for the war, and perhaps made unnecessary many more specific appeals.

How German women reacted to the appeals addressed to them is a fascinating and difficult question. While no conclusive answer is possible at this point, the evidence suggests that the failure of the female labor force to increase during the war years can be attributed, at least in part, to a lack of response from women. Even before the war, Gertrud Scholtz-Klink issued a warning to women who tried to spare their daughters the rigors of the Duty Year: "Now I should like to say a word or two to our mothers! If your daughter desires or is obliged to adopt this course you should not endeavour to oppose her with absurd fears or principles. You do honour neither to yourself nor to your daughter if you insert advertisements couched in terms on the following lines: '*Wanted—suitable position where my daughter can spend her compulsory "Year."—Conditions: central heating, running hot water—no children!*' "[101]

Literature on the Labor Service admitted that some women opposed their daughters' decision to enter, and even

<hr />

Archives, Stanford, California; and the posters included in the Records of the NSDAP (T-81), Roll 24, Frames 21743-22084.

[101] Gertrud Scholtz-Klink, *Tradition is Not Stagnation But Involves a Moral Obligation: Women's Conference at the National Congress of Great Germany* (Nuremberg: The Deutsches Frauenwerk, 1938), p. 9.

admitted that some daughters went reluctantly.[102] Many women apparently feared becoming slaves to their Labor Books, and so stayed out of employment altogether.[103] Even after the passage of the compulsory registration decree in 1943, women avoided registering and were subjected to appeals and threats.[104] Nazi literature admitted that women feared and avoided factory work.[105] The Security Service of the SS, which compiled and distributed reports on public opinion during the war, noted the reluctance of women to take war jobs and regularly recommended the implementation of conscription.[106] The reluctance of women to register

[102] See Arnold, *So schaffen wir!* An article in the N.S. *Frauen-Warte*, 3 (1934?), mentioned the resistance of mothers to sending their daughters away in an agricultural labor service. Lydia Schürer-Stolle, "Wie stehen die Eltern zu uns?" *Das Deutsche Mädel*, n.d. [1936-37], p. 19, dealt with parental attitudes toward the Jungmädel, and concluded that the attitude of the home depended on that of the mother. A story called "Entscheidung" by Lisa Barthel-Winkler, in *Unsere Zeit und wir: Das Buch der deutschen Frau*, ed. Elsbeth Unverricht, 4th ed. (Gauting b. Munich: Verlag Heinrich A. Berg, n.d. [1935]), pp. 215-242, told of a young woman who went against the wishes of her parents and fiancé to join the Labor Service.

[103] See reports in Singer, "German War Economy," *Economic Journal*, 52 (1942), 22; and 53 (1943), 129.

[104] See reports in ibid., 53 (1943), 247-248; and 54 (1944), 209. See also "The Effects of General Mobilisation on the Employment of Women in Germany," *International Labour Review*, 50 (Sept. 1944), 357; Gersdorff, *Frauen im Kriegsdienst*, pp. 56-60. Some reports of shirking are included in the Records of the NSDAP (T-81), Roll 118, Frame 139220, 139224.

[105] See, for example, "Der erste Schritt," in Magda Menzerath, *Kampffeld Heimat: Deutsche Frauenleistung im Kriege* (Stuttgart: Allemannen Verlag A. Jauss, 1944), pp. 32-35; J. Schimmelpfennig, "Die deutsche Frau im Arbeitseinsatz," *Aufklärungs- und Redner-Informationsmaterial*, July/Aug. 1943.

[106] These reports, known as *Meldungen aus dem Reich*, are included in the Records of the Reich Leader of the SS and Chief of the German Police (T-175), Rolls 258-266. On this source, see Heinz Boberach, *Meldungen aus dem Reich: Auswahl aus den geheimen Lageberichten des Sicherheitsdienst der SS 1939-1944* (Neuwied and Berlin: Hermann Luchterhand Verlag, 1965), p. 148. See also the

111

at the employment offices or take up unfamiliar factory work, and the opposition of mothers to their daughters' enlistment in the Labor Service, is certainly understandable. War and Nazi policy imposed tremendous changes on traditional family life, changes which were sure to be resisted or regretted by many.

Statistical evidence indicates that American women entered the labor force while German women did not. Yet there is some indication that the United States government was not entirely pleased with the response of American women to the recruitment campaigns. Certainly the government manifested great concern. The Bureau of Intelligence and the Bureau of Special Services in the Office of War Information kept closely informed about public opinion, preparing confidential reports throughout the war on many subjects, including women's attitudes toward employment.[107]

---

section entitled "Frauenarbeitseinsatz im Spiegel von SD-Berichten," in Gersdorff, *Frauen im Kriegsdienst*, pp. 56-60.

[107] There is an enormous amount of material on public opinion in the Records of the Office of Government Reports, RG 44, in the Washington National Records Center, Suitland, Maryland. Government reports on attitudes toward the employment of women include: "Do War Plants Need Married Women?—Women Consider the Problem," Special Memorandum no. 54, Surveys Division, Bureau of Special Services, OWI, June 3, 1943, RG 44, Box 1802; "Manpower Problems Raise Questions," Division of Research, Report no. C 15, Bureau of Special Services, OWI, Oct. 9, 1943, RG 44, Box 1718; "Public Attitudes Toward the Manpower Situation," Special Memorandum no. 120, Surveys Division, Bureau of Special Services, OWI, June 23, 1944, RG 44, Box 1803; "Willingness of Women To Take War Jobs," Special Memorandum no. 93, Surveys Division, Bureau of Special Services, OWI, Nov. 22, 1943, RG 208, Box 587, File "Womanpower"; "Women and the War: Special Intelligence Report," Bureau of Intelligence, OWI, Aug. 19, 1942, RG 44, Box 1805; "Women and the War: A summary of women's attitudes toward domestic and foreign issues in the first eight months of the war," Extensive Surveys Division, Bureau of Intelligence, OWI, Aug. 6, 1942, RG 44, Box 1798. In addition, weekly intelligence reports included information on attitudes toward the employment of women. These examples represent only a tiny fraction of the OWI material on public opinion.

One report, based on an October 1943 survey of women's reactions to homefront problems, showed that a majority of American women were aware of the labor shortage, thought more women were needed in the labor force, recognized the importance of civilian service jobs—but seventy-three percent of nonemployed women were unwilling to take a full-time war job.[108] The report also offered, with apparent astonishment, the conclusion that the "poor are more willing to take a war job than the prosperous." Based on these conclusions, which are duplicated in other reports, the March 1944 campaign reflected the government's belief that "the basic *restraining factor* on recruitment now is NOT that the woman does not know *what* to do, but that she is not interested in doing *anything*."[109] Another OWI report commented on the failure of considerable numbers of women "to respond to the propaganda urging them to aid in the war effort."[110] And yet another named as the basic problem of all recruiting efforts the "APATHY arising from lack of understanding."[111] Clearly, the government was not completely satisfied with the response of women to the recruitment campaigns.

In spite of these doubts, the American government decided not to conscript women for war work, but to sell them the idea of taking a war job. Despite controversies within the government over labor recruitment and "information" policy, the WMC and the OWI cooperated in launching a series of promotional campaigns that reached large portions of the population. These campaigns had a profound impact on the public image of women during the war years. The German government, beset by conflicting views among top officials over the need for total mobilization, did not enforce the

[108] "Willingness of Women to Take War Jobs," RG 208, Box 587.
[109] "OWI Women in the War Campaign," RG 208, Box 591.
[110] "Analysis of Editorial Opinion," Division of Research, Bureau of Special Services, OWI, March 24, 1944, RG 208, Box 587, File "News Bureau, Womanpower."
[111] "Women in the War . . . For the Final Push to Victory," RG 208, Box 168.

existing conscription measures and did not devote large-scale propaganda efforts to the task of mobilizing women. But the public image of women created by the Nazis before the war had envisioned the German woman as a "mother of the *Volk*," prepared at all times to sacrifice her comforts and her interests for the welfare of her people. This image lived on, with slight adjustments to the wartime situation. Women in both Germany and the United States were expected to join in the war effort, but this expectation created greater disturbances in the American ideal than in the German one.

5

Munitions for Their Sons:
Nazi Mobilization Propaganda

Earlier I buttered bread for him, now I paint
grenades and think, this is for him.
woman worker in a munitions factory

The ideal German woman, according to the prewar image,
was above all a mother, a spiritual mother of her people as
well as an actual or future biological mother. Her duties as
mother of the *Volk* included, besides the usual responsibilities of a housewife and mother, sacrifice of her own interests for the sake of the German people. In spite of such
useful ideological justification, the German government
decided not to conscript women for war work and did not
launch intensive recruitment campaigns designed to increase
the number of women in the labor force. Despite the lack
of concentrated propaganda campaigns, the material about
women, published by party or state offices, or by nongovern-
mental sources with the tacit approval of the government,
urged and exhorted women to participate in the war effort.
Such official and unofficial propaganda did not have to alter
drastically the prewar image of women in response to the
war. Rather, it incorporated the demands of the war into the
existing Nazi conception of women, shifting certain emphases
but changing the basic outlines little.

Hitler called on women to join the war effort at the very
start of the war, in his Reichstag speech on September 1,
1939. In a much-quoted statement, he made known his expectation that every German woman would join the "fighting
community" with "exemplary iron discipline."[1] The war of

[1] *Hitler: Reden und Proklamationen 1932-1945*, ed. Max Domarus
(Würzburg: Max Domarus, 1963), II, p. 1317. A quotation from
Hitler's statement appeared in many Nazi publications. See, for

1914-1918 served the Nazis as a model and warning in the Second World War, and many works approvingly cited the contributions of German women in the lost war.[2] "It has always been an honorable page in the annals of German womanhood, that in times of war women willingly and with self-sacrifice take the places of men. It was so in the World War, and so it is again today."[3] But there were differences, in the eyes of Nazi writers, between the new war and all those that had gone before. One was the existence of National Socialism. The commentary of a slide show on women in the war effort pointed out that women in the earlier war had worked for money, not for their country. Only National Socialism gave women responsibility for the existence of the state, called for their sacrifices and accomplishments, and made the war an immediate struggle for Germany's existence.[4]

But it was not only the existence of National Socialism in Germany that made this war seem different from all earlier wars. The Second World War seemed to many of its partici-

---

example, *N.S. Frauen-Warte*, 8 (Oct. 1939), p. 185; *Deutsches Frauenschaffen im Kriege: Jahrbuch der Reichsfrauenführung*, 1940.

[2] See, for example, Lore Bauer-Hundsdörfer, "Fraueneinsatz 1914-1939," *N.S. Frauen-Warte*, 8 (Jan. 1940), 296-297; NSDAP, Amt Lichtbild der Reichspropagandaleitung der NSDAP, *Der Einsatz der deutschen Frau im Kriege: Einziges parteiamtliches Lichtbildvortragsmaterial der NSDAP* (Dresden: Dr. Güntz-Druck, n.d. [1941?]); NS Gemeinschaft "Kraft durch Freude," Amt "Schönheit der Arbeit," *Frauen im Werk: Schönheit der Arbeit erleichtert der Frau das Einleben im Betrieb* (Berlin: Verlag der Deutschen Arbeitsfront, 1940), p. 3; Alice Rilke, "Die Frauenarbeit in der Kriegswirtschaft," *Deutsches Frauenschaffen im Kriege*, 1940, pp. 21-26; Dora Schmidt-Musewald, *Mädel- und Fraueneinsatz in der Eisen- und Metallindustrie* (Berlin: E. Wernitz, 1943), p. 9; Gertrud Scholtz-Klink, "Zeit der Bewährung," *Deutsches Frauenschaffen im Kriege*, 1940, pp. 4-5; Theodor Sonnemann, *Die Frau in der Landesverteidigung, ihr Einsatz in der Industrie* (Oldenburg i. O.: Gerhard Stalling, Verlagsbuchhandlung, 1939).

[3] NS Gemeinschaft "KdF," *Frauen im Werk*, p. 3.

[4] NSDAP, Amt Lichtbild, *Einsatz der deutschen Frau*; see also Scholtz-Klink, "Zeit der Bewährung."

pants to have a new face, to be a total war. The introduction to a collection of photographs of women in the war effort compared the demand for labor to the effects of bombing: both were indiscriminate with regard to age and sex.[5] In total war, the woman became the comrade-in-arms of the man, because she had to take up the work left behind when he went off to war. Often this demanded accomplishments far from her natural talents and inclinations. Performing unaccustomed tasks constituted part of her sacrifice.

Total war called for total participation. The phrases, "total effort" and "total war" appeared in the Nazi literature, in spite of the fact that the German economy was far from a total war economy. An article in the party propaganda agency's monthly publication for speakers in February 1943 noted that, although total war had been talked about for years, real total war called for sacrifices on the homefront.[6] Despite the lack of actual measures, the theory of total war made German women into the backbone of the homefront, the counterpart of the army at the front lines. The war gave them certain duties, transformed them into Hitler's "home army."[7] Gertrud Scholtz-Klink proclaimed: "Our men at the front do their duty in the face of death—we women at home, with the same unflinching courage, go in whatever direction the Führer indicates."[8] Nazi writings on women are sprinkled with such military imagery, although no militarization of women was intended.

A few writers felt that the demands of war—the need for women to take the places of men, the need for total participation and self-sacrifice—created a new ideal woman.[9] But an

---

[5] *Frauen helfen siegen: Bilddokumente vom Kriegseinsatz unserer Frauen und Mütter* (Berlin: Zeitgeschichte-Verlag, 1941).

[6] *Aufklärungs- und Redner-Informationsmaterial der Reichspropagandaleitung der NSDAP und des Reichspropagandaamtes der Deutschen Arbeitsfront,* Feb. 1943.

[7] NSDAP, Amt Lichtbild, *Einsatz der deutschen Frau.*

[8] Scholtz-Klink, "Zeit der Bewährung," p. 5.

[9] See, for example, Else Wentscher, *Deutsche Frauengestalten* (Leipzig: Koehler und Voigtländer Verlag, 1943).

examination of the literature on women reveals how easily the prewar image could be adapted to fit the needs of war. The ideal German woman continued to fill the roles of mother, housewife, and preserver of racial purity, while accepting the new responsibilities given her by the war. Even before the war, the ideal German woman had been willing to eat, dress, travel, and work in ways that were good for the people as a whole.[10] Her tasks in the war might be more onerous, her sacrifices greater, but the difference was quantitative, not qualitative. Ruth Hildebrand summed up the dominant ideal of service to the nation as it applied to women: "As mother of her family she meets the demands of the nation, as housewife she acts according to the laws of the nation's economic order, as employed woman she joins in the overall plan of the national household. That does not mean that for her, free will and the development of her individual talents is out of the question. But her life, like that of the man, is in its major outlines determined by the binding law that everything must be subordinated to the profit of the people."[11]

First and foremost, the German woman fulfilled her duty to her people as a mother. The numerous books, articles, and pamphlets on woman as mother, the exhibition on German mothers which toured the Reich, the emphasis of Frauenschaft films and slide shows on motherhood, the elaborate preparations for the celebration of Mother's Day in the midst of military defeat—all of this indicated that the demands of war did little to lessen the status of mothers in the Nazi image of women.[12]

[10] NSDAP, Reichsfrauenführung, Presseabteilung, *Das weite Wirkungsfeld* (Berlin: Hauptabteilung Presse/Propaganda der Reichsfrauenführung, Docky Hammer, n.d. [1942]), p. 10.

[11] "Die Frauen in der Neuordnung Europas," *Deutsches Frauenschaffen im Kriege*, 1941, p. 16.

[12] Works on women as mothers include: Paul Danzer, "Das Leben muss siegen," *N.S. Frauen-Warte*, 8 (Jan. 1940), 289; Hans Hagemeyer, *Frau und Mutter, Lebensquell des Volkes*, 2nd ed. (Munich: Hoheneichen-Verlag, 1943); Maria Kahle, *Die deutsche Frau und*

While the Frauenschaft boasted that the war had not constricted its maternity courses at all, and collections of stories, poems, and letters continued to praise the German mother, a new type of literature on women also developed. Collections of essays on heroic German women of the past multiplied during the war. Most of the women included in these collections were the mothers or wives of famous men, often great soldiers.[13] The lives of such women were intended to be instructive, to indicate how women could help their men through loyalty and love. One author stated explicitly his hope that the courageous women of his times would find in

---

ihr Volk (Warendorf i. W.: Peter Heine, 1942); Maria Kahle, "Die deutsche Kriegsmutter," *VB*, July 7, 1940; Kathe Lingner, *Die Mutter der Kinder: Vom ewigen Auftrag der deutschen Frau,* Frauen am Werk, Bildungsstoffe für Schule und Leben, no. 2, 2nd ed. (Leipzig: Julius Klinkhardt Verlagsbuchhandlung, 1941); Ingeborg Petersen, *Deutsche Mütter und Frauen* (Frankfurt a. M.: Verlag Moritz Diesterweg, 1941). Hagemeyer's book is a catalog of the exhibition "Frau und Mutter, Lebensquell des Volkes"; see "Frau und Mutter—Lebensquell des Volkes," *N.S. Frauen-Warte,* 8 (Feb. 1940), 326-327. On the Frauenschaft materials, see *Deutsches Frauenschaffen im Kriege,* 1941; and "Filme helfen uns!" *N.S. Frauen-Warte,* 8 (Feb. 1940), 341. On the celebration of Mother's Day, see the directive on Muttertag 1942, Records of the NSDAP (T-81), Roll 117, Frame 137659-137661; and a folder of material on Muttertag 1944, Records of the NSDAP (T-81), Roll 173, Frame 314486-314534.

[13] See Trude Geissler, *Von tapferen Frauen: Zeugnisse aus deutscher Geschichte* (Munich: Albert Langer/Georg Muller, n.d. [1942]); Liane von Gentzkow, *Liebe und Tapferkeit: Frauen um deutsche Soldaten,* 3rd ed. (Essen: Fels-Verlag Dr. Wilhelm Spael K.G., 1941); Lisa Heiss, *Die grosse Kraft: Frauenschaffen für Deutschlands Weltgeltung* (Stuttgart: Union deutsche Verlagsgesellschaft, 1939); Otto Heuschele, *Deutsche Soldatenfrauen: Bildnis-Skizzen,* 3rd ed. (Stuttgart: J. F. Steinkopf, 1943); Christian Jenssen, *Kraft des Herzens: Lebenswege deutscher Frauen* (Hamburg: Broschek und Co., 1940); Hans Kern, *Vom Genius der Liebe: Frauenschicksale der Romantik,* 3rd ed. (Leipzig: Philipp Reclam jun., 1942); Bogislav Selchow, *Frauen grosser Soldaten* (Berlin: Die Wehrmacht, 1939); Wentscher, *Deutsche Frauengestalten.*

his stories examples of noble behavior in difficult circumstances.[14] Another suggested that her sketches outlined an ideal woman who combined warm motherliness, feminine goodness, and the female essence. Although she felt that total war would require a new type of woman, she hoped that her sketches would provide the model.[15]

Nazi films also portrayed the German woman as a heroic war mother or wife.[16] A 1941 film, *Annelie*, told the story of a frivolous woman who was transformed into a brave mother in time of war. Another film released in the same year, *Auf Wiedersehen, Franziska*, portrayed a woman sending off to war her wandering husband who had finally come home to her. The next year, *Die grosse Liebe* told the story of a famous Scandinavian singer who learned what it meant to be a German soldier's wife through her love for an airforce officer.

The image of the German woman as soldier's mother or wife suggests that the war affected the ideal of the woman in an indirect manner. When a woman's son became a soldier, she became a soldier's mother, remaining in essence a mother. Added to her responsibility for bearing, raising, and educating children was the duty of bravely watching her sons go off to war. The celebrations of Mother's Day honored those mothers with many children and the mothers of sons who had given their lives for Germany. In a radio speech at the end of the campaign in Poland, Rudolf Hess called for a national day of thanksgiving and praised the dedication of German mothers, especially those who had given sons for Germany.[17]

The courage of women sending their sons to war corre-

[14] Jenssen, *Kraft des Herzens*, pp. 7-8.

[15] Wentscher, *Deutsche Frauengestalten*, p. 9.

[16] Erwin Leiser, *Nazi Cinema*, trans. Gertrud Mander and David Wilson (N.Y.: Collier Books, 1974), pp. 62, 64, 65. See also David Stewart Hull, *Film in the Third Reich: A Study of the German Cinema, 1933-1945* (Berkeley: University of California Press, 1969).

[17] "Unsere deutschen Frauen vorn in der Front," *VB*, Oct. 2, 1939.

sponded to their courage in bearing children. Pain and the risk of death in childbirth, so often the analogue of battle in prewar writings, gave women the basis for understanding the life of the soldier: "How well can a mother understand the soldiers who are ready to sacrifice their lives for others! Is not every woman who brings a child into the world ready for the same sacrifice, does she not venture into the same danger as the soldier in battle, the danger of losing her life? But she does not question this, because fate demands that she be brave. . . ."[18]

In yet another sense, women in wartime Germany fulfilled their duties as mothers and at the same time played a special role in the great struggle for the existence of the German people. Military victory alone would not be enough without future generations of Germans dedicated to National Socialism. Women owed it to Germany to continue to bear children and to rear them as National Socialists. What German soldiers fought for in the war, future generations would secure and build up. Men might make history through their thoughts and deeds, one writer proclaimed, but the soul of the people lay in the hands of the mothers.[19]

German women might engage in any of a number of activities, but all became, in the public image, extensions of their central function as mothers. As air raid wardens, women fulfilled their most important duty, protection of the family.[20] As workers in munitions factories, women cared for their sons by making the ammunition they needed at the front.[21] Nature, according to Nazi theory, gave women the

---

[18] Kahle, *Deutsche Frau*, p. 55.

[19] Ibid., p. 123. See also Danzer, "Das Leben muss siegen," p. 289; and Gertrud Scholtz-Klink, "Deutsches Muttertum," in NSDAP, *Unser Familien Buch* (Berlin: Verlag Dr. von Arnim, 1941).

[20] Hagemeyer, *Frau und Mutter*, p. 304.

[21] See "Munition für die Sohne," in Magda Menzerath, *Kampffeld Heimat: Deutsche Frauenleistung im Kriege* (Stuttgart: Allemannen Verlag Albert Jauss, 1944), pp. 48-50; and Brunhilde Dähn, "Mit ganzer Kraft," *Das Deutsche Mädel*, Feb. 1943.

mission of giving life and preserving life, an eternal mission which was deeply rooted in their essence. War only altered the means for carrying out this mission. If women went into factories, they went to secure the lives of their fathers, husbands, brothers, and sons with the work of their hands. "For every shell and gun that women at home help to produce increases the security of our soldiers and spares our people unnecessary loss."[22] One woman, working in a factory while her son fought in the army, reportedly summed up her function in this way: "Earlier I buttered bread for him, now I paint grenades and think, this is for him."[23]

The German woman's second major role in the prewar ideal was as housewife. Even before the war, her household activities had implications beyond the family circle, ramifications for the nation as a whole. The German housewife had responsibility not only for her domestic chores, but also for the cultural atmosphere of the home and for the success of national economic policy. Nazi conquests brought territory into the Reich to be "Germanized," and *Volksdeutsch* families, families of German origin living outside the Reich, came to Germany to raise their children as Germans. In both of these situations, Nazi policy charged women with responsibility for creating a German home.[24] In general, however, Nazi writings during the war paid less attention to the housewife's cultural duties and more to her economic ones.

Housewives, as the major consumers, played a crucial role in national economic policy. Before the war, books and pamphlets urged women to support the Four Year Plan in its striving for autarchy by purchasing only those goods which were in plentiful supply. Although rationing and shortages dictated what German women could buy during the war to a

[22] Marta Hess, " 'Frauen helfen siegen,' " *Nachrichtendienst der Reichsfrauenführung*, 10 (Dec. 1941), p. 283.

[23] Menzerath, *Kampffeld Heimat*, p. 49.

[24] Kahle, *Deutsche Frau*, p. 84; Menzerath, *Kampffeld Heimat*, pp. 103-105; and NSDAP, Reichspropagandaleitung, Hauptkulturamt, *Das deutsche Hausbuch* (Berlin: Zentralverlag der NSDAP, 1943).

great extent, the division of the women's organization responsible for national economic policy and home economics continued to advise women on matters of food and clothing. The division distributed information about recipes and other matters through the newspapers and radio, and through the cooperation of the Propaganda Ministry. In general, the division pursued its prewar goal of coordinating the demands of national economic policy with the needs of the German family. In wartime, this meant helping women to help the war effort.[25]

Housewives could support the war effort not only by buying goods in plentiful supply and conserving materials of all kinds, but also through the volunteer work that was traditionally the sphere of women in time of war. Magda Menzerath, in her book on women's contributions to the war, devoted one section to such volunteer work.[26] Women collected clothing and other items for the Wehrmacht, visited soldiers in hospitals, and generally did anything they could to help make life easier for Germany's soldiers. Such work earned the designation, "kriegswichtig" [important for the war effort].[27] In fact, most of the propaganda campaigns concerning homefront activities urged women to discourage loose talk, gather materials for the armed forces, conserve food and other items, write letters to the front, or perform other traditional tasks within the domestic sphere.[28]

[25] See *Deutsches Frauenschaffen im Kriege*, 1940, 1941.

[26] Menzerath, *Kampffeld Heimat*, section I.

[27] See Schmidt-Musewald, *Mädel- und Fraueneinsatz*, p. 10.

[28] See the folder of propaganda directives from the Propaganda Ministry to the Gaupropagandaamt Hessen-Nassau, 1942-1944, Records of the NSDAP (T-81), Roll 24, Frame 21734-22084; and the folder of propaganda directives from the Reichspropagandaleitung to the Gaupropagandaamt Hessen-Nassau, 1941-1944, Records of the NSDAP (T-81), Roll 117, Frame 137407-137979. See also the wartime posters in the Mueller and Graeff Photographic Poster Collection, Box 4, Hoover Institution Archives. Radio programs too emphasized household advice, child care information, health, social conditions, professions for women, and fashion. See Ernst Kris and

Nazi ideology granted women importance not only as mothers and housewives, but also as guardians of racial purity. Essentially this meant that women had responsibility for choosing their husbands carefully with regard to racial qualities. Racial consciousness, the necessary attribute of a guardian of racial purity, had two aspects, a negative and a positive one. The positive side consisted of racial pride, exemplified by interest in ancestry. The publication during the war of a handsome folio volume for the use of families in keeping their records and genealogies is one reflection of racial pride.[29] The negative side was simpler: German women ought not marry non-Germans, particularly, of course, Jews. The Nuremberg Laws, and the increasingly drastic and violent measures enforced against the Jews leading up to "the final solution," left little choice to the German woman in the matter of marriage with a Jew. But Hitler's decision to bring foreign workers into the Reich rather than conscript women opened up a whole new source of worry for the advocates of racial consciousness. German women became involved in sexual relationships with foreign workers or prisoners of war often enough to warrant concern on the part of the authorities.[30] This is not so surprising, considering that women often worked alongside foreign workers, especially in agriculture, while almost all able-bodied German men were in the army.

The educational office of the Sudetenland Gau, in coopera-

Hans Speier, *German Radio Propaganda: Report on Home Broadcasts during the War* (London: Oxford University Press, 1944), p. 77.

[29] NSDAP, *Unser Familien Buch.*

[30] See, for example, a letter from the Ortsfrauenschaftsleiterin to the Kreisfrauenschaftsleiterin in Kochem, June 4, 1943, concerning "Verkehr eines deutschen Mädchens mit einem polnischen Zivilarbeiter," Records of the NSDAP (T-81), Roll 75, Frame 86346; and the weekly report of the Kreisleiter (Rheingau-St. Goarshausen), Feb. 16, 1944, Records of the NSDAP (T-81), Roll 119, Frame 140637. See also Edward L. Homze, *Foreign Labor in Nazi Germany* (Princeton: Princeton University Press, 1967), pp. 290-298.

tion with the Frauenschaft and the Bund deutscher Mädel, published a pamphlet exhorting women to guard their racial purity and warning against sexual intercourse with foreign workers or prisoners of war.[31] The pamphlet informed women that Hitler had not brought foreigners into the Reich in order to create one great European family, but in order to meet the serious labor shortage. It recognized that women who saw the foreigners every day, working just as well as German men, often wondered why they should not be friendly with them. German women need not despise these workers, but must be proud of their German blood and keep it pure. As a handy summary, the back cover carried twelve rules for German women, rules instructing them to secure the existence of their people by having numerous children, to keep their German blood pure, to maintain a respectful reserve toward foreigners, to be proud to be German. This pamphlet betrays an extremely defensive stance, admitting that German women might be drawn to foreigners, insisting that preservation of racial purity served the interests of all valuable races, and arguing that the protection of German blood was not a sign of scorn for other peoples. In trying to reach the populace, at least some Nazi officials apparently felt that denunciations of other races as inferior or subhuman would not be the best approach.

The war not only brought foreigners into the Reich, it also took German men away, and this created another problem the Nazis considered a part of the general area of racial consciousness. This was the problem of German mothers without husbands. Early in the war, Rudolf Hess published an open letter in the *Völkischer Beobachter* to a young woman expecting a child by her fiancé who had died in the Polish campaign.[32] Hess admitted that the family was the basic cell of

---

[31] NSDAP, Gau Sudetenland, Gauschulungsamt, *Gedenke, dass du ein Deutscher bist!* (Reichenberg: Roland Verlag, n.d.).

[32] "Rudolf Hess an eine unverheiratete Mutter," *VB*, Dec. 26, 1939. See also *Soziale Praxis*, 52 (May 1943), 148-150. On unmarried motherhood, see Hans Peter Bleuel, *Sex and Society in Nazi Ger-*

the state, but argued that in wartime, the people could not afford to renounce any means of preserving and increasing its racially healthy stock. The existence of the people was more important than custom or morality, and the highest service of women was to give the nation racially healthy children.

The German woman might help the war effort as mother, housewife, and guardian of racial purity, but often this was not enough. Her first and most important task was the correct rearing of her children, but if the nation demanded more of her she would have to take on new tasks without neglecting the old ones.[33] And the nation at war demanded that many German housewives take up employment in industry. It was in the question of employment that the greatest changes occurred in the Nazi expectations of women, in spite of the unwillingness to conscript them and the lack of intensive propaganda campaigns. Yet even the demand that women take up factory work changed the image of women relatively little. In the prewar ideal, the Nazi woman was employed, if at all, in "womanly work," but this ideal contained within it the seeds of the wartime image. Employment in "unwomanly work" was simply another form of sacrifice for the state.

In a book published shortly before the outbreak of war by the German Labor Front, the author insisted that National Socialism had always approved of employed women, as long as their work did not strain them physically or endanger them spiritually.[34] Prewar Nazi literature confirms this statement. The major difference between prewar and wartime literature

---

many, trans. J. Maxwell Brownjohn, ed. Heinrich Fraenkel (Philadelphia: Lippincott, 1973), pp. 154-156; and Jill Stephenson, *Women in Nazi Society* (N.Y.: Barnes and Noble, 1975), pp. 63-71.

[33] For a brief formulation of this idea, see Erna Linhardt-Röpke, "Stellung und Aufgabe der deutschen Frau im Krieg," *N.S. Frauen-Warte*, 8 (May 1940), 436-437. See also Kahle, *Die deutsche Frau*, pp. 54-55; and Rilke, "Die Frauenarbeit," p. 21.

[34] Hildegard Rauter, *Frauenarbeit in der Industrie der Steine und Erden*, Schriften des Fachamtes Steine und Erden im Zentralbüro der Deutschen Arbeitsfront, vol. 2 (Berlin: Verlag der Deutschen Arbeitsfront, 1939).

on the employment of women is the wartime demand that women take up factory work. Nazi ideology before the war did not entirely ignore the existence of women who worked in factories in order to support their families, but it certainly emphasized women's work in agriculture, domestic work, nursing, social work, and other areas of employment defined as compatible with the essence of womanhood. In general, the demands of the war did not lead to a redefinition of what constituted "womanly work," in spite of such valiant attempts as that of Ruth Köhler-Irrgang to reconcile the traditional view of woman's place with the need for women in factories. She stated that woman's place was in the home, but: "Our home is Germany, wherever we are needed!"[35]

Most writers agreed with Dora Schmidt-Musewald, who pointed out that the employment of women in the metal industries represented a necessary but unwelcome development, in National Socialist eyes.[36] She insisted that National Socialism retained as a basic principle the belief that women could best serve the people in social work, housework, agriculture, and by caring for their families. But the war demanded the total effort of the entire nation. Schmidt-Musewald echoed Hitler's assurances that the old program would be in force once the war was over, and she promised that the return of women to their natural spheres would be one of the first tasks of the nation after the victory.[37]

In the meantime, German propaganda greeted the need for the increased employment of women less as a necessary evil than as a joyously offered sacrifice: "It makes no difference

[35] Ruth Köhler-Irrgang, *Die Sendung der Frau in der deutschen Geschichte* (Leipzig: Hase und Koehler Verlag, 1940), p. 235.

[36] Schmidt-Musewald, *Mädel- und Fraueneinsatz*, p. 10; see also Dähn, "Mit ganzer Kraft." These two writers were explicit on this point, unlike most other writers who implicitly assumed that factory work for women was necessary but unfortunate.

[37] Schmidt-Musewald, *Mädel- und Fraueneinsatz*, p. 12; excerpts from Hitler's speech to the Kriegs-Winterhilfswerk, Oct. 3, 1941, are printed in NSDAP, Reichspropagandaleitung, Hauptkulturamt, *Das deutsche Hausbuch*, p. 6.

where the German woman joins the war effort; whether in the munitions factory, or in the workshop, whether in the office or behind the counter, whether in work with the railroad, the post office, or with the street car service, everywhere she fulfills her duty joyfully and does not forget to laugh."[38]

For women not willing to take on extra burdens with the proper spirit of self-sacrifice came admonitions that idle women aided the enemy. Gertrud Scholtz-Klink warned that not helping in the war brought the greatest dishonor. The commentary of a slide show on women in the war effort prepared by the party charged women who were not employed or fully occupied at home with the crime of helping the enemy.[39]

The employed woman might still help the war effort by engaging in "womanly work." Agriculture was an eminently suitable sector, since the employment of women in agricultural work not only corresponded to their feminine "essence" and satisfied the "blood and soil" wing of the Nazi movement, but also counteracted the much-lamented "flight from the land." Agriculture remained a highly recommended occupation for young women, along with nursing and social work.[40] Hermann Göring declared in 1940 that he felt deep

[38] NSDAP, Amt Lichtbild, *Einsatz der deutschen Frau.*

[39] See the quotation from Scholtz-Klink in Menzerath, *Kampffeld Heimat*, p. 7; and NSDAP, Amt Lichtbild, *Einsatz der deutschen Frau.*

[40] See Käthe Delius and Susanna Michael, *Wegweiser durch die ländlichen Frauenberufe: Ratgeber für den ländlichen Nachwuchs, für Eltern, Lehrer und Berufsberator,* 2nd ed. (Berlin: Verlag von Paul Parey, n.d. [1941]); Hans Hajek, *Ländliche Berufe für Mädel* (Berlin: Verlag der "Reichs-Elternwarte," Heinrich Beenken, 1942); Hans Hajek, *Landwirtschaftliche Berufe für Mädel: Was kann unser Mädel werden?* (Berlin: Verlag der "Reichs-Elternwarte," Heinrich Beenken, 1941); Lene Neufeind, *Frauenberufe in der Sozialarbeit* (Stuttgart: Muth'sche Verlagsbuchhandlung, 1940); Lene Neufeind, *Frauenberufe in Wirtschaft und Sozialarbeit, in Haus- und Landwirtschaft* (Stuttgart: Muth'sche Verlagsbuchhandlung, 1939); Lydia Reimer, "Die Berufswahl unserer Jugend in Kriegszeiten," *N.S. Frauen-Warte,* 8 (Jan. 1940), 323.

respect and gratitude for the work of farm women, adding that Germany could never perish with such women.[41] Magda Menzerath felt that when the war was over, and people spoke of those who had given the most, they would name the soldiers and the farm women.[42] Collections of photographs showed sturdy farm women, running their farms with the help of women from the Labor Service; the text accompanying these photographs praised women for helping to feed the nation and putting their husbands' minds to rest about their ability to manage.[43] The April 1940 cover of the *N.S. Frauen-Warte*, the magazine of the Frauenschaft, showed a peasant woman plowing, with factories in the background, and looming above everything the profile of a soldier. This cover, done in the style of "poster art," represents the German woman engaged in "womanly work" and helping the war effort to her utmost.

Although "womanly work," especially agriculture, could be vital to the war effort, work in factories earned the designation "kriegsentscheidend" [decisive for the war effort], in distinction to the "kriegswichtig" work of housewives.[44] A book published by the German Labor Front organization, "Strength Through Joy," declared: "In wartime the woman is not only active in the occupations usually reserved for her, the occupations corresponding with her essence, rather she stands today in the munitions factory itself. The lives of our soldiers depend on the neatness and exactness of her work, on her accomplishment and her love of her work."[45]

[41] See the quotation in Lydia Reimer and Anne-Marie Koeppen, "Die Bäuerin in Kriegszeiten," *N.S. Frauen-Warte*, 8 (March 1940), p. 384.

[42] Menzerath, *Kampffeld Heimat*, p. 83.

[43] See *Frauen helfen siegen*; NSDAP, Amt Lichtbild, *Einsatz der deutschen Frau*; Hans Retzlaff, *Arbeitsmaiden am Werk* (Leipzig: Verlag E. A. Seeman, 1940).

[44] Schmidt-Musewald, *Mädel- und Fraueneinsatz*, p. 10.

[45] NS Gemeinschaft "KdF," *Frauen im Werk*, p. 3.

4. A Nazi woman at work in wartime. Cover of the journal of
the Frauenschaft, April 1940

Nazi propaganda compared the situation of a woman working in a factory to that of the soldier. Both had set aside their normal occupations for the duration. Gertrud Scholtz-Klink, addressing a meeting of Frauenschaft officials, attacked those who insisted that one could not expect certain women to go to work in the armaments industry: "That is exactly as if one were to say, one cannot expect an academic to become a soldier. Our men are not asked."[46] Women in factories were fulfilling their duty, just as soldiers fulfilled theirs at the front.

Photographic collections showed women engaged in all kinds of factory jobs, determinedly fulfilling their duty to their people.[47] Women in slacks, like the woman in uniform pictured in a recruitment poster for civilian employees of the armed forces, made their appearance without challenging basic Nazi concepts about women.[48] Women in factories made weapons for their men, an extension of their duties as wives and mothers, but also helped to create a true people's community. Nazi officials said that they hoped to eliminate class differences and create solidarity through the recruitment of women of the "better classes" for factory work.[49] Magda Menzerath told a story of the wife of a commanding general who volunteered to replace a factory worker, in order to allow the worker to take a vacation.[50] The woman's proud gait was the only clue to her exalted position in life.

[46] Gertrud Scholtz-Klink, "Kriegseinsatz der werktätigen Frau," *Sonderdruck zum Nachrichtendienst der Reichsfrauenführung*, Aug. 1940, p. 4. See also NS Gemeinschaft "KdF," *Frauen im Werk*, p. 3.

[47] See *Frauen helfen siegen*; NSDAP, Amt Lichtbild, *Einsatz der deutschen Frau*; NS Gemeinschaft "KdF," *Frauen im Werk*.

[48] See the recruitment posters in Ursula von Gersdorff, *Frauen im Kriegsdienst 1914-1945* (Stuttgart: Deutsche Verlags-Anstalt, 1969).

[49] See Scholtz-Klink's speech, "Kriegseinsatz der werktätigen Frau," pp. 3, 4; and the directive to speakers on the special campaign, "Deutsche Frauen helfen siegen," Records of the NSDAP (T-81), Roll 117, Frame 137924.

[50] "Der verräterische Schritt," in Menzerath, *Kampffeld Heimat*, pp. 56-57.

Few writers seemed to doubt the ability of women to work with machinery and engage in every kind of factory work. Yet Menzerath, in making her case for the ability of women to master machines, indicated that there was at least some doubt in the public mind. She made her argument by pointing out that women were experienced at running sewing machines and using typewriters.[51] Schmidt-Musewald revealed that employers and male employees resisted the employment of women when she urged them to hire and cooperate with women as their contribution to the war effort.[52]

Nazi propaganda did express great concern with protecting women from physical or mental strain that might endanger them as mothers. The German Labor Front insisted that factories were no longer dirty and terrible, claiming that the office "Beauty of Work" had made them comfortable, safe, sunny, airy, and clean.[53] Women might have to sacrifice the pleasure and satisfaction of their normal lives, but they would not have to take any risks by accepting employment in factories. The Labor Front published a collection of photographs of the "new factory," showing women relaxing around a fountain in a garden during a break, looking more like patrons of a fashionable vacation resort than factory workers.[54]

German women might be riveters, welders, or crane operators, but even the most "unwomanly" occupation could be seen as an extension of their primary duties as wives and mothers in time of war. Long before the outbreak of war, the Bund deutscher Mädel and the women's Labor Service

[51] "Meistern Frauen Maschinen?" in Menzerath, *Kampffeld Heimat*, pp. 35-40.

[52] Schmidt-Musewald, *Mädel- und Fraueneinsatz*, p. 12.

[53] NS Gemeinschaft "KdF," *Frauen im Werk*. The protection of women was a common theme; see, for example, Menzerath, *Kampffeld Heimat*; NSDAP, Amt Lichtbild, *Einsatz der deutschen Frau*; Alice Rilke, "Einsatz und Betreuung der werktätigen Frauen," *N.S. Frauen-Warte*, 8 (Oct. 1939), 214-215.

[54] NS Gemeinschaft "KdF," *Frauen im Werk*.

had chosen the image of the heroic woman in wartime as a model for the new German woman. These two organizations, consisting as they did of enthusiastic and idealistic young women, many of them indoctrinated with National Socialist principles at a young age, relentlessly propagated the image of the new German woman throughout the existence of the Third Reich. BDM and Labor Service propaganda projected an ideal in 1944 little changed since 1934.[55] Women in the Labor Service left behind their normal lives and went to work for Germany, just as soldiers did. Yet Konstantin Hierl, the head of the Labor Service, was sensitive to charges of militarization or masculinization in regard to the women's Labor Service and insisted that it produced "genuine German women." In addition, he argued that the Labor Service leaders had done more toward attaining equality for women than the "protesting, demonstrating, and ridiculously masculine feminists of other countries."[56]

The Labor Service or BDM woman was strong, capable, physically fit, athletic, and willing to sacrifice herself for her country. Even the Jungmädel, the youth group for girls from

[55] See Ilse Arnold, *So schaffen wir! Mädeleinsatz im Pflichtjahr* (Stuttgart: Union Deutsche Verlagsgesellschaft, 1941); Hilde Haas, *Ich war Arbeitsmaid im Kriege: Vom Einsatz des Reichsarbeitsdienstes der weiblichen Jugend nach Berichten von Arbeitsmaiden*, 3rd ed. (Leipzig: "Der nationale Aufbau" Verlag Günther Heinig, 1941); Günther Kaufmann, *Das kommende Deutschland: Die Erziehung der Jugend im Reich Adolf Hitlers*, 3rd ed. (Berlin: Junker und Dünnhaupt, 1943); Hilde Munske, *Das bunte Jungmädelbuch* (Berlin: Junge Generation Verlag, 1940); NSDAP, Reichsjugendführung, *Mädel im Dienst: BDM-Sport*, 3rd ed. (Potsdam: Ludwig Voggenreiter Verlag, 1942); NSDAP, Reichsjugendführung, *Mädel im Dienst: Jungmädelsport* (Potsdam: Ludwig Voggenreiter Verlag, 1944); Irmgard Perzl, *Jungmädel auf dem Köllinghof* (Reutlingen: Ensslin und Laiblin, n.d. [1941]); Retzlaff, *Arbeitsmaiden am Werk*; Frieda Sopp, *Der Reichsarbeitsdienst der weiblichen Jugend* (Berlin: Zentralverlag der NSDAP, 1944); Else Stein, *Unser Jahr: Arbeitsmaiden berichten* (Berlin: Junge Generation Verlag, 1943); *Wir folgen: Jahrbuch der Jungmädel; Wir helfen: Kriegsjahrbuch der Mädel; Wir schaffen: Jahrbuch des BDM*.

[56] Quoted in Retzlaff, *Arbeitsmaiden am Werk*, p. 6, 7.

ten to fourteen years of age, propagated this image. These young women contributed to the war effort by preparing themselves in school for employment in agriculture or in factories, and expressed the desire to become known as the bravest, most capable, most beautiful, and proudest women on earth.[57] They rejoiced in healthy discipline, and in the training of their bodies through sport.[58] An official publication of the BDM, speaking for its members, declared: "Our bodies do not belong to us alone, but to our people. Just as the nation needs healthy, productive boys who will develop into men fit for military service, so it also needs healthy, productive girls who will develop into healthy and beautiful women."[59]

The BDM and Labor Service ideal was the model of the new German woman. The propaganda emanating from these two organizations gives the impression that committed young Nazi women consciously viewed themselves as the vanguard of a new type. During the war, both aspects of the prewar ideal, the young athlete-worker and the older married woman and mother, retained their basic outlines within the context of wartime society. The primary obligation of the German mother remained care of her family, but the mother recast her conception of duty to include such "unwomanly" tasks as making grenades for her son. The housewife continued her prewar efforts to create a German home environment and support national economic policy through her function as the major consumer in German society. The ideal German woman continued to serve as guardian of the race by maintaining her racial pride in all dealings with foreigners. The employed woman put aside her own preferences and inclinations and pitched in with whatever work most needed to be done. If she worked at a job alien to

[57] "Meine Mädel!" *Wir helfen: Kriegsjahrbuch der Mädel*, 1944, p. 92.

[58] See Munske, *Das bunte Jungmädelbuch.*

[59] NSDAP, Reichsjugendführung, *Mädel im Dienst: BDM-Sport*, p. 9.

her "womanly essence," this was her sacrifice in the struggle for the existence of the people. The woman in all of her roles created the spirit out of which the strength of the army grew.[60]

The one new major element in the wartime image of women grew directly out of the circumstances of the time. This was the courage of women. To send one's husband or son off to war, to take up unaccustomed work, to face the terror of air raids, to bring up one's children alone, to cope with the difficulties of life in a wartime situation—all of this required tremendous courage. Otto Heuschele wrote a memorial to the unknown soldier's wife who bore all of her trials stoically.[61] The year book of the Jungmädel noted in 1944 that little had been written about the courageous deeds of women because they usually occurred within the domestic sphere and so never reached the public. But women were no longer confined to the home: "Today, when the war leaps over the front and attacks the homeland in the cruelest way, there are thousands of women who, paying no attention to machine gun fire or the dropping of bombs, help and save to the best of their ability. When history closes the book of this war, these nameless women, along with the faithful mothers and beneficent nurses, will fill pages with their quiet heroism."[62]

The courage, the constancy, the readiness, the will to resist that characterized the ideal woman made her the equal of the soldier at the front. While suffering through air raids and waiting for news of her husband, she continued to bear children, and to bring them up to be happy and healthy.[63] In the air raids, women displayed extraordinary courage that

[60] See "10 Kriegsregeln für die deutsche Frau," *Nachrichtendienst der Reichsfrauenführung*, 9 (March 1940), 76-77.

[61] "Die unbekannte Soldatenfrau," in Heuschele, *Deutsche Soldatenfrauen*, pp. 187-192.

[62] "Tapfere Frau," *Wir helfen: Kriegsjahrbuch der Mädel*, 1944, p. 15.

[63] See Menzerath, *Kampffeld Heimat*, p. 150.

135

would put many men to shame, courage that earned them the designation, "soldiers of the homeland."[64]

The party propaganda agency told German women: "We know that the war is pitilessly hard for women, because sons, brothers, fathers sometimes do not return. . . . 'Fallen on the field of honor.' These words are deeply engraved on the heart of the woman who hears them. It is heroism to bear the pain and the torment and to be silent. Life demands more, and it is as if the voice of the fallen hero rises in a chorus and resounds through the land: 'Mother, what was my highest goal must be yours too, serve the Fatherland.' So all women help and serve the Fatherland."[65]

This was the ideal. The statistics clearly show that not all women helped and served the Fatherland. Hitler's opposition to the conscription of women, strengthened by his confidence in a quick victory, resulted in confused government policy toward the mobilization of women and an absence of concerted propaganda campaigns. But the lack of response from women to the pleas for greater participation in the war effort cannot be explained by the Nazi conception of woman's place. Nazi women, in the public image, belonged wherever they were needed. In spite of the absence of intensive propaganda campaigns on the American model, Nazi propagánda proclaimed that woman's place was in the war.

[64] See "Bombennächte," in Menzerath, *Kampffeld Heimat*, pp. 110-117, especially p. 110.

[65] NSDAP, Amt Lichtbild, *Einsatz der deutschen Frau*. The ellipses are in the original.

· 6 ·

Rosie the Riveter:
American Mobilization Propaganda

In the next twelve months, the American housewife must show that she can keep her head and her
temper and roll up her sleeves at one and the same
time. If she can't, her menfolk fighting on distant
atolls are likely to get slaughtered in the hot sun for
lack of ammunition.

J. C. Furnas, 1942

The ideal American woman in the prewar image was not
at all prepared to participate in the war effort. Above all a
wife and mother, she might ponder the possibility of combining marriage and a career, but she knew where her first
responsibilities lay. She might be expected to devote her
leisure time, if any, to public service, but this involved community work which fit easily into her schedule of caring for
her children, cooking, cleaning, chauffeuring, sewing, laundering, shopping, and entertaining. The idea of sacrifice for
her country, so central to the German ideal, was foreign
to her world. Not that she was unpatriotic, but her lack
of concern for world affairs mirrored the mood of isola-
tion that had descended on the United States after the First
World War. Her devotion to home and family might keep
alive American ideals in time of war, but it was difficult to
see how she would aid the war effort beyond complying
with rationing and salvage drives, doing volunteer Red Cross
work, and buying war bonds.

Clearly, the image would have to change if the government expected to launch recruitment campaigns. Mobilization propaganda could not ignore the fact that industry
needed women in jobs previously reserved for men, jobs
such as riveting and welding which had no place in the pre-

137

war image. The War Manpower Commission and the Office of War Information forged ahead with their policy of selling the war to women, and in the process the image of American women underwent major transformations. Yet these changes were in a larger sense superficial, because they were meant by the government, and understood by the public, to be temporary. It was a tremendous change for Rosie the Riveter, who was always a housewife in the public image, to leave behind her peaceful home existence and take up riveting, but everyone understood that it was only for the duration. Rosie was still primarily a wife and mother, and her factory job could be viewed as an extension of these duties. Just as the German woman made grenades for her son, so the American woman worked to bring her man home sooner. The difference was that the prewar German ideal had already demanded of German women a readiness to take up unusual tasks. Pearl Harbor found the American image, like the American people, totally unprepared for war.

The War Manpower Commission, in spite of its decision to recruit women for war work through intensive promotional campaigns, expressed its belief that a woman's first duty was to her children. The WMC directed that no women with dependent children be encouraged or compelled to seek employment until all other sources had been exhausted, and if such women had to be employed, that adequate care be provided for the children.[1] This was, of course, a policy statement, and did not mean that women with young children were not recruited in labor shortage areas, or that adequate care was provided, by the federal government or anyone else. Paul McNutt, head of the WMC, explained the rationale behind this aspect of government policy: "Even in a national emergency as critical as this, the welfare of our children must be of paramount importance, since it is for

[1] See "WMC Policy on Recruitment, Training and Employment of Women Workers," Appendix B to "U.S. Government OWI Womanpower Campaigns," RG 208, Box 156. See also U.S. OWI, *War Jobs for Women* (Washington: OWI, Magazine Section, 1942), p. 19.

them that our civilization is to be preserved and by them that it will be maintained and bettered."[2]

McNutt was not alone in stressing the importance of women's traditional responsibilities. Although the image of women as workers became important during the war, the prewar image of women as wives and mothers by no means disappeared. A government publication on women's participation in defense activities noted that "great events have always carried women foreward [sic] in their quest to find a secure place in the fields of labor," but added that ". . . their primary instinct has been, and still is, to cherish their greater interest in the protection of the home, the family, and the community."[3] In 1942, the Catholic periodical *Commonweal* lamented "the perilous lack of stress today upon the home and upon woman's function therein."[4] A job and marriage manual for women, although designed to give advice on war work, assumed that the woman's primary role in life was as wife and mother: "The mother stands at the heart of life. She it is who will create the world after the war."[5] Mrs. Leverett Saltonstall, wife of the governor of Massachusetts, summed up the view that women, in spite of the war, were still mothers above all: "Men's work is fighting the battles; women's is the task of keeping homes warm and true, of seeing that little children eat their oatmeal, that their elbows are patched and that they say their prayers."[6]

Even material intended for government recruitment cam-

[2] McNutt was quoted in J. C. Furnas, "Womanpower," *LHJ*, 59 (Nov. 1942), 21.

[3] Lucille Foster McMillin, *The First Year: A Study of Women's Participation in Federal Defense Activities* (Washington: U.S. Government Printing Office, 1941), p. 5.

[4] "Women and War," *Commonweal*, 35 (March 27, 1942), 549.

[5] Gulielma Fell Alsop and Mary F. McBride, *Arms and the Girl, A Guide to Personal Adjustment in War Work and War Marriage* (N.Y.: Vanguard, 1943).

[6] Mrs. Leverett Saltonstall, "Winning on the Home Front," *LHJ*, 60 (June 1943), 31.

paigns sometimes glorified the American housewife. The exhibitor's sales guide for an RKO picture, *Women at Arms*, carried a suggested press release with the headline, "Housewives are Women at Arms Too."[7] The text told of Mrs. Larkin, "just plain housewife," who would like to join the WAACS or work on a farm or in a factory, but had two young children and a house to look after. What could Mrs. Larkin do? "In 'Women at Arms' you see the answer that representative women of America have given that question. You see Mrs. Larkin's answer—that if she goes right on being a good housewife, she's among the strongest, bravest and most valuable of America's women-at-arms. She's the keeper of the Home, the thing we're all fighting for."

Another case of glorification of the American housewife suggests that as the government recruitment campaigns intensified, the supporters of the traditional sphere became more defensive. In response to the major campaign launched in September 1943, *American Home* published an article ostensibly part of the campaign but in reality subversive of the government's intentions.[8] Although the article reported the need for women workers and urged full support of the government's program, it paid sympathetic tribute to the woman who stayed at home to handle a job just as tough as any factory job, and just as necessary to the war effort: "I may be on dangerous ground, but I think that too many women with families are today defining patriotism as 'money-making activities outside the home.' There is another kind of patriotism, less glamorous and more difficult, but upon which rests the future of the country. It is the patriotism practiced daily by those mothers who turn down the attractions of a man's job to stay at home and do a woman's vital work!"

Those who believed that the war demanded nothing of

---

[7] " 'Women at Arms.' Exhibitor's Sales Guide," RG 208, Box 587, File "Graphics: Womanpower."

[8] Ethel McCall Head, "It's Harder to Stay at Home!" *American Home*, 30 (Sept. 1943), 4.

women beyond their normal duties were, however, relatively rare. Most writers expected, at the very least, that women would engage in the kinds of volunteer activities and wartime housekeeping traditionally part of women's sphere. Susan B. Anthony II, grandniece of the suffragist, denounced housekeeping-as-usual as sabotage, calling on women at least to revise their normal housekeeping practices to conform to the demands of the war.[9] Neither Anthony nor the majority of writers on women in the war effort thought that volunteer work or wartime housekeeping was really enough for most women. Anthony objected to the War Manpower Commission policy making the first responsibility of women the care of their young children at home. She, and in her opinion the majority of American women, believed that the first responsibility of all women was to join the war effort wherever and whenever they were needed.[10] The government designed its campaigns not only to urge wartime housekeeping, but to convince housewives to take war jobs as well, as this recommended radio spot suggests: "This is (name) speaking . . . speaking earnestly to the housewives of (city).

[9] Susan Brownell Anthony II, *Out of the Kitchen—Into the War: Woman's Winning Role in the Nation's Drama* (N.Y.: Stephen Daye, 1943), p. 156. Government posters and pamphlets, books and articles called on women to practice wartime housekeeping and take up volunteer work. See the posters in RG 44-PA, housed in the Audio-Visual Department of the National Archives; and Government Information Program Booklets, Dec. 1942-June 1945, RG 208, Box 165. Books and articles include: Keith Ayling, *Calling All Women* (N.Y.: Harper, 1942); Margaret Culkin Banning, *Women for Defense* (N.Y.: Duell, Sloan and Pearce, 1942); Dorothy Dunbar Bromley, "Women on the Home Front," *Harper's*, 183 (July 1941), 188-199; Stella Akulin Koenig, "Mrs. John Doe We Need You!" *WHC*, 69 (July 1942), 51; Josephine R. Robertson, "How Stay-at-Home Mothers Can Help," *Parents' Magazine*, 18 (June 1943), 23; Saltonstall, "Winning"; Toni Taylor, "She Also Serves . . . ," *McCall's*, 70 (July 1943), 44; Dorothy Thompson, "Women and Army Morale," *LHJ*, 58 (Sept. 1941), 6. See the chapter on volunteer activities in Eleanor F. Straub, "Government Policy Toward Civilian Women During World War II," Ph.D. diss., Emory University, 1973, pp. 64-102.

[10] Anthony, *Out of the Kitchen*, p. 130.

I'm a housewife, too . . . never worked outside my home until this year. Feeding my family and buying war bonds just didn't seem enough. So I got an 8-hour-a-day job, and managed to run my home· besides. My husband's proud of me . . . and I've never been happier. I feel I'm *really* helping to make the war end sooner . . . and maybe saving the life of just one boy from home."[11]

All of the government campaigns addressed housewives with little or no experience of employment. Any mention of what Sheila Tobias and Lisa Anderson called "the other Rosie," the woman who had worked before the war, was extremely rare.[12] The government paid no attention to women already employed. No doubt the opening to women of high-paying factory jobs led working women to exchange their usual low-status and low-paying jobs for jobs in defense industries whenever they were able. The government expended no effort convincing women to move from inessential to essential jobs, doubtless because the effort was unnecessary; the government campaigns inadvertently fulfilled the function of informing women already employed of the need for women in war industry. Only in 1943, when the shortage of labor for essential service jobs became acute, did the government turn its attention to the unglamorous, underpaid, low-status jobs that no one wanted to fill. The

---

[11] 1-minute spot no. 12, "Womanpower Spots," RG 208, Box 587.

[12] See Sheila Tobias and Lisa Anderson, "What Really Happened to Rosie the Riveter: Demobilization and the Female Labor Force, 1945-47," MSS Modular Publications, Module 9 (1974). I am grateful to Sheila Tobias for sending me a copy of an unpublished paper by Tobias and Anderson, "New Views of Rosie the Riveter," in which they attempted to resurrect "the other Rosie," the women employed prior to Pearl Harbor. See also Paddy Quick, "Rosie the Riveter: Myths and Realities," *Radical America*, 9 (July-Oct. 1975), 115-131; and J. E. Trey, "Women in the War Economy—World War II," *Review of Radical Political Economics*, 4 (July 1972), 40-57. During the war, Elizabeth Gurley Flynn, a Communist, wrote about working class women and black women, but these women were practically invisible to the public eye. See Flynn's pamphlet, *Women in the War* (N.Y.: Workers Library Publications, 1942).

employed woman before the war, especially the woman employed in factory work or a low-status service industry, had no place in the public image, and the war paid her no further attention.

As a result of the government campaigns, the housewife-turned-factory-worker came into the limelight. Because the prewar image had ignored working women, and because official and unofficial propaganda concentrated on women in industry rather than in other sectors, the war transformed the image of American women. That the ideal woman in 1943 worked at all was a change. But that she worked in a factory, in a job previously defined as "masculine," was unprecedented. In spite of the fact that most women did not work in factories, that the need for women to replace men in other jobs, such as teaching, was also great—the woman in the factory dominated the wartime public image. The women in the armed forces, too, received a great deal of publicity, although their numbers were so small. Magazine illustrations and advertisements pictured women in uniform to an extent out of all proportion to their actual numbers. The woman in uniform was, of course, a new and exciting phenomenon, and military recruitment relied greatly on the supposed glamour of service with the armed forces. Like the WAC, the housewife-factory worker was a fascinating phenomenon. Books and articles informing women of the need for their labor abounded.[13] Numerous guides told wom-

13 A few examples of such books and articles include: Beulah Amidon, "Arms and the Women," *Survey Graphic*, 31 (May 1942), 244-248; Katherine Glover, *Women at Work in Wartime*, Public Affairs Pamphlet no. 77 (N.Y.: Public Affairs Committee, 1943); "How Are You Helping?" *WHC*, 70 (June 1943), 20; "The Key to Victory," *WHC*, 69 (July 1942), 6-9; Thelma McKelvey, *Women in War Production*, America in a World at War, no. 22 (N.Y.: Oxford University Press, 1942); Paul V. McNutt, "Wake Up and Work," *WHC*, 70 (May 1943), 40-41; Paul V. McNutt, "Why You Must Take a War Job," *American Magazine*, 136 (Dec. 1943), 24-25; "More Women Must Go to Work as 3,200,000 New Jobs Beckon," *Newsweek*, 22 (Sept. 6, 1943), 74; Frances Frisbie O'Donnell, "The War

en in great detail how to choose and get a war job.[14] Photographs of women in work clothes adorned the covers and texts of major magazines. Hollywood movies, such as *Swing Shift Maisie*, began to portray working women.[15] Songs about women workers, such as "The Lady at Lockheed," "We're the Janes Who Make the Planes," and, of course, "Rosie the Riveter," flourished.[16] The war spawned a new genre, the woman's wartime narrative. Women housewives, teachers, or students described their experiences in the factory.[17] Even *Real Confessions* published an account entitled

Needs Women," *Parents' Magazine*, 18 (Sept. 1943), 24-26; "Output: Ladies Welcome," *Newsweek*, 20 (Nov. 30, 1942), 56; Frances Perkins, "Women's Work in Wartime," *Monthly Labor Review*, 56 (April 1943), 661-665; Mary Elizabeth Pidgeon, *Women's Work and the War*, American Job Series, Occupational Monographic no. 36 (Chicago: Science Research Associates, 1943); "Woman's Place," *Business Week*, May 16, 1942, p. 20.

[14] See Laura Nelson Baker, *Wanted: Women in War Industry: The Complete Guide to a War Factory Job* (N.Y.: E. P. Dutton, 1943); Herbert Burstein, *Women in War, a Complete Guide to Service in the Armed Forces and War Industries* (N.Y.: Service Publishing Co., 1943); Shelby Cullom Davis, *Your Career in Defense* (N.Y.: Harper, 1942); Mary Rebecca Lingenfelter, *Wartime Jobs for Girls* (N.Y.: Harcourt Brace, 1943); U.S. OWI, *War Jobs for Women*; Evelyn M. Steele, *Wartime Opportunities for Women* (N.Y.: E. P. Dutton, 1943); William Vilmos, *1943 War Job Guide for Women* (N.Y.: Kenmore Publishing Co., 1943).

[15] See Molly Haskell, *From Reverence to Rape: The Treatment of Women in the Movies* (Baltimore: Penguin, 1974), pp. 189-230; Richard Lingeman, *Don't You Know There's a War On?* (N.Y.: G. P. Putnam's Sons, 1970); and Marjorie Rosen, *Popcorn Venus* (N.Y.: Avon, 1973), pp. 201-220.

[16] See Lingeman, *Don't You Know*, p. 270.

[17] See Constance Bowman, *Slacks and Callouses* (N.Y.: Longmans, Green, 1944); Augusta H. Clawson, *Shipyard Diary of a Woman Welder* (N.Y.: Penguin Books, 1944); Beatrice Gray Cook, "Mother—1943 Model," *American Home*, 29 (March 1943), 29; Gene Dickson, "Housewife-War Worker," *New Republic*, 109 (Oct. 18, 1943), 518-519; Mable R. Gerken, *Ladies in Pants: A Home Front Diary* (N.Y.: Exposition Press, 1949); Nell Giles, *Punch In, Susie! A Woman's War Factory Diary* (N.Y.: Harper, 1943); Eliza-

"I Take Part in the War Effort."[18] One would have thought it was the first time the factory gates had opened to women. Women had, of course, been doing factory work for years, but employment had never loomed so large in the public image of women. The public Rosie underwent a sudden transformation. She now set off to work, perhaps even on the night shift, clad in overalls and carrying a dinner pail. In a certain sense, the work clothes and new lifestyle of the working housewife evoked the bobbed hair and easy manners of the flapper of the 1920's. Rosie, like the flapper, seemed a radically new phenomenon and elicited much comment. Certainly there were those who believed that everything had changed because of the war, who saw Rosie the Riveter as a "new woman." An underwear ad proclaimed: "There's a new woman today doing a man's job so that he may fight and help finish this war sooner."[19] Some men expressed in print their fears that women had become tough and competent and would challenge men in all spheres after the war.[20] *Scholastic Magazine* reported the results of a stu-

---

beth Hawes, "My Life on the Midnight Shift," *WHC*, 70 (Aug. 1943), 24; Ruth Tracy Millard, "53 Hours a Week," *SEP*, 215 (June 12, 1943), 22; Ann Pendleton [pseud. of Mary Beatty Trask], *Hit the Rivet, Sister* (N.Y.: Howell, Soskin, Publishers, 1943); Josephine Von Miklos, *I Took a War Job* (N.Y.: Simon and Schuster, 1943); Virginia Snow Wilkinson, "From Housewife to Shipfitter," *Harper's*, 187 (Sept. 1943), 328-337.

[18] This article appeared on an OWI list of articles which supported the womanpower campaigns. See "Magazine Editorials, Articles and Fiction Stories on Programs Being Promoted By OWI," RG 208, Box 1699.

[19] Munsingwear ad, *Life*, Sept. 20, 1943, p. 60.

[20] Corporal Marion Hargrove, "Girls We're Going to Marry When the War Is Done," *GH*, 115 (Nov. 1942), 39; Harold L. Ickes, "Watch Out for the Women," *SEP*, 215 (Feb. 20, 1943), 19; Raymond Knight, "A Lass—But Still a Lack," *Independent Woman*, 21 (Oct. 1942), 299. Such articles were often intended to be humorous, but expressed nevertheless the conviction that women had moved into male spheres to stay. Hargrove wrote sketches for his hometown paper which he collected in 1942 for a book, *See Here, Private Hargrove*, which became a big seller and later a film.

dent opinion poll in an article entitled, "High School Girls Deny That Woman's Place is in the Home."[21] Other writers saw the "new woman" as responsible, proud, independent, with a strong sense of citizenship, straightforward, sincere, still feminine but not fluttering or "vampy"; she wore simple clothes and sensible shoes, used lipstick, powder, and rouge, fixed her hair in a short, smooth, neat style, and did not indulge as much as she had before the war in coffee drinking, smoking, or gossiping.[22] Dorothy Parker proclaimed it "the day of the strong and the sure; the day of the girl who comes marching down to cases like a soldier."[23] She felt that this new strong woman replaced the "glamour girl" of the past. Elizabeth Field agreed with Parker: "The Glamour Girl is practically interred, along with the Gibson girl and the Flapper, and the Boom Town Girl is here for the duration. And—after the war? Well, she's not worrying about that. She's got a job to do right now that's *mighty* important—and she's doing it!"[24]

Unquestionably, the image of the "boom town girl" was new, but the image was in part an adaptation of the "glamour girl" to wartime conditions. Not all photographs and drawings showed young beautiful women war workers. Norman Rockwell's *Saturday Evening Post* cover featuring Rosie the Riveter pictured a large, tough woman with powerful arms, a copy of *Mein Kampf* under her feet and an enormous rivet gun resting across her overall-clad thighs.[25] An advertisement for the Pennsylvania Railroad showed "Mrs. Casey

[21] *Scholastic Magazine*, 46 (March 5, 1945), 26.

[22] See "I Am A Woman," *WHC*, 70 (Feb. 1943), 4; Meloney, "Foreword," in *American Women at War*, p. 5; Violet Moss, "New Women in a New World," *Independent Woman*, 22 (Oct. 1943), 293; "Women in War Work," *The* [Franklin] *Institute News*, 7 (March 1943), 1.

[23] Dorothy Parker, "Are We Women or Are We Mice?" *Reader's Digest*, 43 (July 1943), 72.

[24] Elizabeth Field, "Boom Town Girls," *Independent Woman*, 21 (Oct. 1942), 298.

[25] *SEP*, 215 (May 29, 1943).

Jones," a smiling middle-aged woman in overalls and bandana wielding a sledge hammer and a wrench.[26] Neither Rockwell's Rosie nor Mrs. Casey Jones was a glamour girl. But the vast majority of publicity concerning women workers emphasized glamour. Nell Giles, a reporter for the *Boston Globe* who took a war job in order to write the glamour out of war, complained about such coverage: "Too many articles about women in war written by people who've never been a woman in war . . . too many pictures of beautiful girls posed on the wings of planes with a glowing caption to make you think that war is glamorous . . . and that all the women who go to war, whether it's on the production bench or elsewhere, are young and lovely and fresh from college."[27]

Magazines featured fashion articles on work clothes and debate on the role of glamour in war.[28] A guide to war work in industry addressed women bluntly: "You must admit, for it is a well established fact, that you are a vain creature. And all the factory jobs in the country, whatever their other compensations, would not appeal to you if you had to appear before your fellow workers wearing some 'simply horrid looking thing!' "[29]

Woman's Home Companion took four women war workers to Hollywood, where they were outfitted, made-up, and photographed to show that women workers could be as beautiful as any other women.[30] The resulting article proclaimed proudly that American women were learning not only how to put together tanks, read blueprints, weld, and rivet—but also how to look smart in overalls and be

[26] *Life*, Sept. 6, 1943, p. 19.

[27] Giles, *Punch In, Susie!*, pp. 1-2.

[28] See Wilhela Cushman, "Now It's Woman's Work," *LHJ*, 59 (May 1942), 28-29; Fannie Hurst, "Glamour As Usual?" *The N.Y. Times Magazine*, March 29, 1942, pp. 10-11; Mrs. Horace L. Harrison, "Glamour As Usual: Reply," *The N.Y. Times Magazine*, April 26, 1942, p. 33.

[29] Baker, *Wanted: Women in War Industry*, p. 89.

[30] Virginia Bennett Moore, "Begrimed—Bewitching or Both," *WHC*, 70 (Oct. 1943), 80-81.

5. Norman Rockwell's famous Rosie the Riveter. Reprinted with permission from *The Saturday Evening Post* © 1943 The Curtis Publishing Company

Meet **MRS.** Casey Jones

CASEY'S gone to war . . . so Mrs. Jones is "working on the railroad!"

She is putting in a big day's work oiling and swabbing down giant engines, cleaning and vacuuming cars, handling baggage, selling tickets, moving through the aisles as a trainman.

In fact, she is doing scores of different jobs on the Pennsylvania Railroad — and doing them well. So the men in the armed forces whom she has replaced can take comfort in the fact Mrs. Casey Jones is "carrying on" in fine style.

Since the war began, Pennsylvania Railroad has welcomed thousands of women into its ranks of loyal, busy and able workers. They are taking a real part in the railroad's big two-fold job of moving troops and supplies and serving essential civilian needs during the war emergency.

You will find these women, not merely i expected places, such as offices, telephor exchanges and ticket windows . . . you wi find them out where "man-size" jobs have r be done: in the round house, in the shop in the yards, in the terminals, in the car

We feel sure the American public will tai pride in the way American womanhood h pitched in to keep the Victory trains rollin

BUY UNITED STATES
WAR BONDS AND STAMPS

PENNSYLVANIA RAILROAD
Serving the Nation

★ ★ ★ ․․․ in the Armed Forces   ★ 30 have given their lives for their country

6. Mrs. Casey Jones. "Casey's gone to war . . . so Mrs. Jones is 'working on the railroad!' " From *Life*, September 6, 1943. Reprinted with the permission of the Penn Central Transportation Company and the Al Paul Lefton Company Inc.

glamorous after work. Articles, wartime narratives, and especially war-related advertisements insisted that women war workers could be beautiful in their coveralls.[31] Pond's skin cream continued its series of advertisements featuring young engaged women who used Pond's to remain lovely, but now many of the women worked in war industry, including Hilda Holder, "adorably pretty, adorably in earnest about her war job."[32]

Mary Jackson, director of counseling for Consolidated Vultee Aircraft Corporation, made a study of women workers and concluded: "Women are primarily interested in being women. Their interest in any other kind of success runs a bad second." She continued, however, with a most perceptive comment: "Maybe it could be said with equal truth that men are primarily interested in being men—but being a man *includes* making good in a man's world. Being a successful woman seldom includes that at all."[33]

The glamour girl was working in an emergency, and the war work she did led to the creation of a new image of American women. The change was startling. Women in the public eye now wore bluejeans and safety boots, and carried dinner pails. Official and unofficial propaganda might insist that women workers were "cute" with grease smears on their cheeks, and emphasize that they had only to wash their hands and powder their noses to be as beautiful as any woman in an evening gown, but it could not ignore their

[31] This theme runs throughout the literature. A few examples include: Steve King, "Danger! Women at Work," *American Magazine*, 134 (Sept. 1942), 40-41; James C. Lynch, "Trousered Angel," *SEP*, 215 (April 10, 1943), 23; a Sanforized ad in *Life*, Jan. 19, 1942, p. 58, with the lines: "Oh, aren't we cute and snappy/ in our coveralls and slacks?/ And since the tags say 'Sanforized'/ we'll stay as cute as tacks!"; and an ad for Woodbury facial soap in *Life*, Aug. 9, 1943, p. 67, with the caption, "She turned her back on the Social Scene and is finding Romance at work!"

[32] Ad for Pond's in *Life*, Jan. 31, 1944, p. 89.

[33] Gretta Palmer, "They Learned About Women," *Reader's Digest*, 45 (Sept. 1944), 106.

existence. The public read articles about women recklessly wearing tight sweaters and Veronica Lake hairstyles.[34] Such items gave the impression that women cared more about glamour than safety. But, as Clare Boothe Luce pointed out in the *Woman's Home Companion,* women knew that glamour was more easily found in evening dresses than in overalls.[35] Perhaps the glamorizing of war work signified an attempt to ease the transition from the apron-clad housewife of the prewar image to the woman war worker in pants. Rosie the Riveter, like the flapper, was exotic in appearance, even perhaps in lifestyle. But the new image did not mean that the ideal American woman had changed beyond recognition. Beneath her begrimed exterior, she remained very much a traditional woman.

Ladies' Home Journal distributed questionnaires on women to soldiers, sailors, and marines and compiled the results to furnish the "blueprint for a dream girl, 1942 model."[36] The blueprint showed how little Rosie's wartime image challenged traditional expectations. The ideal woman of American fighting men was short, healthy, and vital, devoted to her home and children, able to participate in at least one outdoor sport, and fond of a moderate amount of dancing. Her skill in cooking was far more important than "braininess" or business ability, and her figure and disposition more important than her face. Most of the men preferred that their wives not work after marriage unless an emergency made it desirable.

The "dream girl, 1942 model" envisioned by American

[34] See, for example, "Sex in the Factory," *Time,* 40 (Sept. 14, 1942), 21; "Veronica Lake," *Life,* March 8, 1943, pp. 39-40. Veronica Lake changed her hairstyle at the urging of the WMC in order to encourage women workers to do likewise.

[35] Clare Boothe Luce, "Victory is a Woman," *WHC,* 70 (Nov. 1943), 121. Other criticism of the glamour approach can be found in: "More Women Must Go to Work," p. 76; and "Women—Now!" *Business Week,* Jan. 9, 1943, p. 72.

[36] Louise Paine Benjamin, "What Is Your Dream Girl Like?" *LHJ,* 59 (March 1942), 114.

men indicated that the new image of women as muscular riveters or beautiful welders was a temporary phenomenon. After all, the image of the woman as worker coexisted throughout the war with the famous American pin-up. Various factors in mobilization propaganda—the concept of women's abilities, the appeals addressed to women, and the concern for the postwar world—made Rosie's transitory nature abundantly clear. She was exotic, but only on the surface and only for the duration.

In the public image, Rosie took up factory work for the first time during the war. The government, ignoring the fact that women had worked in factories since the beginnings of industrialization, suggested that mobilization propaganda liken factory work to housework in an attempt to convince women that they could handle it. Just as Magda Menzerath assured her German readers that women experienced with sewing machines and typewriters could master machines, so the American propaganda took up the Office of War Information's suggestion, and reported that women took to factory machines "as easily as to electric cake-mixers and vacuum cleaners."[37] Such comparisons, although meant to reassure women, only reinforced the idea that women's talents lay primarily in homemaking. The unfortunate conviction that women excelled at repetitive jobs requiring finger dexterity and a large measure of patience, furthered by Women's Bureau studies, stereotyped women as capable of the least skilled jobs.[38] Rosie had left the kitchen for the factory,

[37] Mary Hornaday, "Factory Housekeeping," in *American Women at War, By 7 Newspaper Women* (N.Y.: National Association of Manufacturers, 1942), p. 35. See also Glover, *Women at Work*, p. 1; and Peggy McEvoy, "Gun Molls," *Reader's Digest*, 42 (March 1943), 48.

[38] See "Big Field is Seen for Women in War," *The New York Times*, Dec. 23, 1941, p. 28; Pidgeon, *Women's Work and the War*, p. 9; U.S. OWI, *War Jobs for Women*, p. 21; U.S. Women's Bureau, *Effective Industrial Use of Women in the Defense Program*, Special Bulletin no. 1 (Washington: U.S. Government Printing Office, 1940); "Women in War Work," *The* [Franklin] *Institute News*, 7 (March 1943), 1.

but the public image of the work she did made it clear that she was not intended to become a permanent part of the labor force.

The appeals used to recruit women for war work strengthen the impression that the public Rosie was, inside her coveralls, the same prewar woman who cooked, cleaned, and cared for her family. Men had to be persuaded to give up some of their comforts and perhaps even pitch in and help a bit with the housework, temporarily, of course. Government propaganda appealed to men to encourage their wives to take war jobs. One poster, showing a woman worker and her husband standing in front of an American flag, proclaimed: "I'm proud . . . my husband *wants* me to do my part."[39] An article entitled "I'm Proud of My Wife's War Job" advised men to give up some of their comforts and the satisfaction of supporting their families by themselves and to feel the same pride when their wives took war jobs as they felt when their sons went off to war.[40] Perhaps men were expected to feel the same twinge of fear or anxiety that must have affected even the proudest father when his son went off to fight. The assumption clearly was that many women refused to take war jobs because their husbands did not approve. Susan Anthony II was more critical of men than the government propaganda, mincing no words in calling on them to realize that victory in the war depended on women and men working together: "At present, the majority of you think of women as either sex machines or glorified domestic servants whose job it is to feed you, wash for you, and nurse you. I must be fair and acknowledge that it is not deliberately your fault that you think this. You have been subjected to the same movies, the same books, the same newspapers that we have since childhood."[41]

[39] This poster is part of the National Archives Collection, RG 44-PA. Another poster, with the caption, "Should Your Wife Take a War Job?" is included in RG 208, Box 168.

[40] Toni Taylor, "I'm Proud of My Wife's War Job," *McCall's*, 70 (Sept. 1943), 41. See also Millard, "53 Hours a Week."

[41] Anthony, *Out of the Kitchen*, pp. 204-205.

7. American recruiting poster. Courtesy of the National Archives

As Anthony pointed out, recruitment propaganda had to overcome the popular conceptions of sex roles in order to persuade both men and women that women should join the war effort. A Washington woman involved in recruiting expressed no surprise that women who had never worked before hesitated to take war jobs, since they had "been reared wrong."[42] Theresa Wolfson, writing in the *Annals of the American Academy*, tried to explain why women were slow to enter industry and why men resented their entrance, even under the pressure of national need: "It is not easy to forget the propaganda of two decades even in the face of a national emergency."[43] What these women and others realized was that mobilization propaganda would have to change the public image of women. But they underestimated the ability of propaganda to create a new surface image without challenging basic assumptions about peacetime sex roles.

The appeal that the Office of War Information recommended as most useful for persuading women to take war jobs reveals the underlying conviction that women were essentially housewives and mothers, and workers only "for the duration." The government originally recommended an emphasis on high wages, but retreated in fear of increased consumer spending leading to inflation. Throughout the campaigns, the major appeal was to women's sense of patriotism. In a statement of general recommendations on all material for the womanpower campaigns, the government declared: "The copy should be pitched on a highly emotional, patriotic appeal."[44] In fact, much propaganda insisted that women worked only out of patriotism, not for money at all.[45]

[42] Quoted in J. C. Furnas, "Woman Power," p. 147.

[43] Theresa Wolfson, "Aprons and Overalls in War," *Annals*, 229 (Sept. 1943), 47.

[44] "Preliminary Supplement (A) to the U.S. Government Campaign on Manpower," RG 208, Box 166.

[45] See Bowman, *Slacks and Callouses*, p. 171; Clawson, *Shipyard Diary*, p. ix; Cook, "Mother—1943 Model," p. 29; "Elizabeth Appraises Average Woman," *Manpower Review*, July 1943; King,

The patriotic appeal had two aspects, the positive "do your part" approach and the negative "a soldier may die if you don't do your part" warning. The campaign slogan, "The More Women at Work—The Sooner We'll Win," promised women that their contributions could bring their men home sooner. The picture of a soldier and an empty machine, captioned "This soldier may die *unless* you man this machine," warned that if women did not take war jobs, their men might not come home at all.[46] But in either case, the appeal to patriotism usually took on a personalized cast, urging women to work for their men rather than for their country. Such an appeal made use of a concept of extended motherhood identical to that found in Nazi propaganda. The difference between American and Nazi propaganda, however, was that Nazi propaganda also utilized the abstract ideal of sacrifice for one's country, while the great majority of American appeals to women were couched in personal terms.

Clare Boothe Luce believed that the women in war factories were in fact there for patriotic reasons, on a personal level—for their husbands or brothers or fathers in the armed forces.[47] Whether or not this was so, the recruitment propaganda took up the concept of personalized patriotism with gusto. One poster showed a melancholy woman clutching a letter to her breast; the caption read, "Longing won't bring him back sooner . . . GET A WAR JOB!"[48] An advertisement for DuBarry Beauty Preparations promised that "One woman can shorten this war!"[49] An article in

---

"Danger! Women at Work," p. 119; Lingenfelter, *Wartime Jobs for Girls*, p. 223; Luce, "Victory is a Woman," p. 121; "More Women Must Go to Work," p. 76. Pendleton, *Hit the Rivet, Sister*, indicated that most of the women with whom she worked were in it for the money, but such an admission was a rare exception.

[46] "Answers to Questions Women Ask About War Work," RG 208, Box 582, File "Women in War Work."

[47] Luce, "Victory is a Woman," p. 121.

[48] Poster in the National Archives Collection, RG 44-PA.

[49] *Life*, Sept. 6, 1943, p. 113.

Ladies' Home Journal warned: "In the next twelve months, the American housewife must show that she can keep her head and her temper and roll up her sleeves at one and the same time. If she can't, her menfolk fighting on distant atolls are likely to get slaughtered in the hot sun for lack of ammunition."[50] A film called *Conquer the Clock* warned women not only to get a job, but to do it right. It told the story of a woman defense worker who left the assembly line to smoke a cigarette, thus causing the death of a soldier because in her absence some cartridges went out without primers.[51]

Other posters proclaimed that "'The girl he left behind' is still behind him," or called on women to "Do the job he left behind."[52] A Bristol-Myers advertisement for Sal Hepatica, under the query, "What *can* you say?" pictured a woman worker meeting an acquaintance who had just lost her only son. The worker wondered what to say, then finally blurted out, "If there was only something I could do." The sorrowing mother looked at the woman's slacks and lunchbox and replied, "You're doing it."[53] In a statement reminiscent of the German mothers making munitions for their sons, an American newspaperwoman wrote of the "deep satisfaction which a woman of today knows who has made a rubber boat which may save the life of her aviator husband, or helped to fashion a bullet which may avenge her son!"[54]

The Rosie who worked to bring her husband home sooner, in the meantime making him proud of her contribution to the war, was the same Rosie who dressed in masculine clothes and led a strange and exhausting life, working in a factory at night and performing her domestic chores by day. The fact that she worked out of personalized patriotism helped

[50] Furnas, "Woman Power," p. 20.

[51] See Lingeman, *Don't You Know*, p. 229.

[52] Posters in the National Archives Collection, RG 44-PA; and RG 208, Box 587, File "Graphics: Womanpower."

[53] *Life*, Oct. 16, 1944, p. 13.

[54] Mrs. William Brown Meloney, "Foreword," in *American Women at War*, p. 6.

8. American recruiting poster. Courtesy of the National Archives

9. An advertiser participates in the recruitment effort. "One woman can shorten this war! You're that woman. Yes, *you!*" From *Life*, September 6, 1943. Reprinted with the permission of DuBarry Cosmetics—Texas Pharmacal Division of Warner-Lambert

to allay her strangeness. Women in wartime had to step out of their usual roles, the propaganda insisted, but the war did not have to bring any basic changes to society. An important influence on the public image of women during the war was the concern for postwar society, which cropped up quite early in the war, as soon as eventual victory seemed assured. In Germany, concern for women's status after the war was rare, while in the United States it was a major issue. No doubt this situation resulted from the very different prospects of the two countries by mid-war. In Germany, the onset of losses in Russia and North Africa perhaps made the postwar world increasingly remote. After the tide turned for the United States in the Pacific war, thoughts turned from victory to the immediate future. Women's role in postwar society was of course only a small part of the discussion. But the fact that Americans could look beyond the end of the war to the reestablishment of a peacetime society certainly influenced the public image of women in the midst of the war. Those who expected that housewives-turned-riveters would leave their jobs to the returning veterans at the end of the war naturally did not view women in factories as "new women" or permanent workers.

Toward the end of the war, critics concerned with women's role in the postwar world began to assess their performance in the war. A *Life* editorial in January 1945 denounced women for failing to earn the respect paid them during the war years.[55] Admitting that some women were brave and competent, the editorial argued that too many others were slack, unfocused, helpless, and hopeless. While some women worked in factories and on farms, others shopped, went to movies, and played bridge. Too many were lazy, apathetic, and ill-informed. The editorial, which provoked both negative and positive response from readers, regretted that the government could not draft the pioneer grandmothers of American women rather than rely on the sad performance

[55] "American Women," *Life*, Jan. 29, 1945, p. 28.

of women of the 1940's. *Life* spoke for other critics who believed that women had let their country down in its hour of need.[56]

Life's harsh criticism, when the war was winding down and women were already worried about losing their jobs, suggests an attempt to belittle the contributions of American women to the approaching victory. For while some writers condemned women for failing to take war jobs quickly enough, others began to fear that those who had would not leave them in proper haste at the end of the war. But the majority of writers seemed to assume that women would want to leave their jobs when the war was over. Although the research of Sheila Tobias and Lisa Anderson has shown that a majority of women wanted to keep on working after the war, this particular piece of reality played little part in the public image.[57] A *Woman's Home Companion* poll showed that seventy-five percent of the magazine's "reader-reporters" thought that women should relinquish their war jobs after the victory.[58] *Ladies' Home Journal* reported the results of a national study which showed that most new women workers wanted to go home after the war.[59] Nell Giles summed up the results as follows: "If the American woman can find a man she wants to marry, who can support her, a job fades into insignificance beside the vital business of staying at home and raising a family—three children is the ideal number, she thinks."

It is not clear why the *Ladies' Home Journal* survey came

[56] See "Females in Factories," *Time*, 44 (July 17, 1944), 60; J. C. Furnas, "Are Women Doing Their Share in the War?" *SEP*, 216 (April 29, 1944), 12-13; Patricia Davidson Guinan, "A Long War is Paved With Good Intentions," *House Beautiful*, 85 (Sept. 1943), 30-31; Jean Tigar, "Portrait of a Woman," *House Beautiful*, 86 (May 1944), 106-107.

[57] Tobias and Anderson, "Whatever Happened to Rosie the Riveter?"

[58] "Give Back Their Jobs," *WHC*, 70 (Oct. 1943), 6-7.

[59] Nell Giles, "What About the Women?" *LHJ*, 61 (June 1944), 22-23.

up with results contradictory to those of a Women's Bureau survey cited by Tobias and Anderson. Perhaps the two surveys asked different questions which influenced the outcome of the results, or perhaps the groups of women surveyed were not comparable. In any case, Tobias and Anderson present convincing evidence to show that about half of all new women workers who had been housewives before the war, and three-quarters of those who had been in school, wanted to remain in the labor force after the war. A puzzling finding of the *Ladies' Home Journal* survey may help to reconcile the two studies. Giles pointed out that seventy-nine percent of new working women thought working more fun than staying at home, and that seventy percent of married working women agreed. Giles could offer no explanation for the fact that they intended to quit their jobs anyway, unless they had only temporarily been taken in by the propaganda urging them to escape the drudgery of housework and take a war job. This explanation makes little sense. Perhaps what the survey showed was that a majority of new working women liked working but expected to lose their jobs at the war's end.

Some writers, particularly women, believed that women could and should remain in the labor force after the war.[60] Others wanted women to have the choice of retaining their jobs, but supposed that most would not want to keep them.[61]

[60] See Anthony, *Out of the Kitchen*; Lucy Greenbaum, "The Women Who 'Need' to Work," *The N.Y. Times Magazine*, April 29, 1945, p. 16; Elizabeth Meyer, "Ma's Making Bombers!" *Reader's Digest*, 41 (Nov. 1942), 49-53; Dorothy Thompson, "Women and the Coming World," *LHJ*, 60 (Oct. 1943), 6.

[61] See Ruth M. Leach, *Women and the Top Jobs* (N.Y.: National Association of Manufacturers, 1944); and Dorothy Thompson, "The Stake of Women in Full Postwar Employment," *LHJ*, 61 (April 1944), 6. Thompson's articles are somewhat contradictory. In the article cited in the previous footnote, she noted that she knew of no case in which a group of people who had expanded the area of their lives had been persuaded later to restrict it again; thus, she argued that the school and factory would have to take over some of the functions of the home in order to free women for employment. In

But the majority of popular pronouncements saw women returning to their domestic chores with little regret. Mary Jackson, director of counseling at Consolidated Vultee Aircraft, believed that women would be better homemakers after the experience of working in factories.[62] They would understand how tired a man is when he comes home from work, they would know the value of money, and their experience of the importance of system and order would improve their housekeeping. Dorothy Canfield Fisher agreed that women would not go "back" to housekeeping, but forward to a new and better system of homemaking.[63]

The approaching end of the war brought the lament that women were losing their femininity, as well as a denunciation of modern women as emotionally unstable feminists, and a warning that women were, if not the inferior sex, the dangerous one.[64] But in a sense, these were only indications that little had changed in the public definition of sex roles. The anxiety about women's place in the postwar world, like the nature of the appeals addressed to women, indicates that the image of Rosie the Riveter, the housewife who wielded a rivet

---

the April 1944 article cited in this footnote, Thompson argued that all women should have the choice of working or not, but that many women would leave their jobs: "The ideal of every normal woman is to find the right husband, bear and rear his children, and make with his earnings, for him and for them, a cozy, gay, happy home." Such contradictions parallel the paradoxes in Thompson's life.

[62] Palmer, "They Learned About Women," p. 107.

[63] "From the Lathe to the Hearth," *The N.Y. Times Magazine*, Dec. 5, 1943, p. 16.

[64] Joseph H. Fichter, "The Decline of Femininity," *Catholic World*, 161 (April 1945), 60-63; Marynia F. Farnham and Ferdinand Lundberg, "Men Have Lost Their Women," *LHJ*, 61 (Nov. 1944), 23; John Erskine, "'The World Will Belong to the Women,'" *The N.Y. Times Magazine*, March 14, 1943, p. 15. The Farnham and Lundberg article presented the argument of the authors' much-discussed book, *Modern Woman: The Lost Sex* (N.Y.: Harper, 1947). Chafe called this book the most sophisticated presentation of the antifeminist point of view in the postwar period. See Chafe, *American Woman*, pp. 202-206.

Women Want Homes Like This!

A FRIENDLY doorway that always says "Welcome"... a lovely door-garden where sunshine and flowers suggest the happiness and contentment inside... not just a house, but a *home* where you have time to relax and enjoy life.

These are things we all want.

And in these days of tired bodies and troubled minds it's good for one to think about them now and then—about the new

kind of home *you* will have after victory. Cooking, dishwashing, laundry and house-cleaning will still go on, of course, but they will be done the easy, efficient, electrical way without drudgery... there'll be time to fuss with flowers.

But just now new home things must wait—there's a war to win first. So put your money in war bonds—buy another and another and another. Each extra dollar does an extra bit

to speed victory. And each dollar you spend *after* victory will help provide jobs for the soldiers returning to peace-time industry.

Until the war is won General Electric will continue making only "tools of victory". But when that job is finished we will go back with added enthusiasm to the job we like best—making better electrical equipment for your home that will bring you better living at less cost.

GENERAL ⊛ ELECTRIC

10. Preparing for the postwar world. From *Life*, February 7, 1944. Reprinted with permission of General Electric Company

164

gun, was a temporary phenomenon, a result of wartime up-
heavals. Still, the change in image, however transient, was
important. For the first time, the working woman dominated
the public image. Women, for the duration, were riveting
housewives in slacks, not mothers, domestic beings, or
civilizers. Although German women were also pictured as
factory workers in slacks, the change in the American image
was much greater than in the German.

It is interesting to note that American propaganda concentrated so heavily on the image of the riveting housewife,
ignoring other historical American images that might have
proved useful. Neither Molly Pitcher, the revolutionary war
heroine who took her husband's place on the battlefield, nor
the heroic pioneer woman whose courage and capability
helped to win the west found any place in mobilization
propaganda. *Life* magazine pined for the pioneer grandmothers of American women, but the government and the
other creators of the public image had either forgotten or
chose not to use such models from the American past.

The tone of much of the American mobilization propaganda directed at women was much less serious than the
German. The Nazi government envisioned the war as a struggle to the death between the forces of light and dark, and
while the war was important to the United States, the participation of women could be handled in a humorous vein. German propaganda followed the line set up before the war by
the most militant of the writers on women; American propaganda transformed the prewar public image of women.
It is interesting that the Nazis, who certainly never intended
a militarization of women, used military imagery fairly fre-
quently when describing the role of women in the war. Yet
this too was a recasting of the prewar theme of women in
childbirth as soldiers of the state. In contrast, although the
American government enlisted women in the armed services,
and magazines, advertisements, and posters pictured women
in uniform, military imagery was unusual in American
mobilization propaganda. A poster of three women workers

with the caption, "Soldiers *without* guns," is a rare example of the use of such imagery.[65] The War Manpower Commission and the Office of War Information envisioned the woman worker as "the girl behind the man behind the gun" rather than the soldier of the homefront.

Because German propaganda could draw on the prewar image of Nazi women, it continued to devote attention to all of the major themes in prewar ideology. Women were important as workers for the Reich, but they remained important as guardians of racial purity, mothers, housewives, and bearers of the cultural heritage as well. American propaganda, in contrast, played down woman's role as wife and mother while emphasizing her new functions. But in both cases, propaganda challenged basic assumptions about women's nature as little as possible. The German woman took up "unwomanly" tasks in her capacity as "mother of the *Volk*," in the spirit of sacrifice for her country. The American woman stepped into the unaccustomed world of factory work in order to bring her man home sooner. A newspaper might ask in 1943, "Who still dares to say 'a woman's place is in the home?' " since everyone knew that a woman's place was in the war.[66] But, as a woman worker with a sense of humor asserted, only for the duration.[67] Mobilization propaganda, in both countries, made use of prewar images when possible, created new images when necessary, but intended no permanent change in ideas about "woman's place."

[65] See the poster in the National Archives Collection, RG 44-PA.
[66] "Women in War Work," p. 1.
[67] Pendleton, *Hit the Rivet, Sister.*

· 7 ·

Conclusion:
Mobilizing Women for War

The relationship between propaganda and the success or failure of mobilization is a complex one, as illustrated by the
cases of Nazi Germany and the United States. In spite of
significant similarities in the nature of the propaganda addressed to women, the scope of propaganda and the results
of mobilization efforts were different in the two countries.
Germany did not launch large-scale propaganda campaigns,
in spite of the suitability of Nazi ideology for use in mobilization propaganda, and ultimately did not mobilize women.
Although the prewar image of women assumed readiness to
take up "unwomanly" work for the good of Germany, women
were not subjected to the kind of steady practical propaganda
urging them to take war jobs which the American government
utilized. The United States made extensive use of propaganda
to urge women to join the war effort and succeeded in
mobilizing them.

But the relationship between propaganda and mobilization
is not as simple as this might suggest. The correlation between intensive propaganda and successful mobilization does
not mean that women entered or did not enter the labor force
solely in response to propaganda. A number of factors, and
particularly the financial incentive, influenced women in their
decisions. Propaganda operated in conjunction with these
factors by stressing or ignoring appeals that touched on wom-
en's actual concerns. Although the disseminators of propaganda may have assumed that they controlled women's
responses, in fact the relationship was not that direct. Propagandists intend to persuade, but they may in fact serve the
function of informing the public.

To suggest that propaganda played some role in mobiliza-

167

tion does not necessarily imply that women were simply manipulated into, and out of, the labor force. The concept of manipulation, accepted by some historians of women in the war and vehemently rejected by others, assumes that women were passive objects with no motivation or will of their own.[1] But those who reject the idea that women were manipulated have concentrated entirely on women who had worked before the war, arguing that they worked because they had to, and such a conclusion cannot explain the motivations of the women who joined the labor force for the first time during the war.[2] Certainly the women who had always worked, and who suddenly had the chance to move into high-paying factory work, are an important element in the history of women during the war. But they were not the women addressed by official and unofficial propaganda, and their motivations do not explain the relationship between propaganda and mobilization.

Financial incentive is the most important factor influencing women's decision to enter the labor force. Although women may seek employment for reasons of self-actualization or out of boredom (a factor which may have motivated some childless married women whose husbands were away in the armed forces), money is, for both women and men, the major reason for working.

The different situation in Germany and the United States with regard to financial incentives is probably the most important reason why American women entered the labor force and German women did not. Although the United States government policy of equal pay for equal work did not mean

[1] J. E. Trey, "Women in the War Economy—World War II," *Review of Radical Political Economics*, 4 (July 1972), 41-57, treated the history of women in the American labor force during the war as a case study of manipulation. Paddy Quick, "Rosie the Riveter: Myths and Realities," *Radical America*, 9 (July-Oct. 1975), 115-131, rejected the model of manipulation.

[2] See Quick, "Rosie"; and Sheila Tobias and Lisa Anderson, "What Really Happened to Rosie the Riveter," MSS Modular Publications, Module 9 (1974).

in practice that women received the same wages as men in identical positions, war industry did offer American women higher wages than they could ordinarily command. In contrast, German industry paid poorly and made no pretense of instituting an equal pay policy, in spite of the Frauenschaft's support for such a principle.[3]

In addition, the two governments differed in policy toward allowances to dependents of men in the armed forces. Allowances were far more generous, in relative terms, in Germany than in the United States.[4] Furthermore, the German government gave a smaller allowance to dependents who worked, while the United States did not penalize dependents for working. The German system provided no financial incentive to encourage women to take employment. In any case, there were few goods to buy in Germany as the war went on. Although shortages also plagued consumers in the United States, the government made some attempt to appeal to women by stressing high wages which could be put into war bonds and used after the war.

The entire question of financial incentive must be considered in light of the different employment situations in the two countries previous to the war. The German economy had reached full employment by 1936, while only entrance into the war ended the lingering effects of the Depression in the United States. What this meant for many American women was that the war provided the first real chance for employment. German women who sought jobs had found greater opportunities in the labor shortage that had developed as Hitler made his early preparations for war.

[3] See Eleanor F. Straub, "Government Policy Toward Civilian Women During World War II," Ph.D. diss., Emory University, 1973, pp. 239-258; and Gerhard Bry, *Wages in Germany, 1871-1945* (Princeton: Princeton University Press, 1960). On the Frauenschaft's support of equal pay for equal work, see *Deutsches Frauenschaffen: Jahrbuch der Reichsfrauenführung*, 1937, p. 50.

[4] Clarence D. Long, *Labor Force in War and Transition: Four Countries*, Occasional Paper no. 36 (N.Y.: National Bureau of Economic Research, 1952), pp. 41-43.

In light of the importance of financial incentives, one would expect propaganda that emphasized wages to succeed in encouraging women to enter the labor force. The Nazi government, in a situation of low wages for women, never used such an appeal, which in any case would have sounded very "individualistic" in propaganda emphasizing service for the nation so heavily. Propaganda policy in the United States was more confused on this point. The Office of War Information recommended an appeal based on high wages rather hesitantly, fearful of encouraging inflation. This recommendation resulted in some appeals to women to earn, buy savings bonds, and in this way save for the postwar period. But the appeal based on wages was never central or even especially prominent. The lack of appeals to women's needs or desires to earn money in both countries strengthens the impression that wartime propaganda avoided challenging traditional assumptions about women. By ignoring or playing down economic motivation, it was possible to view women as wives and mothers responding to the needs of the country or of their men rather than as workers.

Although financial incentive was probably the most important factor in encouraging women to accept employment, other factors influenced them as well. High wages may attract a woman to employment, but one would expect that her decision to enter the labor force, if she has children, would be affected by her child care responsibilities and the availability of child care facilities. Yet the evidence indicates that this factor does not help to explain the difference in response between German and American women. The child care burden on women was greater in the United States than in Germany, although the number of children per woman outside the labor force was higher in Germany.[5] In any case, child care facilities in the United States were not sufficient, in terms of quantity or quality, to explain the influx of women into the labor force.[6] Federally funded child care centers, built

[5] Ibid., p. 43.
[6] See William H. Chafe, *The American Woman: Her Changing*

with Lanham Act funds, cared for only 120,000 children at their peak in 1944, and community- and industry-sponsored child care was not extensive. In contrast, German day nurseries numbered 32,000 by 1944 and cared for 1,200,000 children.[7] The Frauenschaft, in conjunction with the Nazi welfare organization, operated "harvest kindergartens" for the children of farm women. The Labor Service, too, sent women to care for the children of rural women. In addition, children entered the Hitler Youth at an early age and youth activities took up much of their spare time. The idea of institutionalized child care was more acceptable to the Nazi state than to American society, in spite of Nazi ideology's emphasis on motherhood, because of the Nazi practice of indoctrination through a thorough organization of society.

Whether one emphasizes the child care burden on all women (which was higher in the United States) or the child care burden on women outside the labor force (which was higher in Germany), the existence of child care facilities cannot explain the difference in response between American and German women. The OWI recognized that the provision of adequate child care would encourage women to accept employment, but the government chose to continue appealing to women's personal patriotism rather than develop and advertise child care facilities on a large scale for women workers. The Nazi government made much of its facilities, but not in conjunction with appeals to women to enter the labor force.

Social, Economic, and Political Role, 1920-1970 (N.Y.: Oxford University Press, 1972), pp. 159-172; Howard Dratch, "The Politics of Child Care in the 1940's," *Science and Society*, 38 (1974-75), 167-204; Virginia Kerr, "One Step Forward—Two Steps Back: Child Care's Long American History," in *Child Care—Who Cares?* ed. Pamela Roby (N.Y.: Basic Books, 1973); Margaret O'Brien Steinfels, *Who's Minding the Children? The History and Politics of Daycare in America* (N.Y.: Simon and Schuster, 1973); Straub, "Government Policy," pp. 259-306.

[7] See Long, *Labor Force in War*, p. 43.

The level of employment, if not affected by the child care burden, was clearly influenced by what might be termed "status barriers." The Nazi government complained that women of the middle and upper classes of society were leaving the burden of war work to women of the lower classes. Perhaps these complaints and the much commented upon fear of factory work in Germany help to explain the reluctance of women to take war work. Germany, unlike the United States, had a strong socialist tradition which had resulted, before 1933, in a division of the women's movement into bourgeois and socialist camps. Perhaps this division in particular, and the socialist dichotomy between working class and bourgeoisie in general, led to a strong reluctance among middle and upper-class women to take on work they associated with the lower classes. That this was so is indicated by Gertrud Scholtz-Klink's denunciation of middle-class women for failing to respond to the call of the nation in need. Perhaps the status barrier in the minds of middle-class women was too powerful for them to overcome.

Middle-class American women, of course, were not accustomed to working in factories either, but government propaganda worked hard to make factory work seem exciting and highly respectable. Although German propaganda issued by the Labor Front did try to convince women that factories were clean and comfortable, no campaigns comparable to the American ones glorified factory work as a glamorous duty. The United States government recognized the existence of status barriers in 1943 when it analyzed the reasons for the shortage of women in poorly paying and low-status service jobs. The attempt to persuade women to accept such jobs was less successful than the propaganda urging women to take up factory work.

Both countries, in different fashions, appealed to the patriotism of women, and certainly patriotism motivated some women to enter the labor force. Here again propaganda played a role. It is impossible to conclude anything definite about levels of support for the two governments solely from

172

the response of women to mobilization propaganda, but the lack of response from German women shows that they were not the fanatic supporters of the regime depicted in Nazi propaganda. Nazi propaganda failed to persuade women to take the jobs they had no financial incentive to seek out of a spirit of sacrifice for the nation. The Nazi government had been calling for sacrifice since 1933, making it difficult to create a sense of crisis with the outbreak of the war. In contrast, the war descended on the American people with the bombing of Pearl Harbor, inducing national solidarity in the face of imminent danger. American women, not yet weary of calls for sacrifice, responded in the American tradition of voluntarism. The authoritarian Nazi system overplayed the sacrifice theme and thereby discouraged voluntary responses.

A comprehensive explanation of German failure and American success in mobilizing women must consider not only government policy, but also these factors which influenced women's availability for, and motivation to seek, employment. The United States relied on intensive propaganda campaigns based primarily on appeals to personalized patriotism to inform and persuade women, while the Nazi government displayed hesitation and conflict over mobilization in general and the mobilization of women in particular, resulting in propaganda less intensive than the American. The financial incentive of relatively high wages and low allowances to dependents of men in the armed forces in the United States, combined with the propaganda's successful legitimization of factory work for middle-class women and its powerful appeal to patriotism in the voluntaristic tradition, encouraged women to enter the labor force. Lack of adequate child care certainly made the situation of the working mother difficult, but most women managed to meet the demands of a job as well as the demands of a family. In Germany, the lack of financial incentive, the failure of propaganda to overcome status barriers to factory work by middle-class women, the government's overuse of the theme of sacrifice for the state, and uncertain government policy which undoubtedly gave women conflicting messages, discouraged women from entering the labor force.

The success of propaganda must be evaluated according to its own goals and expectations. German propaganda, however hesitantly, called for sacrifice and service for the nation, and by these standards failed. The indications of small-scale resistance—refusal to enter the Labor Service or register with the employment offices—joined with the undeniable statistical data on labor force participation strongly suggests that the Nazi regime could not or would not exercise its theoretically totalitarian power. Likewise, an examination of appeals to women shows that the legendary Nazi propaganda machine was in fact less effective, in this area, than the Office of War Information in the United States. American propaganda was far more intensive and pervasive, at least in part because of the powerful role played by the advertising industry in supporting the war effort. But in any case, propaganda in both countries was less important in persuading women to take war jobs than it was in adapting public images to the wartime situation without challenging basic assumptions about women's roles in society.

An analysis of mobilization propaganda reveals the interplay between economic need and public images. A modern industrialized society at war requires the participation of women, and this means that the public image of women must adapt in order successfully to meet this need. The American example indicates that the needs of war can transform the ideal in an extremely short period of time. Public images, unlike basic beliefs about woman's nature, can change quickly in response to economic need. The economic role and the popular image of women may change drastically in the course of a modern war, but basic ideas about women's proper sphere, characterized by cultural lag even in the case of long-term economic developments, change little. Of course, the war was too short a span of time to expect fundamental changes in people's attitudes. The German and American cases show that public images can adapt to the need for women in jobs previously reserved for men without challenging traditional assumptions.

In the German case, mobilization propaganda made use of the Nazi ideal of sacrifice for one's nation, drawing on the prewar conception of women as "mothers of the *Volk*" to urge women to participate in the war effort. In the American case, the employed woman, previously invisible in the public image, made her appearance and the housewife-turned-riveter became commonplace for the duration. Official and unofficial mobilization propaganda met the demands of the war by changing the public image as much or as little as necessary to bring it into line with the need for women in the war economy. American propaganda did not find the change difficult or uncomfortable. Public images reflect deeply held convictions, but are themselves susceptible to rapid transformation.

It is clear that the wartime changes expanded the options of women in a way intended by the propagandists as temporary. The mode of adaptation of public images assured that the wartime range of options would contract once again in peacetime. The postwar situation in Germany was complicated by the defeat and occupation, but the history of the postwar period in the United States is instructive. Historians and others have wondered at the legendary total domesticity of the 1950's following on the heels of the supposedly "liberating" war. In *The Feminine Mystique*, Betty Friedan explained the 1950's as a reaction to "emancipation," a reaction dominated by the postwar creation of the "mystique."[8] But if one looks beneath the surface of wartime imagery, the 1950's make more sense. The feminine mystique was no new creation, but simply the 1950's version of the traditional wife and mother. The postwar image of women did not have to make tremendous adjustments. Rosie simply stepped out of her overalls, still wearing her apron underneath.

[8] *The Feminine Mystique* (N.Y.: Dell, 1963).

The idea that wars "liberate" women, that wars bring about social revolution, overlooks the fact that societies in time of war accept changes normally considered undesirable on a permanent basis. William Chafe, in his book on American women in the twentieth century, argued that the war forced on the American people a change in behavioral patterns (increased labor force participation of women) which eventually resulted, in the 1960's, in a change of attitudes towards women's role in society.[9] This theory explains social change as a result of involuntary changes in actual behavior, and points to the war as a watershed in the history of American women.

I agree with Chafe that direct experience is probably the most effective means of dispelling prejudice, but I am not convinced by his argument that the war began this process. It is true that the patterns of labor force participation changed in the period 1940 to 1960: the female participation rate as a whole increased, and the participation rate of older and married women rose sharply.[10] But, as Graph IV shows, the tremendous increase in the number of women in the labor force during the war had no permanent impact on the trend in the size of the female labor force. The participation rate, however, shown in Graph V, provides a better indication of changes in the female labor force.[11] While there are difficulties with an analysis of female participation rates over time as a result of possible inadequacies in the census data, the evidence does not support the contention that the Second World War was responsible for permanent changes in

[9] Chafe, *American Woman.*

[10] See Valerie Kincade Oppenheimer, *The Female Labor Force in the United States*, Population Monograph no. 5 (Berkeley: Institute of International Studies, 1970).

[11] See the appendix. In Graph V, I have adjusted the yearly figures for 1940-1950 downward by 3 percent in order to bring them into line with the decennial figures. The decennial figures are based on census data, the yearly figures on data from current population reports.

176

the participation rate.[12] Female labor force participation increased throughout the period 1890 to 1960, more sharply in the later decades, as goods and services once produced within the home were taken over by the market economy and as the service sector of the economy expanded. Thus the demand for female labor increased, matched by an increase in the supply of female labor (the addition of older and married women to the labor force). The influx of women into the labor force during the war had nothing to do with these long-term changes, and had no permanent impact on the female labor force.

Chafe's theory of social change can be applied to the United States in the 1960's and 1970's to explain shifts in attitudes as the employment of women became commonplace, but the war did not set the process of social change in motion. The American public perceived the war as an extraordinary situation and accepted many temporary changes it would not tolerate in peacetime. The mobilization propaganda directed at women allowed the public to accept the participation of women in unusual jobs without challenging basic beliefs about women's roles. Wartime opinion polls on the public's acceptance of the employment of married women show that the proportion approving increased tremendously during the war if the question was phrased in terms of employment in war industry. In 1945, an American Institute of Public Opinion poll showed little change since a 1937 poll in the attitudes of Americans toward the employment of married women who could be supported by their husbands.[13] Understandably, the public accepted the need for the employment of married women in the wartime crisis,

[12] On the debate over participation rates, see W. Elliot Brownlee and Mary M. Brownlee, *Women in the American Economy: A Documentary History, 1675-1929* (New Haven: Yale University Press, 1976), pp. 4-8, especially p. 5, footnote 2; and Oppenheimer, *Female Labor Force.*

[13] See Oppenheimer, *Female Labor Force,* p. 47.

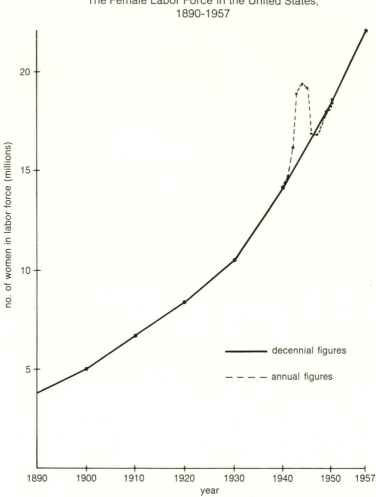

GRAPH IV

The Female Labor Force in the United States,
1890-1957

no. of women in labor force (millions)

year

——— decennial figures

– – – – annual figures

GRAPH V

The Female Participation Rate in the United States, 1890-1960

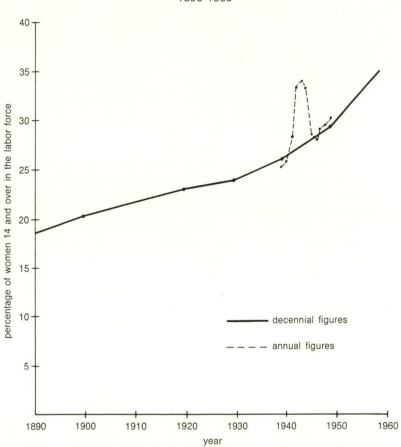

decennial figures

— — — — annual figures

but this does not indicate that the war experience had any permanent impact on attitudes.

In accordance with traditional attitudes, women were laid off in great numbers after the war and pushed out of the sacred male precincts which they had invaded for the first time. Not until the mid-1950's did the number of women in the labor force reach the level of the wartime peak. The war may have served as a preview of the kind of changes Chafe discussed, but not until the 1960's did the public have to confront the disparity between attitudes toward women and experiences with women in the labor force on a permanent basis.

Although the German case is much confused by defeat and division, there is some evidence that the same kind of tension between attitudes and reality existed in the Federal Republic in the 1960's.[14] The war resulted in a large surplus of women over men, which meant that the demand for labor would have to be met in large part by women. After the war, most German families needed the income of the woman in order to survive. As the economic situation improved, the primary motive for married women in the labor force became the desire to improve the family's standard of living. By the 1960's, one-third of all married women had jobs. Yet the public remained ambivalent about the propriety of working mothers. Helge Pross reported that two-thirds of all German women advocated a law forbidding the employment of mothers with children under ten years of age.[15] Another

[14] See Ursula Lehr and Hellgard Rauh, "Male and Female in the German Federal Republic," in *Sex Roles in Changing Society*, ed. Georgene H. Seward and Robert C. Williamson (N.Y.: Random House, 1970), pp. 220-239; and Helge Pross, "West Germany," in *Women in the Modern World*, ed. Ralph Patai (N.Y.: The Free Press, 1967), pp. 247-266. Alfred Katzenstein, "Male and Female in the German Democratic Republic," in *Sex Roles*, ed. Seward and Williamson, pp. 240-256, argued that relations between the sexes in East Germany are egalitarian.

[15] Pross, "West Germany." Pross did not cite a source for this statement.

study pointed out that sociological works on German women assumed the perpetuation of traditional sex roles. Although the concept of the "old patriarch" was gone, that of the "good housemother" remained.[16]

Such tension between attitudes and reality was nonexistent during the war. The adaptation of public images to the demands of war allowed both the German and the American public to accept the employment of women in "unwomanly" occupations without challenging basic ideas about "woman's place." Propaganda in both countries proclaimed that "woman's place is in the war." The disseminators of propaganda could do this without challenging deeply held beliefs only because it was wartime. The Nazi woman making munitions for her son, like Rosie the Riveter, had no permanent impact on women's status in society. The war was not a social revolution, for society generally or for women in particular. As long as women had a "place," in the home or in the war, little had changed.

[16] Lehr and Rauh, "Male and Female," p. 221.

181

Appendix

EXPLANATION OF STATISTICS

This appendix brings together from various sources the statistics used in the text and in constructing the graphs.

SOURCES: The prewar German statistics come from the *Statistisches Jahrbuch für das deutsche Reich*, 1941-1942, p. 33, the last of this series published by the Statistisches Reichsamt. The wartime statistics come from the United States Strategic Bombing Survey study, *The Effects of Strategic Bombing on the German War Economy*, pp. 202-207. The Survey staff used figures published by the Statistisches Reichsamt for 1939-1944 as *Kriegswirtschaftliche Kräftebilanz*.

The American figures come from the United States Bureau of the Census, *Historical Statistics of the United States, Colonial Times to 1957*, pp. 8, 9, 71, 72; and *Statistical Abstract of the United States*, 1949, p. 174. There are no figures for 1910 because the 1910 census is not considered comparable with other censuses.

AREA: The German statistics cover varying areas. The early years through the first set of figures for 1939 cover the territory known as Old Germany, the territory prior to the acquisitions of the Third Reich. The figures for 1939 (second set) through 1944 cover the area known as Prewar Germany, Germany as of September 1, 1939 (including the Saar, the Sudetenland, and Austria). I have not included postwar figures because the available statistics covering occupied Germany, the Democratic Republic, and the Federal Republic are meaningless in comparison with the prewar and wartime figures. The absolute numbers cannot be compared throughout the period covered, but the relative figures, expressed in percentages, remain useful.

182

THE LABOR FORCE CONCEPT: The U.S. Bureau of the Census developed the concept of the labor force and applied it to all post-1940 census returns. Previously an individual was included in the labor force if he or she expressed willingness and ability to work. In 1940, the test became actual activity, and an individual was included in the labor force only if he or she was working or actively looking for work. Pre-1940 figures are not exactly comparable to post-1940 statistics because of this difference. The labor force includes the employed (those working for pay or profit; or working at least fifteen hours as unpaid family workers in business or on a farm; or those not at work or seeking work but who had jobs from which they were absent for reasons of illness, bad weather, vacation, or labor disputes), and the unemployed (those actively seeking work; or waiting to be called back to work or to start new employment; or those who would seek work but were ill or expressed the belief that no jobs were available). The United States labor force figures include only those over fourteen years of age, because the number of those under this age in the labor force is insignificant. The figures for the female labor force include women in the armed forces.

The German statistics use basically the same concept, including the employed (including employers, the self-employed, salaried employees, wage earners, and unpaid helping family members) and the unemployed, and excluding students, housewives, retired persons, persons living on their own means, and persons wholly dependent. Beginning in 1925, the German statistics included women who considered their main subsistence to derive from participation in the business of the head of the household. The figures for the female labor force include women employed by the armed forces.

PARTICIPATION RATE: The participation rate is the percentage of the female population of working age in the labor force.

183

My figures for the U.S. participation rate come from *Historical Statistics of the U.S.*, p. 71, and are based on the decennial census for 1890, 1900, 1920, 1930, 1940, and 1950 (the figures in parentheses are decennial census figures for 1940 and 1950), and on *Current Population Reports* for the years 1940-1957. These figures express the female labor force as a percentage of the female population fourteen and over. The German figures are not comparable to the American, because they express the female labor force as a percentage of the total female population. Figures for the German female population fourteen and over are not available. Because of this difference, the German participation rate is understated. But the German rate is higher than the American, as explained in the text, because of the large number of German women who were unpaid helping family members in agriculture. In 1939, 40 percent of all women in the labor force were engaged in agriculture, and 75 percent of these were unpaid helping family members. In the United States, the proportion of women engaged in agriculture was very small, 8.1 percent in 1940. This difference is important because women engaged in agriculture on family farms, although they usually worked longer hours than other employed women, were not employed in the same sense as women who worked in offices or factories, in part because they could care for their children and did not have to leave their homes.

SHARE OF THE LABOR FORCE: The female share of the labor force measures the number of women in the labor force as a percentage of the entire labor force. The female labor force in the United States includes women in the armed forces. The German figures include women employed as civilians with the armed forces. They do not include women in the Labor Service, but they do include women employed in agriculture or domestic service in fulfillment of their Duty Year obligation.

Germany: Female Participation Rate
and Share of Labor Force (in percentages)

Year	Participation Rate	Share of Total Labor Force	Share of Civilian Labor Force[a]	Share of German Civilian Labor Force[b]
1882	24.4	30.0		
1907	30.5	34.5		
1925	35.6	35.9		
1933	34.2	35.5		
1939	36.3	37.1		
1939	36.0	35.9	37.1	37.4
1940		34.6	40.0	41.3
1941		32.7	39.2	42.7
1942		32.7	40.6	46.1
1943	35.6	32.1	40.5	48.9
1944		32.8	41.0	51.1

[a] Including foreign labor.
[b] Excluding foreign labor.

185

U.S.: Female Participation Rate
and Share of Labor Force (in percentages)

Year	Participation Rate	Share of Total Labor Force	Share of Civilian Labor Force
1890	18.2	17.0	
1900	20.0	18.1	
1920	22.7	20.4	
1930	23.6	21.9	
1940	27.9	25.2	25.8
	(25.7)		
1941	28.5	25.4	25.6
1942	31.0	26.7	28.8
1943	35.8	29.1	34.1
1944	36.5	29.3	35.4
1945	35.9	29.5	35.1
1946	31.1	27.6	29.8
1947	30.8	27.4	28.6
1948	31.7	28.0	29.1
1949	32.2	28.3	29.7
1950	32.8	28.8	30.0
	(29.0)		
1957	35.5	31.2	33.0

Germany: Female Population
and Labor Force (in thousands)

Year	Female Population	Total Labor Force	Civilian Labor Force	Female Labor Force	Foreign Labor Force
1882	20,333	16,495		4,954	
1907	27,884	24,637		8,501	
1925	32,214	32,009		11,478	
1933	33,533	32,296		11,479	
1939	35,029	34,269		12,700	
1939	40,613	40,781	39,415	14,626	301
1940		41,583	35,983	14,386	1,154
1941		43,377	36,177	14,167	3,033
1942		44,160	35,525	14,437	4,224
1943	41,613	46,084	36,529	14,806	6,260
1944		45,210	36,110	14,808	7,126

U.S.: Female Population and Labor Force
(in thousands)

Year	Female Population[a]	Total Labor Force	Civilian Labor Force	Female Labor Force (including armed forces)	Female Armed Forces
1890	30,711	21,833		3,704	
1900	37,226	27,640		4,999	
1920	52,171	40,282		8,229	
1930	60,780	47,404		10,396	
1940	65,770	56,180	54,870	14,160	0
1941	66,482	57,530	54,980	14,640	0
1942	67,263	60,380	55,880	16,120	10
1943	68,194	64,560	54,860	18,810	110
1944	69,020	66,040	54,220	19,370	200
1945	69,893	65,290	54,180	19,270	240
1946	70,757	60,970	56,450	16,840	
1947	72,180	61,758	59,120	16,915	
1948	73,502	62,898	60,524	17,599	
1949	74,853	63,721	60,835	18,048	
1950	76,153	64,749	62,183	18,680	
1957	86,371	70,746	66,951	22,097	574

[a] These figures include the entire female population, not just women fourteen and over. For this reason, the participation rate figures cannot be calculated from this table.

Selected Bibliography

PRIMARY SOURCES

1. Archival Sources

GERMAN

Library of Congress Poster Collection. Prints and Photographs Division, Library of Congress, Washington, D.C.
Mueller and Graeff Photographic Poster Collection. Hoover Institution Archives, Stanford, California.
Records of the National Socialist German Workers Party. T-81. Captured German Documents deposited at the National Archives, Washington, D.C.
Records of the Reich Leader of the SS and Chief of the German Police. T-175. Captured German Documents deposited at the National Archives, Washington, D.C.
Terramare Office Records. Hoover Institution Archives, Stanford, California.
Theodore Abel Collection. Hoover Institution Archives, Stanford, California.

AMERICAN

Records of the Office of Government Reports. RG 44. Washington National Records Center, Suitland, Maryland.
Records of the Office of Government Reports. Audiovisual Records. RG 44-PA. National Archives, Washington, D.C.
Records of the Office of War Information. RG 208. Washington National Records Center, Suitland, Maryland.

2. Published Documents, Speeches, Statistical Sources

GERMAN

Hitler, Adolf. *Hitler, Reden und Proklamationen, 1932-1945.* Ed. Max Domarus. 2 vols. Würzburg: Max Domarus, 1963.

Hitler, Adolf. *Hitler's Table Talk*. Trans. Norman Cameron and R. H. Stevens. London: Weidenfeld and Nicholson, 1953.

——. *The Speeches of Adolf Hitler*. Ed. Norman H. Baynes. 2 vols. London: Oxford University Press, 1942.

International Military Tribunal. *Trial of the Major War Criminals Before the International Military Tribunals*. 42 vols. Nuremberg: International Military Tribunal, 1947-49.

Reichsministerium des Innern. *Reichsgesetzblatt*. Berlin: Reichsverlagsamt, 1933-45.

Statistisches Reichsamt. *Statistik des deutschen Reichs*. Berlin: Verlag für Sozialpolitik, Wirtschaft und Statistik, Paul Schmidt, 1933, 1939.

Statistisches Reichsamt. *Statistisches Jahrbuch für das Deutsche Reich*. Berlin: Verlag der Reimar Hobbing, 1933-42.

U.S. Chief of Counsel for the Prosecution of Axis Criminality. *Nazi Conspiracy and Aggression*. 10 vols. Washington: U.S. Government Printing Office, 1946-48.

U.S. Strategic Bombing Survey. *The Effects of Strategic Bombing on the German War Economy*. Overall Economic Effects Division, October 31, 1945.

AMERICAN

U.S. Bureau of the Census. *Historical Statistics of the United States, Colonial Times to 1957*. Washington: U.S. Government Printing Office, 1960.

U.S. Bureau of the Census. *Statistical Abstract of the United States*. Washington: U.S. Government Printing Office, 1940-50.

U.S. Statutes at Large.

3. Newspapers, Periodicals

GERMAN

Aufklärungs- und Redner-Informationsmaterial der Reichspropagandaleitung der NSDAP und des Reichspropagandaamtes der Deutschen Arbeitsfront.

Das Deutsche Mädel: Die Zeitschrift des Bundes Deutscher Mädel in der Hitler-Jugend.
Deutsches Frauenschaffen: Jahrbuch der Reichsfrauenführung.
Deutsches Frauenschaffen im Kriege: Jahrbuch der Reichsfrauenführung.
Jahrbuch des Reichsarbeitsdienstes.
Nachrichtendienst der Reichsfrauenführung.
N.S. Frauen-Warte: Die Einzige Parteiamtliche Frauenzeitschrift.
Soziale Praxis: Zentralblatt für Sozialpolitik und Wohlfahrtspflege.
Unser Wille und Weg: Monatsblätter der Reichspropagandaleitung der NSDAP.
Völkischer Beobachter. (VB).
Die Werktätige Frau: Mitteilungsdienst des Frauenamts der Deutschen Arbeitsfront.
Wir folgen: Jahrbuch der Jungmädel.
Wir helfen: Kriegsjahrbuch der Mädel.
Wir schaffen: Jahrbuch des BDM.

AMERICAN

Employment Security Review.
Employment Service Review.
Independent Woman.
Life.
Manpower Review.
New York Times.
Saturday Evening Post.

4. Books, Articles, Pamphlets, Dissertations

GERMAN

Alexander, Lucie. *Unser der Weg: Vom Kampf der Jugend unserer Tage.* Berlin: Verlag H. W. Rödiger, 1935.
"Alfred Rosenberg und die deutsche Frau." *Völkischer Beobachter (VB)*, March 27/28/29, 1932.
"Amerikanische Frauenerziehung." *VB*, June 10/11, 1928.

Ammon, Kurt. "Zur Frage des Doppelverdienertums." *Soziale Praxis (SP)*, 42 (Sept. 1933), 1139-41.

"Antwort an Frau Dr. Hadlich." *VB*, April 4, 1926.

"Die Arbeit der Lichtbild-Propaganda im Kriege." *Unser Wille und Weg*, Jan. 1940, pp. 4-5.

Arnold, Ilse. *So schaffen wir! Mädeleinsatz im Pflichtjahr.* Stuttgart: Union Deutsche Verlagsgesellschaft, 1941.

B., Josefine von. "Die deutsche Frau im Kampf für Deutschlands Freiheit." *VB*, Feb. 6, 1926.

Bauer-Hundsdörfer, Lore. "Fraueneinsatz 1914-1939." *N.S. Frauen-Warte*, 8, no. 13 (Jan. 1940), 296-297.

Baumann, Gerhard. "Nationalsozialistische und 'demokratische' Propagandagrundsätze." *Unser Wille und Weg*, Nov. 1940, pp. 124-125.

Bäumer, Gertrud. *Familienpolitik: Probleme, Ziele und Wege.* Berlin: Verlag für Standesamtswesen, 1933.

―――. *Die Frau im deutschen Staat.* Berlin: Junker und Dünnhaupt, 1932.

―――. *Die Frau im neuen Lebensraum.* Berlin: F. A. Herbig, 1931.

―――. *Die Frau in der Krisis der Kultur.* Berlin: F. A. Herbig, 1926.

Baumgart, Gertrud. *Die altgermanische Frau und wir.* Heidelberg: C. Winters Universitätsbuchhandlung, 1935.

―――. *Frauenbewegung, gestern und heute.* Heidelberg: C. Winters Universitätsbuchhandlung, 1933.

Belmede, August Friedrich. *Hausbuch der deutschen Jugend.* Berlin: Junge Generation Verlag, n.d.

Benz, Edith. *Frauenarbeit.* Bildung und Nation, Schriftenreihe zur nationalpolitischen Erziehung, no. 10. Leipzig: Eichblatt-Verlag (Max Zedler), 1934.

Bernsee, Hans. "Das Problem der ledigen Mutter und die deutsche Volksgemeinschaft." *SP*, 46 (May 1937), 579-582.

Beyer, Karl. *Die Ebenbürtigkeit der Frau im nationalsozialistischen Deutschland: Ihre erzieherische Aufgabe.* Leipzig: Armanen-Verlag, 1932.

————. *Familie und Frau im neuen Deutschland.* Langensalza: Verlag von J. Beltz, 1936.

Boehm-Stoltz, Hilde. "Die Nationalsozialistin und die Familie." *VB*, Jan. 20, 1932.

Boger-Eichler, Else. *Von tapferen, heiteren und gelehrten Hausfrauen.* Munich: J. F. Lehmanns Verlag, 1937.

Bohe, Walter. "Die Aufgaben der Frauenwelt in der NSDAP." *VB*, June 18, 1927.

Bohnstedt, Werner. "Sozialpolitik des Nationalsozialismus." *SP*, 44 (Sept. 1935), 1090-98.

Bosch, Elisabeth. *Es ist kein Ende der Liebe.* Munich: Deutscher Volksverlag, 1941.

————. *Vom Kämpfertum der Frau.* Stuttgart: Alemanen-Verlag, 1938.

Bühler, Dr. "Totaler Krieg." *SP*, 52 (Feb. 1943), 49-50.

Buresch-Riebe, Ilse. *Frauenleistung im Kriege.* Berlin: Zentralverlag der NSDAP, 1941.

Caesar-Weigel, Hildegard. *Das Tagewerk der Landfrau.* Berlin: Reichsnährstand-Verlag, 1940.

Castell-Rüdenhausen, Clementine. *Glaube und Schönheit: Ein Bildbuch von den 17-21 jährigen Mädeln.* Munich: Zentralverlag der NSDAP, n.d. [1940].

Dähn, Brunhilde. "Mit ganzer Kraft." *Das Deutsche Mädel,* Feb. 1943.

Danzer, Paul. "Das Leben muss siegen." *N.S. Frauen-Warte,* 8, no. 13 (Jan. 1940), 289.

Darré, R. Walther. *Das Bauerntum als Lebensquell der nordischen Rasse.* 2nd ed. Munich: J. F. Lehmanns Verlag, 1933.

————. *Neuadel aus Blut und Boden.* Munich: J. F. Lehmanns Verlag, 1930.

Delius, Käthe and Michael, Susanna. *Wegweiser durch die ländlichen Frauenberufe: Ratgeber für den ländlichen Nachwuchs, für Eltern, Lehrer und Berusberator.* 2nd ed. Berlin: Verlag von P. Parey, n.d. [1941].

Deutsche Arbeitsfront. Arbeitswissenschaftliches Institut. *Die Frauenarbeit im Blickfeld der Krankenstatistik.* Berlin: Arbeitswissenschaftlichen Verlag, 1941.

Deutsche Arbeitsfront. Frauenamt. *Tagewerk und Feiera-bend der schaffenden deutschen Frau.* Leipzig/Berlin: Verlag Otto Beyer, 1936.

Diehl, Guida. *Die deutsche Frau und der Nationalsozialis-mus.* 5th ed. Eisenach: Neulandverlag, 1933.

Diers, Marie. "Frau ohne Politik—mit Herz!" *VB*, April 16/17, 1933.

————. "Frauenfrage und Frauenantwort." *Kampfpause: Beilage zum Nationalen Sozialisten*, Feb. 1, 1930. Re-printed in *Die nationalsozialistische Linke 1925-1930.* Ed. Reinhard Kühnl. Meisenheim am Glan: Hain, 1966.

Edel, Fritz. *German Labour Service.* Berlin: Terramare Office, 1938.

Eggener, Elfriede. *Die organische Eingliederung der Frau in den nationalsozialistischen Staat.* Diss. Leipzig, 1938. Borna-Leipzig: R. Noske, 1938.

Ehrle, Gertrud. *Leben spricht zu Leben: Wirklichkeitsbilder aus dem Alltag der Frau.* 3rd ed. Freiburg i. B.: Herder, 1941.

Eichhoff, Theodore. "Frauenwirken am Wiederaufbau Deutschlands." *SP*, 42 (Dec. 1933), 1425-28.

————. "Nationalsozialistische Stimmen zur Frauenfrage." *SP*, 43 (Oct. 1934), 1244-48.

————. "Neuere Literatur zur Frauenfrage." *SP*, 43 (Feb. 1934), 232-236.

Erbrich, Ilse-Maria. *Typische Frauenarbeiten in der Indus-trie.* Diss. Heidelberg, 1938. Karlsruhe: Buchdruckerei Paul Fröscher, 1938.

" 'Ersatz' von Männerarbeit durch Frauenarbeit?" *SP*, 47 (Sept. 1938), 1094-95.

Estorff, Gustav von. *Dass die Arbeit freude werde! Ein Bild-bericht von den Arbeitsmaiden.* Berlin: W. Andermann, 1938.

"Fest bleiben!" *VB*, Feb. 20, 1926.

"Filme helfen uns!" *N.S. Frauen-Warte*, 8, no. 16 (Feb. 1940), 341.

"Die Frau im Beruf." *N.S. Frauen-Warte*, 1 (Nov. 1932), 194.

"Die Frau im deutschen Arbeitsleben." *Das Deutsche Mädel*, Jan. 1939, pp. 2-3.

"Frau und Mutter—Lebensquell des Volkes." *N.S. Frauen-Warte*, 8, no. 15 (Feb. 1940), 326-327.

"Frauen der Deutschen Volkspartei verunglimpfen!" *VB*, Feb. 9, 1932.

Frauen helfen siegen: Bilddokumente vom Kriegseinsatz unserer Frauen und Mütter. Berlin: Zeitgeschichte-Verlag, 1941.

Freiin von Brand, Marie; Kisker, Ida; Roeske, Lucie; and Walter, Toni. *Die Frau in der deutschen Landwirtschaft. Deutsche Agrarpolitik*, vol. 3. Ed. M. Sering and C. von Dietze. Berlin: Verlag Franz Vahlen, 1939.

Frick, Wilhelm. *Die deutsche Frau im nationalsozialistischen Staate.* Fr. Manns Päd. Magazin, no. 1400. Langensalza: Hermann Beyer und Söhne (Beyer und Mann), 1934.

Friedrich, Theodor. *Formenwandel von Frauenwesen und Frauenbildung.* Leipzig: Armanen-Verlag, 1934.

Frobenius, Else. *Die Frau im dritten Reich: Eine Schrift für das deutsche Volk.* Berlin-Wilmersdorf: Nationaler Verlag J. G. Huch, n.d. [1933].

Frühauf, Ludwig. *Deutsche Frauentum, deutsche Mütter.* Hamburg: Hanseatische Verlag, 1935.

Gallus, Arth. "Moderne Wahnideen." *VB*, Feb. 20, 1926.

Ganzer-Gottschewski, Lydia. See Gottschewski, Lydia.

Garbe, Ulrike. *Frauen des Merowingerhauses: Königinnen und Mägde, Heilige und Dirnen, ein Beitrag zur Sittengeschichte der Zeit des Kulturbruchs.* Reden und Aufsätze zum nordischen Gedanken, no. 38. Leipzig: Adolf Klein Verlag, 1936.

———. *Frauenschicksal—Frauengrösse: Lebens- und Charakterbilder germanischer Frauen von der Frühzeit bis zur Gegenwart.* 2nd ed. Stuttgart: Union Verlag, 1936.

"Das Gehirn bei Mann und Weib." *VB*, March 27/28, 1927.

Geissler, Trude. *Von tapferen Frauen, Zeugnisse aus deutscher Geschichte.* Munich: A. Langen/G. Müller, n.d. [1942].

Gentzkow, Liane von. *Liebe und Tapferkeit: Frauen um deutsche Soldaten.* 3rd ed. Essen: Fels-Verlag Dr. Wilhelm Spael K.G., 1941.

Germany Speaks, by 21 Leading Members of Party and State. London: Thornton Butterworth Ltd., 1938.

"Girls." *VB,* Oct. 16, 1926.

Goebbels, Joseph. *Michael: Ein deutsches Schicksal in Tagebuchblättern.* Munich: Zentralverlag der NSDAP, 1929.

Goebbels, Magda. *Die deutsche Mutter: Rede zum Muttertag, gehalten im Rundfunk am 14. Mai 1933.* Heilbronn: Eugen Salzer Verlag, 1933.

Gottschewski, Lydia. *Das deutsche Frauenantlitz: Bildnisse aus allen Jahrhunderten deutschen Lebens.* Munich: J. F. Lehmanns Verlag, 1939.

―――. *Männerbund und Frauenfrage: Die Frau im neuen Staat.* Munich: J. F. Lehmanns Verlag, 1934.

―――. "Die Nationalsozialistin in Volk und Staat." *N.S. Frauen-Warte,* 1 (Sonderaufgabe, n.d.), 2-5.

Graf, Ruth. "Neuorientierung in der Wirtschaftsfürsorge." *SP,* 45 (April 1936), 402-408.

Groote, Paula Siber von. See Siber von Groote, Paula.

Haas, Hilde. *Ich war Arbeitsmaid im Kriege: Vom Einsatz des Reichsarbeitsdienstes der weiblichen Jugend nach Berichten von Arbeitsmaiden.* 3rd ed. Leipzig: "Der Nationale Aufbau" Verlag Günther Heinig, 1941.

Haase-Mahlow, Liselotte. "Gruss der deutschen Frauen an den Führer." *VB,* April 16/17, 1933.

Hadeln, Charlotte. *Deutsche Frauen, deutsche Treue, 1914-1933: Ein Ehrenbuch der deutschen Frau.* Berlin: Traditions-Verlag Kolk, 1935.

Hadlich [Emma]. "Aufgaben der deutschen Frau in der Gegenwart." *VB,* Jan. 12, 1926.

―――. "Aufgaben der deutschen Frau in der Gegenwart." *VB,* Jan. 23, 1926.

―――. "Frauenfrage?" *VB,* April 4, 1926.

Hagemeyer, Hans. *Frau und Mutter, Lebensquell des Volkes.* 2nd ed. Munich: Hoheneichen-Verlag, 1943.

Hajek, Hans. *Ländliche Berufe für Mädel.* Berlin: Verlag der "Reichs-Elternwarte," H. Beenken, 1942.

————. *Landwirtschaftliche Berufe für Mädel: Was kann unser Mädel werden?* Berlin: Verlag der "Reichs-Elternwarte" H. Beenken, 1941.

Hamm, F. "Augen auf, deutsche Frau!" *VB*, Dec. 28, 1931.

————. "Frauenberuf und Nationalsozialismus." *VB*, Feb. 24, 1932.

Hansen, Henrich. *Das Antlitz der deutschen Frau.* Dortmund: Westfalen-Verlag, n.d. [1934].

Harms, Suse. *Die deutschen Frauenberufe.* Berlin: Junker und Dünnhaupt Verlag, 1939.

Hecht, Thilda. "Gedanken zur Frauenfrage." *VB*, Feb. 6, 1926.

Heiss, Lisa. *Die grosse Kraft: Frauenschaffen für Deutschlands Weltgeltung.* Stuttgart: Union deutsche Verlagsgesellschaft, 1939.

Hess, Luise. *Die deutschen Frauenberufe des Mittelalters.* Beiträge zur Volkstumsforschung, vol. 6. Munich: Neuer Filser-Verlag, 1940.

Hess, Marta. " 'Frauen helfen siegen.' " *Nachrichtendienst der Reichsfrauenführung*, 10 (Dec. 1941), 282-284.

Hess, Rudolf. "Die Aufgaben der deutschen Frau." *VB*, May 27, 1936.

————. "Rudolf Hess an eine unverheiratete Mutter." *VB*, Dec. 26, 1939.

Heuschele, Otto. *Deutsche Soldatenfrauen: Bildnis-Skizzen.* 3rd ed. Stuttgart: J. F. Steinkopf, 1943.

Hildebrand, Ruth. "Die Frauen in der Neuordnung Europas." *Deutsches Frauenschaffen im Kriege*, 1941, pp. 8-17.

————. *Frauenaufgaben im Krieg: Was die deutsche Frau heute wissen muss.* Berlin: Verlag H. W. Rödiger, n.d. [194-].

Hitler, Adolf. *Mein Kampf.* Trans. Ralph Manheim. Boston: Houghton Mifflin, 1943.

Hoerner, Suse von. *Mädels im Kriegsdienst: Ein Stück Leben.* Leipzig: Von Hase und Koehler Verlag, 1934.

Hoffmann-Linke, Eva Elisabeth. *Idee oder Schicksal? Ein Wort an die deutsche Frau.* Leipzig: R. Voigtländer, 1933.

Holzmann, Hans. *Die Verkäuferin in der Bäckerei.* Berlin: Handwerker-Verlagshaus H. Holzmann, 1943.

Höpfner, Frau. "Streit der Geschlechter?" *VB*, Feb. 20, 1926.

Jaeger, Seraphine. *BDM in Bamberg.* Bayreuth: Gauverlag Bayerische Ostmark, 1936.

Jänchen, Gabriele. "Über den Kriegsarbeitseinsatz der deutschen Frau." *N.S. Frauen-Warte*, 9, no. 21 (May 1941), 338-339.

Jenssen, Christian. *Kraft des Herzens: Lebenswege deutscher Frauen.* Hamburg: Broschek, 1940.

Jenssen, Christian. *Licht der Liebe: Lebenswege deutscher Frauen.* Hamburg: Verlag Broschek, 1938.

Junk, Margarete. *Mädelberufe in vorderster Front: Über Hauswirtschaft, Säuglings- und Krankenpflege zur Volkspflege.* Stuttgart: Union Deutsche Verlagsgesellschaft, 1940.

Kahle, Maria. *Akkordarbeiterin: Aus meinem Tagebuch.* 2nd ed. Warendorf i. W.: P. Heine, 1937.

———. *Die deutsche Frau und ihr Volk.* Warendorf i. W.: P. Heine, 1942.

———. "Die deutsche Kriegsmutter." *VB*, July 7, 1940.

Kaiser, Helena. *Der Einfluss industrieller Frauenarbeit auf die Gestaltung der industriellen Reservearmee in der deutschen Volkswirtschaft der Gegenwart.* Diss. Leipzig, 1933. Leipzig: Buchdruckerei A. Teicher, 1933.

Kallsperger, Anna. *Nationalsozialistische Erziehung im Reichsarbeitsdienst für die weibliche Jugend.* Diss. Heidelberg, 1939. Leipzig: Grossdruckerei Oskar Leiner, 1939.

"Kann eine Arbeiterfrau Marxisten sein?" *VB*, June 24, 1931.

Kaufmann, Günter. *Das kommende Deutschland: Die Erziehung der Jugend im Reich Adolf Hitlers.* 3rd ed. Berlin: Junker und Dünnhaupt, 1943.

Kern, Hans. *Vom Genius der Liebe: Frauenschicksale der Romantik.* 3rd ed. Leipzig: P. Reclam, 1942.

Kienle, Else. *Frauen, aus dem Tagebuch einer Ärztin.* Berlin: G. Kiepenheurer, 1932.

Klaje-Wenzel, Dorothea. *Die Frau in der Volksgemeinschaft.* Leipzig: Adolf Klein Verlag, 1934.

Koeberle-Schönfeldt, Charlotte. "Matriarchat?" *N.S. Frauen-Warte,* 1 (Sept. 15, 1932), 122.

Koeppen, Anne Marie. *Das deutsche Landfrauenbuch.* Berlin: Reichsnährstand Verlags-G.m.b.H., 1937.

Köhler-Irrgang, Ruth. *Die Sendung der Frau in der deutschen Geschichte.* Leipzig: Hase und Koehler Verlag, 1940.

Leers, Johann von. "Die berufstätige Frau." *Das Deutsche Mädel,* n.d. [Feb. 1935?], pp. 8-9.

Leistritz, Hans Karl. *Deutsches Volkshandbuch.* Berlin: A. Sudau, 1939.

Lemke, Hilde. *Deutscher Frauenarbeitsdienst in der Kurmark.* Berlin: H. W. Rödiger, 1936.

Ley, Robert. *Wir alle helfen dem Führer: Deutschland braucht jeden deutschen.* Munich: Zentralverlag der NSDAP, 1940.

Lingner, Käthe. *Die Mutter der Kinder: Vom ewigen Auftrag der deutschen Frau.* Frauen am Werk, Bildungsstoffe für Schule und Leben, no. 2. 2nd ed. Leipzig: J. Klinkhardt Verlagsbuchhandlung, 1941.

Linhardt-Röpke, Erna. "Stellung und Aufgabe der deutschen Frau im Krieg." *N.S. Frauen-Warte,* 8, no. 21 (May 1940), 436-437.

Lowitsch, Vera. *Die Frau als Richter.* Berlin: C. Heymann, 1933.

Ludendorff, Mathilde. *Des Weibes Kulturtat: Zwei Vorträge mit Aussprache, gehalten auf dem ersten Allgemeinen Frauenkonzil von M. von Kemnitz.* Garmisch: Verlag von M. von Kemnitz, 1920.

Lüders, Else. "Deutsche Frauenleistung in Kriegszeiten." *SP,* 50 (Aug. 1941), 581-586.

———. "Die Dienstpflicht der Frau." *SP,* 47 (Nov. 1938), 1347-58.

Lüders, Marie Elisabeth. *Volksdienst der Frau.* Berlin-Tempelhof: H. Bott Verlag, 1937.

199

Lukas, Oskar. *Das deutsche Frauenbuch: Ein Buch für Werktag und Feierabend.* Karlsbad-Drahowitz: A. Kraft, 1938.

"Mädel am Werk: Eine Bildberichtfolge von Berufen und Arbeitsmöglichkeiten." *Das Deutsche Mädel,* n.d. [June 1936?], pp. 14-15.

Mallmann, Margarete. "Für die politische Erziehung." *Das Deutsche Mädel,* n.d. [Jan. 1935?], pp. 2-3.

Marawske-Birkner, Lilli. *Der weibliche Arbeitsdienst: Seine Vorgeschichte und gegenwärtige Gestaltung.* Leipzig: "Der nationale Aufbau" Verlag G. Heinig, 1942.

Maresch, Maria. "Zur Frage der Frauenarbeit." *SP,* 43 (Sept. 1934), 1134-36.

Meerheimb., Freifrau von. "Berechtigung von Frauenforderungen?" *VB,* Feb. 20, 1926.

Meichner, Fritz. *Die Stunde der Entscheidung: Schicksale deutscher Mütter und Frauen.* Weimar: Der Neue Dom, 1938.

"Meine Mädel!" *Wir helfen,* 1944, p. 92.

Meister, Angela. *Die deutsche Industriearbeiterin.* Jena: Verlag von Gustav Fischer, 1939.

Mende, Clara. *Deutsches Frauenstreben: Die deutsche Frau und das Vaterland.* Stuttgart: Deutsche Verlags-Anstalt, n.d. [193-].

Mentzel, Hilde. *Der helle Morgen: Ein Buch für junge Mädchen.* Essen: Fels-Verlag, 1941.

Menzerath, Magda. *Kampffeld Heimat: Deutsche Frauenleistung im Kriege.* Stuttgart: Allemannen Verlag Albert Jauss, 1944.

Merschberger, Gerda. *Die Rechtsstellung der germanischen Frau.* Leipzig: Curt Kabitzsch Verlag, 1937.

Müffling, Wilhelm von. *Wegbereiter und Vorkämpfer für das neue Deutschland.* Munich: J. F. Lehmanns Verlag, 1933.

Müller, August. *Ich will mehr lernen: Ein besinnliches Buch für die deutsche Frau und Mutter.* Kaiserslautern: H. Kayser, n.d. [1938].

Munske, Hilde. *Das bunte Jungmädelbuch.* Berlin: Junge Generation Verlag, 1940.

Mutter: Ein Buch der Liebe und der Heimat für Alle.
Berlin: Mutter und Volk Verlagsgesellschaft, 1934.

NSDAP. *Unser Familien Buch.* Berlin: Verlag Dr. von
Arnim, 1941.

NSDAP. Amt Schriftumspflege. *Ausstellung "Frau und Mutter—Lebensquell des Volkes."* Berlin: W. Limpert, n.d.
[193-].

NSDAP. Deutsches Frauenwerk. *Die Frau für ihr Volk.*
Berlin: Hauptabteilung Presse-Propaganda der Reichsfrauenführung, n.d.

NSDAP. Gau Oberdonau. *Propagandisten-Fibel.* Wels:
Leitner, n.d. [193-].

NSDAP. Gau Sudetenland. Gauschulungsamt. *Gedenke, dass
du ein Deutscher bist!* Reichenberg: Roland Verlag, n.d.
[1940].

NSDAP. Reichsfrauenführung. Presseabteilung. *Das deutsche
Frauenbuch: Ein Wegweiser für die deutsche Mutter und
Hausfrau mit Kalendarium.* Dortmund: Westfalen-Verlag,
n.d. [1939].

NSDAP. Reichsfrauenführung. Presseabteilung. *Nationalsozialistische Frauenschaft.* Schriften der Deutschen Hoch-
schule für Politik, Der organisatorische Aufbau des Dritten Reiches, no. 15. Berlin: Junker und Dünnhaupt,
1937.

NSDAP. Reichsfrauenführung. Presseabteilung. *Das weite
Wirkungsfeld.* Berlin: Hauptabteilung Presse/Propaganda
der Reichsfrauenführung, Docky Hammer, n.d. [1942].

NSDAP. Reichsjugendführung. *Mädel im Dienst: BDM-
Sport.* 3rd ed. Potsdam: L. Voggenreiter Verlag, 1942.

NSDAP. Reichsjugendführung. *Mädel im Dienst: Jungmädelsport.* Potsdam: L. Voggenreiter Verlag, 1944.

NSDAP. Reichsjugendführung. *Mädel im Gesundheitsdienst.*
Munich: J. F. Lehmanns Verlag, 1941.

NSDAP. Reichspropagandaleitung. *Propaganda.* Munich:
Leopold-Druckerei, n.d. [192-].

NSDAP. Reichspropagandaleitung. Amt Lichtbild. *Der
Einsatz der deutschen Frau im Kriege: Einziges parteiamt-*

liches Lichtbildvortragsmaterial der NSDAP. Dresden: Dr. Güntz-Druck, n.d. [1941?].

NSDAP. Reichpropagandaleitung. Hauptkulturamt. *Das deutsche Hausbuch.* Berlin: Zentralverlag der NSDAP, 1943.

NSDAP. Reichspropagandaleitung. Hauptkulturamt. *Deutsche Kriegsweihnacht.* Munich: Zentralverlag der NSDAP, 1941.

NSDAP. Reichspropagandaleitung. Hauptkulturamt. *Ich kämpfe.* Munich: Zentralverlag der NSDAP, 1943.

"Nationalsozialistiche Frauenarbeit." *VB,* Oct. 2, 1926.

"Die N.S.-Frauenschaften rüsten zum Endkampf." *VB,* March 27/28/29, 1932.

Nationalsozialistische Gemeinschaft "Kraft durch Freude." Amt "Schönheit der Arbeit." *Frauen im Werk: Schönheit der Arbeit erleichtert der Frau das Einleben im Betrieb.* Berlin: Verlag der Deutschen Arbeitsfront, 1940.

Naujoks, Hans. *Die Wandlung der deutschen Frau.* Stuttgart: F. Enke Verlag, 1935.

Naumann, Ida. *Altgermanisches Frauenleben.* Jena: E. Diederichs Verlag, 1937.

―――. *Germanische Frauen der Völkerwanderungszeit.* Berlin: F. A. Herbig Verlagsbuchhandlung, 1930.

Netter, Irmgard. *Germanisches Frauentum.* Leipzig: Quelle und Meyer, 1936.

Neuefeind, Lene. *Frauenberufe in der Sozialarbeit.* Stuttgart: Muth'sche Verlagsbuchhandlung, 1940.

―――. *Frauenberufe in Wirtschaft und Sozialarbeit, in Haus- und Landwirtschaft.* Stuttgart: Muth'sche Verlagsbuchhandlung, 1939.

Nöllenburg, Lies. "Zwischen Stahl und Maschinen." *Das Deutsche Mädel,* April 1940, pp. 4-5.

Overweg, Freya. *Erzählungen und Bilder aus dem Leben im Reichsarbeitsdienst für die weibliche Jugend.* Wolfenbüttel: G. Kallmeyer, 1938.

"Die 'Parole der Woche.'" *Unser Wille und Weg,* Jan. 1940, pp. 6-8.

Passow, Helene. "Rechte und Pflichten." *VB*, March 19, 1926.

Peikow, Richard. *Die soziale und wirtschaftliche Stellung der deutschen Frau in der Gegenwart*. Diss. Berlin, 1937. Berlin-Charlottenburg: K. v. R. Hoffmann, 1937.

Perzl, Irmgard, *Jungmädel auf dem Köllinghof*. Reutlingen: Ensslin und Laiblin, n.d. [1941].

Petersen, Ingeborg. *Deutsche Mütter und Frauen*. Frankfurt a. M.: Verlag Moritz Diesterweg, 1941.

Plumeyer, Karl. "Soll die Frau Richter werden?" *VB*, April 16/17, 1933.

Pohl, Wolfgang. "Zehn Jahre nationalsozialistische Sozialpolitik." *SP*, 52 (Jan. 1943), 1-8.

Pranz, Erna. "Berufserziehung der weiblichen Jugend." *SP*, 48 (Dec. 1939), 1255-60.

Rabe, Sofia. *Die Frau im national-sozialistischen Staat*. Broschurenreihe der Reichs-Propaganda-Leitung der NSDAP, no. 18. Munich: Zentralverlag der NSDAP, 1932.

Rauter, Hildegard. *Frauenarbeit in der Industrie der Steine und Erden*. Schriften des Fachamtes Steine und Erden in Zentralbüro der Deutschen Arbeitsfront, vol. 2. Berlin: Verlag der Deutschen Arbeitsfront, 1939.

Reber-Gruber, Auguste. *Weibliche Erziehung im Nationalsozialistischer Lehrerbund*. 2 vols. Leipzig: Teubner, 1934-36.

"Rede der Reichsfrauenführerin Frau Gertrud Scholtz-Klink im Sportspalast in Berlin am 13. Juni 1940." *N.S. Frauen-Warte*, 9, no. 2 (July 1940), 24-25.

Rees, Hanna. *Frauenarbeit in der NS-Volkswohlfahrt*. Berlin: Zentralverlag der NSDAP, 1938.

Reichenau, Irmgard. *Deutsche Frauen an Adolf Hitler*. Leipzig: Adolf Klein Verlag, 1933.

Reimer, Lydia and Koeppen, Anne-Marie. "Die Bäuerin in Kriegszeiten." *N.S. Frauen-Warte*, 8, no. 18 (March 1940), 384-385.

Reimer, Lydia. "Die Berufswahl unserer Jugend in Kriegszeiten." *N.S. Frauen-Warte*, 8, no. 14 (Jan. 1940), 323.

Reinhardt, Lore. *Die deutsche Frau als Quelle völkischer Kraft und sittlicher Gesundung.* Leipzig: Adolf Klein Verlag, 1934.

"Die Reserve an weiblicher Arbeitskraft." *Die Wirtschaftskurve*, 20 (1941), 148-150.

Retzlaff, Hans. *Arbeitsmaiden am Werk.* Leipzig: Verlag E. A. Seeman, 1940.

Reuss zur Lippe, Marie Adelheid. *Nordische Frau und nordischer Glaube.* Flugschriften der Nordischen Glaubensbewegung, no. 2. Berlin: Verlag von Struppe und Winckler, n.d. [1935].

Rheden, Hildegard von. "Die Weltanschauung der Bäuerin im dritten Reich." *N.S. Frauen-Warte*, 3 (April 1935), 684-685.

Rieffert, Christine. *Die deutsche Frau.* Bochum i. W.: Verlag F. Kamp, 1938.

Rilke, Alice. "Einsatz und Betreuung der werktätigen Frauen." *N.S. Frauen-Warte*, 8, no. 8 (Oct. 1939), 214-215.

————. "Die Frauenarbeit in der Kriegswirtschaft." *Deutsches Frauenschaffen im Kriege*, 1940, pp. 21-26.

————. "Der Fraueneinsatz in der Kriegswirtschaft." *N.S. Frauen-Warte*, 8, no. 20 (April 1940), 416-418.

Rogge-Börner, P. Sophie. "Neue Erkenntnisse." *N.S. Frauen-Warte*, 1 (Jan. 15, 1933), 313-315.

————. *Nordischer Gedanke und Verantwortung.* Leipzig: Adolf Klein Verlag, n.d.

————. *Zurück zum Mutterrecht?* Leipzig: Adolf Klein Verlag, n.d.

Rosenberg, Alfred. *Der Mythus des 20. Jahrhunderts: Eine Wertung der seelisch-geistigen Gestaltenkämpfe unserer Zeit.* Munich: Hoheneichen-Verlag, 1930.

————. "Nachwort der Schriftleitung." *VB*, Jan. 23, 1926.

————. "Der Staat, der Mann, die Frau." *VB*, April 4, 1926.

Rosikat, Margarete. "Offener Brief an Frau Hadlich." *VB*, Feb. 6, 1926.

Rühle-Gerstel, Alice. *Das Frauenproblem der Gegenwart.* Leipzig: Hirzel, 1932.

Salburg, Edith. "Die Entsittlichung der Frau durch die jüdische Mode." *VB*, June 18, 1927.

Schaper-Haeckel, Margarete. *Die Germanin: Körper, Geist und Seele.* Berlin: C. V. Engelhard, 1943.

Scheffen, Luise. *Adelheid und ich: Briefe an eine junge Freundin.* Gotha: L. Klotz Verlag, 1935.

Schickedanz, Margareta. *Deutsche Frau und deutsche Not im Weltkrieg.* Leipzig: B. G. Teubner, 1940.

————. *Das Heimatheer der deutschen Frauen im Weltkrieg.* Leipzig: B. G. Teubner, 1936.

Schimmelpfennig, J. "Die deutsche Frau im Arbeitseinsatz." *Aufklärungs- und Redner-Informationsmaterial,* July/Aug. 1943.

Schlick, Dr. "Hauswirtschaftliche Schulung—ein Gebot der Stunde." *SP*, 45 (Jan. 1936), 17-20.

Schmidt-Musewald, Dora. *Mädel- und Fraueneinsatz in der Eisen- und Metallindustrie.* Berlin: Verlag Emil Wernitz, n.d. [1943].

Scholtz-Klink, Gertrud. *Aufbau des Deutschen Frauenarbeitsdienstes.* 2nd ed. Leipzig: "Der Nationale Aufbau" Verlagsgesellschaft, n.d. [1934].

————. "Die Berufung der schaffenden Frau im Arbeitsleben unseres Volkes." *N.S. Frauen-Warte*, 3 (Jan. 1935), 453.

————. "Deutsch sein—heisst stark sein." *N.S. Frauen-Warte*, 4 (Jan. 1936), 501.

————. *Einsatz der Frau in der Nation.* Berlin: Deutsches Frauenwerk, 1937.

————. "Kriegseinsatz der werktätigen Frau." *Sonderdruck zum Nachrichtendienst der Reichsfrauenführung,* August 1940, pp. 1-11.

————. *Tradition is not Stagnation but Involves a Moral Obligation: Women's Conference at the National Socialist Congress of Great Germany.* Nuremberg: The Deutsche Frauenwerk, 1938.

Scholtz-Klink, Gertrud. *Verpflichtung und Aufgabe der Frau im nationalsozialistischen Staat.* Berlin: Junker und Dünnhaupt, 1936.

———. "Zeit der Bewährung." *Deutsches Frauenschaffen im Kriege,* 1940, pp. 4-5.

Schultes, Richard. "Die deutsche Frau und ihre Stellung zum Mann." *VB,* Feb. 6, 1926.

Schulze-Langendorff, Johanna. "Mode und Zeitgeist." *VB,* March 11/12, 1928.

Schünemann, Frau L. "Deutsche Kleidung für die deutsche Frau!" *VB,* July 9, 1927.

Schürer-Stolle, Lydia. "Wie stehen die Eltern zu uns?" *Das Deutsche Mädel,* n.d. [1936-37?], p. 19.

Schwertfeger-Zypries, Gertrud. *Die Arbeitsmaid.* Berlin: Deutscher Verlag, n.d. [1937].

———. *Das ist der weibliche Arbeitsdienst!* Berlin: Junge Generation Verlag, n.d. [1940].

———. *Reichsarbeitsdienst für die weibliche Jugend.* 3rd ed. Berlin: Junker und Dünnhaupt, 1941.

Selchow, Bogislav. *Frauen grosser Soldaten.* Berlin: Die Wehrmacht, 1939.

Semmelroth, Ellen. *N.S. Frauenbuch.* Munich: J. F. Lehmann, 1934.

———. "Die Organisation der deutschen Frauen." *N.S. Frauen-Warte,* 3, no. 2 (Aug. 1934), 130-133.

Siber von Groote, Paula. *Die Frauenfrage und ihre Lösung durch den Nationalsozialismus.* Wolfenbüttel: G. Kallmeyer, 1933.

Sonnemann, Theodor. *Die Frau in der Landesverteidigung: Ihr Einsatz in der Industrie.* Oldenburg i. O.: Gerhard Stalling Verlagsbuchhandlung, 1939.

Sopp, Frieda. *Der Arbeitsdienst der deutschen Mädchen.* Berlin: H. Büttner, n.d. [1941].

———. *Der Reichsarbeitsdienst der weiblichen Jugend.* Berlin: Zentralverlag der NSDAP, 1944.

Stahl-Meding, Hildegard. "Die Fabrik ruft." *N.S. Frauen-Warte,* 9, no. 2 (July 1940), 23.

Stein, Else. *Arbeitsmaiden*. 2nd ed. Berlin: Deutscher Verlag, n.d.

————. *Unser Jahr: Arbeitsmaiden berichten*. Berlin: Junge Generation Verlag, 1943.

Strasser, Gregor. "Die Frau und der Nationalsozialismus." *VB*, April 6, 1932.

————. "Gedanken über Aufgaben der Zukunft." *National-sozialistische Briefe*, June 15, 1926.

Syrup, Friedrich. "Der Arbeitseinsatz in Deutschland im Jahre 1938." *SP*, 47 (Feb. 1938), 129-136.

"Tapfere Frau." *Wir helfen*, 1944, pp. 14-15.

Tasche, Lisa. *Hurra, wir zwingen das Glück: Erlebnisse-Gestalten-Bilder aus dem weiblichen Arbeitsdienst*. Berlin: Verlag für Kulturpolitik, 1935.

Thimm, Frau Dr. L. "Die oberste Aufgabe der national-sozialist. Frauenbewegung." *VB*, Sept. 4, 1926.

Tremel-Eggert, Kuni. *Barb, der Roman einer deutschen Frau*. Munich: Zentralverlag der NSDAP, 1934.

"Und wo warst Du im Kriege?" *N.S. Frauen-Warte*, 9, no. 24 (June 1941), 386.

"Unsere deutschen Frauen vorn in der Front." *VB*, Oct. 2, 1939.

"Unser Gespräch mit der Reichsfrauenführerin." *N.S. Frauen-Warte*, 9, no. 2 (July 1940), 16-17.

Unverricht, Elsbeth. *Unsere Zeit und wir: Das Buch der deutschen Frau*. 4th ed. Gauting b. Munich: Verlag Heinrich A. Berg, n.d. [1935].

Vogel, G. *Die deutsche Frau*. 2nd ed. Schriften zu Deutschlands Erneuerung, nos. 56-58. 3 vols. Breslau: Verlag von Heinrich Handel, n.d. [1936].

Vorwerck, Else. *Die Hausfrau im Dienste der Volkswirt-schaft*. Grundlagen, Aufbau und Wirtschaftsordnung des nationalsozialistischen Staates, vol. 3. Berlin: Industrie Verlag Spaeth und Linde, n.d. [1937].

Wedelstaedt, Clara von. "Die Arbeiterfrau in der völkischen Bewegung." *VB*, Oct. 11, 1926.

Wellinghusen, Lena. [Pseud. of Lena Osswald]. *Die deutsche Frau, Dienerin oder Gefährtin.* Munich: Ludendorffs Verlag, 1933.

"Wenn die Frau doppelten Dienst tut." *VB*, Jan. 28, 1940.

Wentscher, Else. *Deutsche Frauengestalten.* Leipzig: Koehler und Voigtländer Verlag, 1943.

Wenz, Gisela. *Lebensbilder germanischer Frauen.* Leipzig: Quelle und Meyer, 1940.

Wessel, Ingeborg. *Mütter von Morgen.* Munich: F. Bruckmann, 1936.

Wiedenhöft, Bernhard. *Weib unterm Kreuz: Die Stellung der Frau im Christentum.* Stuttgart: Durchbruch-Verlag F. Bühler, n.d. [1936].

Wille, Otto. *Die Frau, die Hüterin der Zukunft: Ein Buch über Welt und Weib.* Leipzig: C. Kabitzsch, 1933.

Willumeit, Elsa. "Sie müssen sich wieder achten lernen." *VB*, March 19, 1926.

Witte, Emma. "Der 'Männerstaat.' " *VB*, March 19, 1926.

"Wo bleiben die Frauenvereine?" *VB*, Feb. 27/28, 1927.

"Wo melden sich Frauen zur Mitarbeit?" *N.S. Frauen-Warte*, 8 (Oct. 1939).

Zander, Elsbeth. "Nationalsozialistische Frauenaufgaben: Ein nationalsozialistisches Frauen- und Mädchenheim." *VB*, July 24, 1926.

———. "Weg und Ziele des Deutschen Frauenordens." *VB*, Jan. 23, 1926.

"Zehn Gebote für die Gattenwahl." *N.S. Frauen-Warte*, 3 (Nov. 1934), 295.

"10 Kriegsregeln für die deutsche Frau." *Nachrichtendienst der Reichsfrauenführung*, 9, no. 6 (March 1940), 76-77.

Zühlke, Anna. *Frauenaufgabe-Frauenarbeit im Dritten Reich. Bausteine zum neuen Staat und Volk.* Leipzig: Verlag von Quelle und Meyer, 1934.

Zypries, Gertrud. *Das Gesicht des Arbeitsdienstes für die weibliche Jugend.* Munich: Zentralverlag der NSDAP, n.d.

AMERICAN

Abbott, Harriet. "What the Newest New Woman Is." *Ladies' Home Journal (LHJ)*, 37 (Aug. 1920), 154.

Adams, Grace. "American Women are Coming Along." *Harper's*, 178 (March 1939), 365-372.

Addams, Jane. *Newer Ideals of Peace.* Chatauqua, N.Y.: The Chatauqua Press, 1907.

Alsop, Gulielma Fell and McBride, Mary F. *Arms and the Girl: A Guide to Personal Adjustment in War Work and War Marriage.* N.Y.: Vanguard Press, 1943.

Altmeyer, Arthur J. "If Legal Controls Should Come." *Employment Security Review*, 9 (Sept. 1942), 20.

"American Women." *Life*, 18 (Jan. 29, 1945), 28.

"American Women." *Life*, 18 (Feb. 19, 1945), 2.

American Women at War, By 7 Newspaper Women. N.Y.: National Association of Manufacturers, 1942.

"American Women Explained." *Living Age*, 337 (Nov. 15, 1929), 381-382.

"American Women of Today and Yesterday." *LHJ*, 40 (Apr. 1923), 34.

Amidon, Beulah. "Arms and the Women." *Survey Graphic*, 31 (May 1942), 244-248.

"And We Learned About Women From Them." *Woman's Home Companion (WHC)*, 47 (March 1920), 9.

Anderson, Mary. "The Growing Army of Women Workers." *Current History*, 17 (March 1923), 1003-08.

———. "Sixteen Million Women at Work: What Will Happen After the War?" *N.Y. Times Magazine*, July 18, 1943, pp. 18-19.

Anthony, Susan B., II. *Out of the Kitchen—Into the War: Woman's Winning Role in the Nation's Drama.* N.Y.: Stephen Daye, 1943.

Austin, Mary. "Woman Looks at Her World: A Review of Feminine Progress for the Past Twenty-Five Years." *Pictorial Review*, 26 (Nov. 1924), 8-9.

Ayling, Keith. *Calling All Women.* N.Y.: Harper, 1942.

Baker, Laura Nelson. *Women in War Industry: The Complete Guide to a War Factory Job.* N.Y.: E. P. Dutton, 1943.

Banning, Margaret Culkin. *Women for Defense.* N.Y.: Duell, Sloan and Pearce, 1942.

Belmont, Mrs. O. H. P. "Women as Dictators." *LHJ*, 39 (Sept. 1922), 7.

Benjamin, Louise Paine. "Hats Off to the Girls in the Factories." *LHJ*, 59 (Oct. 1942), 98.

———. "What Is Your Dream Girl Like?" *LHJ*, 59 (March 1942), 114.

Bent, Silas. "Woman's Place is in the Home." *Century*, 116 (June 1928), 204-213.

Bigelow, William Frederick. "Women are People." *Good Housekeeping (GH)*, 105 (Oct. 1937), 4.

Black, Alexander. "The Truth About Women." *Harper's*, 143 (Nov. 1921), 753-757.

Blair, Emily Newell. "Discouraged Feminists." *Outlook*, 158 (July 8, 1931), 302-303.

———. "What Are We Women Going To Do?" *LHJ*, 36 (May 1919), 47.

———. "Where Are We Women Going?" *LHJ*, 36 (March 1919), 37.

Blood, Kathryn. *Negro Women War Workers.* Washington: Women's Bureau, 1945.

Bodenheim, Maxwell. "Men and Women." *Dial*, 68 (May 1920), 562-564.

Boothe, Viva. "Women in the Modern World." *Annals of the American Academy of Political and Social Science*, 143 (May 1929).

Bowman, Constance. *Slacks and Callouses.* N.Y.: Longmans, Green, 1944.

Breuer, Elizabeth. "What the Future Holds for the American Woman." *Pictorial Review*, 31 (Oct. 1929), 13-14.

Brisbane, Arthur. "As I See Them: Women of 1934." *Pictorial Review*, 36 (Jan. 1935), 18-19.

210

Bromley, Dorothy Dunbar. "Feminist—New Style." *Harper's*, 155 (Oct. 1927), 552-560.

——. "Women on the Home Front." *Harper's*, 183 (July 1941), 188-199.

Brown, Clara M. and Arnesen, Ruth V. *Employment Opportunities for Women With Limited Home Economics Training*. Minneapolis: Burgess Publishing Co., 1944.

Bryn Mawr College. *Women During the War and After*. Philadelphia: Curtis Publishing Co., 1945.

Burstein, Herbert. *Women in War: A Complete Guide to Service in the Armed Forces and War Industries*. N.Y.: Service Publishing Co., 1943.

Butler, Dorothy Sabin. "Men Against Women." *Forum*, 94 (Aug. 1935), 79-84.

Butler, Sara Schuyler. "Women as Citizens." *Review of Reviews*, 69 (June 1924), 642-645.

Calverton, V. F. "Careers for Women: A Survey of Results." *Current History*, 29 (Jan. 1929), 633-638.

"Can a Woman Run a Home and a Job Too?" *Literary Digest*, 75 (Nov. 11, 1922), 40-63.

Canfield, Dorothy. "Women in War—A Recipe." *N.Y. Times Magazine*, March 15, 1942, p. 8.

Cannon, Poppy. "Pin-Money Slaves." *Forum*, 84 (Aug. 1930), 98-103.

Carlisle, N. V. "Calling All Girls." *Scholastic Magazine*, 42 (Feb. 22, 1943), 31.

"Changing Feminine Ideals." *Scribner's Magazine*, 68 (Sept. 1920), 376-377.

Chase, Judith. "The Average Woman." *Collier's*, 111 (Feb. 27, 1943), 74-75.

Claire-Howe [Ruth Howe and Clair Sifton]. "Return of the Lady." *New Outlook*, 164 (Oct. 1934), 34-38.

Clawson, Augusta H. *Shipyard Diary of a Woman Welder*. N.Y.: Penguin, 1944.

Codman, Florence. "Womanpower 4-F." *Independent Woman*, 22 (Sept. 1943), 260.

Cook, Beatrice Gray. "Mother—1943 Model." *American Home*, 29 (March 1943), 29.

Cook, Elizabeth. "The Kitchen-Sink Complex." *LHJ*, 48 (Sept. 1931), 12.

Corbin, John. "The Forgotten Woman." *North American Review*, 216 (Oct. 1922), 455-466.

Crowell, Chester T. "Sisters Under Their Skins?" *Independent*, 104 (Dec. 18, 1920), 390-391.

Cushman, Wilhela. "Now It's Woman's Work." *LHJ*, 59 (May 1942), 28-29.

Davenport, Eugene. "You Can Change the World." *LHJ*, 39 (Jan. 1922), 23.

Davis, Elmer. "New Eve and the Old Adam." *Delineator*, 116 (March 1930), 9.

Davis, Shelby Cullom. *Your Career in Defense*. N.Y.: Harper, 1942.

De Leeuw, Adele. "Do You Have What It Takes?" *Independent Woman*, 22 (April 1943), 103.

Dickson, Gene. "Housewife-War Worker." *New Republic*, 109 (Oct. 18, 1943), 518-519.

Dryer, Sherman H. *Radio in Wartime*. N.Y.: Greenberg Publishers, 1942.

Duffus, Robert L. "Should Young Women Go To Work?" *Collier's*, 72 (Dec. 1, 1923), 32.

Durant, Will. "Men and Women." *American Magazine*, 104 (Sept. 1927), 13-15.

———. "Modern Woman: Philosophers Grow Dizzy as She Passes By." *Century*, 113 (Feb. 1927), 418-429.

Eddy, Don. "Boom Town in Skirts." *American Magazine*, 137 (June 1944), 42-43.

"Elizabeth Appraises Average Woman." *Manpower Review*, July 1943.

"Enrollment Campaign for Women Workers, 1942." *Monthly Labor Review*, 54 (March 1942), 488-489.

Erskine, John. "The World Will Belong to the Women." *N.Y. Times Magazine*, March 14, 1943, p. 15.

Farnham, Marynia F. and Lundberg, Ferdinand. "Men Have Lost Their Women." *LHJ*, 61 (Nov. 1944), 23.

———. *Modern Woman: The Lost Sex.* N.Y.: Harper, 1947.

"Females in Factories." *Time*, 44 (July 17, 1944), 60.

Fichter, Joseph H. "The Decline of Femininity." *Catholic World*, 161 (April 1945), 60-63.

Field, Elizabeth. "Boom Town Girls." *Independent Woman*, 21 (Oct. 1942), 296-298.

Fisher, Dorothy Canfield. "From the Lathe to the Hearth," *N.Y. Times Magazine*, Dec. 5, 1943, p. 16.

Fletcher, Grace Nies. "He Wants My Job!" *Independent Woman*, 14 (May 1935), 154.

Flynn, Elizabeth Gurley. *Women in the War.* N.Y.: Workers Library Publications, 1942.

Franklin Institute. *Women in War Work.* Philadelphia: Curtis Publishing Co., 1943.

Fraser, Sir John Foster. "Is the American Woman Superior to the American Man? As a Britisher Sees Them Both." *LHJ*, 36 (Sept. 1919), 51.

Furnas, J. C. "Are Women Doing Their Share in the War?" *Saturday Evening Post (SEP)*, 216 (April 29, 1944), 12-13.

———. "Woman Power." *LHJ*, 59 (Nov. 1942), 20-21.

Gale, Zona. "Backwash." *Forum*, 70 (Aug. 1923), 1828-35.

Gardner, Mona. "Only Grandmothers Need Apply." *LHJ*, 60 (June 1943), 24-25.

George, W. L. "Hail, Columbia!: The American Woman." *Harper's*, 142 (March 1921), 457-469.

———. "Woman and the Family." *GH*, 68 (March 1919), 40-41.

———. "Woman in the New World." *GH*, 76 (Jan. 1923), 14-15.

———. "Woman in the New World." *GH*, 76 (Feb. 1923), 78.

———. "Woman in the New World." *GH*, 76 (March 1923), 14-15.

George, W. L. "Woman in the New World." *GH*, 76 (April 1923), 79.

―――. "Woman in the New World." *GH*, 76 (May 1923), 90.

Gerken, Mable R. *Ladies in Pants: A Home Front Diary.* N.Y.: Exposition Press, 1949.

Gibbs, Philip. "Some People I Met in America." *Harper's*, 139 (Sept. 1919), 457-471.

Giles, Nell. *Punch In, Susie! A Woman's War Factory Diary.* N.Y.: Harper, 1943.

―――. "What About the Women? Do They Want to Keep Their Factory Jobs When the War is Over?" *LHJ*, 61 (June 1944), 22-23.

Gilman, Charlotte Perkins. "The New Generation of Women." *Current History*, 18 (Aug. 1923), 731-737.

"Girls in Overalls." *Popular Mechanics*, 78 (Sept. 1942), 40-43.

"Give Back Their Jobs." *WHC*, 70 (Oct. 1943), 6-7.

Glover, Katherine. "Women as Manpower." *Survey Graphic*, 32 (March 1943), 68-75.

―――. *Women at Work in Wartime.* Public Affairs Pamphlet no. 77. N.Y.: Public Affairs Committee, 1943.

Gove, Gladys F. "Womanpower Questions from the Grassroots." *Independent Woman*, 22 (Nov. 1943), 337.

Greenbaum, Lucy. "The Women Who 'Need' to Work." *N.Y. Times Magazine*, April 29, 1945, p. 16.

Guinan, Patricia Davidson. "A Long War is Paved With Good Intentions." *House Beautiful*, 85 (Sept. 1943), 30-31.

Hahn, Sylvia M. "Will You Be 'So Nice to Come Home To?' " *Independent Woman*, 23 (March 1944), 69.

Halle, Rita S. "Do You Need Your Job?" *GH*, 95 (Sept. 1932), 24-25.

Hargrove, Marion. "Girls We're Going to Marry When the War is Done." *GH*, 115 (Nov. 1942), 39.

Harriman, Mrs. J. B. "How Meet Today's Crisis? Women,

214

Enlist Now!" *Independent Woman*, 20 (June 1941), 162-163.

Harris, Corra. "The Happy Woman." *LHJ*, 40 (Nov. 1923), 33.

———. "Obsolete Womanhood." *SEP*, 202 (Aug. 24, 1929), 6-7.

Harrison, Mrs. Horace L. "Glamour As Usual: Reply." *N.Y. Times Magazine*, April 26, 1942, p. 33.

Hawes, Elizabeth. "My Life on the Midnight Shift." *WHC*, 70 (Aug. 1943), 24.

———. "Woman War Worker: A Case History." *N.Y. Times Magazine*, Dec. 26, 1943, p. 9.

———. "Woman War Worker: A Case History." *N.Y. Times Magazine*, May 15, 1944.

Head, Ethel McCall. "It's Harder To Stay At Home!"*American Home*, 30 (Sept. 1943), 4.

"Her Infinite Variety." *Reader's Digest*, 31 (Sept. 1937), 96.

"High School Girls Deny That Woman's Place is in the Home." *Scholastic Magazine*, 46 (March 5, 1945), 26.

Hohman, Leslie B. "Can Women in War Industries Be Good Mothers?" *LHJ*, 59 (Oct. 1942), 100-101.

Hollingsworth, Leta S. "The New Woman in the Making." *Current History*, 27 (Oct. 1927), 15-20.

"Hopeless Wails Against the New Woman." *Literary Digest*, 84 (Jan. 17, 1925), 49-50.

"How Are You Helping?" *WHC*, 70 (June 1943), 20.

"How Mobilize Womanpower?" *Independent Woman*, 19 (Nov. 1940), 348.

Howe, E. W. "These Women!" *Forum*, 83 (April 1930), 244-246.

Huntington, Ellsworth. "Why the American Woman is Unique." *Nation*, 125 (Aug. 3, 1927), 105-107.

Hurst, Fannie. "Glamour As Usual?" *N.Y. Times Magazine*, March 29, 1942, pp. 10-11.

"I Am A Woman." *WHC*, 70 (Feb. 1943), 4.

"I Wish I Had Married and Found Life." *GH*, 77 (Nov. 1923), 14-15.

Ickes, Harold L. "Watch Out For the Women." *SEP*, 215 (Feb. 20, 1943), 19.

Jacobs, Downing. "A New Type of Beauty: American." *Delineator*, 96 (Feb. 1920), 16-17.

Jordan, Elizabeth. "Office and the Woman." *LHJ*, 38 (June 1921), 25.

"The Key to Victory." *WHC*, 69 (July 1942), 6-9.

King, Steve. "Danger! Women at Work." *American Magazine*, 134 (Sept. 1942), 40-41.

Kingsley, J. Donald. "Women in the War Effort." *Current History*, NS, 3 (Sept. 1942), 29-32.

Kirkland, Winifred. "The Get-There Sex." *Harper's*, 146 (April 1923), 672-675.

[Klinger, Emmy]. "A German Woman Judges Her American Sisters." *The Living Age*, 340 (April 1931), 215-216.

Knight, Raymond. "A Lass—But Still a Lack." *Independent Woman*, 21 (Oct. 1942), 299.

Koenig, Stella Akulin. "Mrs. John Doe We Need You!" *WHC*, 69 (July 1942), 51.

Lane, Rose Wilder. "Woman's Place Is In the Home." *LHJ*, 53 (Oct. 1936), 18.

Lapin, Eva. *Mothers in Overalls*. N.Y.: Workers Library Publishers, 1943.

Leach, Ruth M. *Women and the Top Jobs*. N.Y.: National Association of Manufacturers, 1944.

Lee, Mabel Barbee. "The Dilemma of the Educated Woman." *Atlantic*, 146 (Nov. 1930), 590-595.

Lerner, Max. *Public Journal: Marginal Notes on Wartime America*. N.Y.: Viking Press, 1945.

Lewis, Sinclair. *Main Street: The Story of Carol Kennicott*. N.Y.: Harcourt, Brace, 1920.

Lewis, Sinclair and Thompson, Dorothy. "Is America a Paradise for Woman?" *Pictorial Review*, 30 (June 1929), 14-15.

Lingenfelter, Mary Rebecca. *Wartime Jobs for Girls*. N.Y.: Harcourt, Brace, 1943.

Lochridge, Patricia. "The Mother Racket." *WHC*, 71 (July 1944), 20-21.

"Lonely Wife." *Life*, 13 (Dec. 21, 1942), 71-73.

Long, Georgia. "I Can't Get a Job." *SEP*, 214 (June 27, 1942), 18.

Luce, Clare Boothe. "Victory is a Woman." *WHC*, 70 (Nov. 1943), 34.

Lyle, Betty. *And So To Work*. N.Y.: The Woman's Press, 1943.

Lynch, James C. "Trousered Angel." *SEP*, 215 (April 10, 1943), 23.

"Ma: Her Day." *Collier's*, 74 (Dec. 20, 1924), 18-19.

McEvoy, Peggy. "Gun Molls." *Reader's Digest*, 42 (March 1943), 47-50.

McKelvey, Thelma. *Women in War Production*. America in a World at War, no. 22. N.Y.: Oxford University Press, 1942.

McMillin, Lucille Foster. *The First Year: A Study of Women's Participation in Federal Defense Activities*. Washington: U.S. Government Printing Office, 1941.

———. *The Second Year*. Washington: U.S. Government Printing Office, 1943.

McNutt, Paul V. "Wake Up and Work." *WHC*, 70 (May 1943), 40-41.

———. "Why You Must Take a War Job." *American Magazine*, 136 (Dec. 1943), 24-25.

Maffett, Minnie L. "Mobilize for Victory!" *Independent Woman*, 21 (Jan. 1942), 1-2.

———. "Mobilizing Womanpower: An Open Letter to the Manpower Commission." *Independent Woman*, 21 (Dec. 1942), 356.

Martin, Edward S. "Aren't These Women Equal Yet?" *Collier's*, 72 (Sept. 29, 1923), 8.

———. "New Freedom and the Girls." *Harper's*, 153 (Aug. 1926), 389-392.

217

"A Mere Man Asks, How Should I Like to be a Woman?" *Literary Digest*, 73 (May 20, 1922), 59-62.

Metz, Harold W. *Is There Enough Manpower?* Pamphlet no. 45. Washington: The Brookings Institution, 1942.

Meyer, Elizabeth. "Ma's Making Bombers!" *Reader's Digest*, 41 (Nov. 1942), 49-53.

"Middle-Class Women." *Nation*, 127 (July 18, 1928), 55.

Millard, Ruth Tracy. "53 Hours a Week." *SEP*, 215 (June 12, 1943), 22.

Moore, Virginia Bennett. "Begrimed—Bewitching or Both." *WHC*, 70 (Oct. 1943), 80-81.

"More Women Must Go to Work as 3,200,000 New Jobs Beckon." *Newsweek*, 22 (Sept. 6, 1943), 74.

Moss, Violet. "New Women in a New World." *Independent Woman*, 22 (Oct. 1943), 293.

Nathan, George Jean. "Once There Was a Princess." *American Mercury*, 19 (Feb. 1930), 242.

Newman, Dorothy K. *The Woman Counselor in War Industries: An Effective System.* Women's Bureau Special Bulletin no. 16. Washington: U.S. Government Printing Office, 1944.

Northwestern University. *College Women and the War: The Armed Services, War Industry, Technical Operations, Community Service.* Evanston, Illinois: Northwestern University, 1942.

"Occupation: Housewife." *Life*, 11 (Sept. 22, 1941), 78-85.

O'Donnell, Frances Frisbie. "The War Needs Women." *Parents' Magazine*, 18 (Sept. 1943), 24-26.

Oglesby, Catharine. "It's Up to the Women." *LHJ*, 50 (March 1933), 46.

———. "It's Up to the Women." *LHJ*, 50 (April 1933), 44.

———. "It's Up to the Women." *LHJ*, 50 (May 1933), 108.

———. "It's Up to the Women." *LHJ*, 50 (June 1933), 51.

"Our American Matriarchs." *Literary Digest*, 96 (Jan. 21, 1928), 13.

"Our Petticoat Government Through German Eyes." *Literary Digest*, 109 (June 27, 1931), 15.

"Output: Ladies Welcome." *Newsweek*, 20 (Nov. 30, 1942), 56.

Palmer, Gretta. "They Learned About Women." *Reader's Digest*, 45 (Sept. 1944), 105-107.

Parker, Dorothy. "Are We Women or Are We Mice?" *Reader's Digest*, 43 (July 1943), 71-72.

Parkhurst, Genevieve. "Is Feminism Dead?" *Harper's*, 170 (May 1935), 735-745.

————. "Women Beware!" *Pictorial Review*, 35 (July 1934), 4.

Parry, Albert. *What Women Can Do to Win the War*. Chicago: Consolidated Book Publishers, 1942.

Pendleton, Ann. [pseud. of Mary Beatty Trask]. *Hit the Rivet, Sister*. N.Y.: Howell, Soskin, Publishers, 1943.

Perkins, Frances. "Women's Work in Wartime." *Monthly Labor Review*, 56 (April 1943), 661-665.

Phelps, William Lyon, "Women." *LHJ*, 42 (Nov. 1925), 16.

Pickel, Margaret Barnard. "Warning to the Career Woman." *N.Y. Times Magazine*, July 16, 1944, p. 19.

Pidgeon, Mary Elizabeth. *Changes in Women's Employment During the War*. Women's Bureau Special Bulletin no. 20. Washington: U.S. Government Printing Office, 1944.

————. *A Preview as to Women Workers in Transition From War to Peace*. Women's Bureau Special Bulletin no. 18. Washington: U.S. Government Printing Office, 1944.

————. *Women's Work and the War*. American Job Series, Occupational Monograph no. 36. Chicago: Science Research Associates, 1943.

Putnan, N. W. and Phillips, H. I. "Weaker Sex, Which?" *American Magazine*, 96 (July 1923), 24-27.

"Recruiting By Air." *Business Week*, July 10, 1943, p. 115.

Richardson, Anna Steese. "The Modern Woman and Her Problems." *WHC*, 57 (June 1930), 25-26.

219

Robertson, Josephine R. "How Stay-at-Home Mothers Can Help." *Parents' Magazine*, 18 (June 1943), 23.

Roosevelt, Eleanor. "American Women in the War." *Reader's Digest*, 44 (Jan. 1944), 42-44.

———. "Defense and Girls." *LHJ*, 58 (May 1941), 25.

Ruck, Berta. "Why I Should Like My Boy to Marry an American Girl—and Why I Shouldn't." *LHJ*, 37 (April 1920), 41.

Sainsbury, Dorothy. "A Woman's World: Reply to J. Erskine." *N.Y. Times Magazine*, April 18, 1943, p. 4.

Saltonstall, Mrs. Leverett. "Winning on the Home Front." *LHJ*, 60 (June 1943), 31.

Schlesinger, Elizabeth Bancroft. "They Say Women Are Emancipated." *New Republic*, 77 (Dec. 13, 1933), 125-127.

Schoonmaker, Nancy M. "Women's Progress in 1924." *Current History*, 21 (Jan. 1925), 563-564.

Scoville, Elinor. "You, America's Leading Lady." *American Home*, 29 (Dec. 1942), 66.

Seldes, Gilbert. "Rx for Revolution." *SEP*, 199 (May 21, 1927), 22-23.

"Sex in the Factory." *Time*, 40 (Sept. 14, 1942), 21.

Shallcross, Ruth. *Should Married Women Work?* Public Affairs Pamphlet no. 49. N.Y.: Public Affairs Committee, 1940.

Siepmann, Charles. *Radio in Wartime.* America in a World at War, no. 26. N.Y.: Oxford University Press, 1942.

Snedden, David. "Probable Economic Future of American Women." *American Journal of Sociology*, 24 (March 1919), 528-565.

Steele, Evelyn M. *Wartime Opportunities for Women.* N.Y.: E. P. Dutton, 1943.

Stern, Edith M. "Facing the Facts of Life." *WHC*, 71 (Dec. 1944), 35.

Stoddard, George D. and Taylor, Toni. "Do You Want a War Job, Girls?" *McCall's*, 70 (Aug. 1943), 37.

Taft, William Howard. "As I See the Future of Women." *LHJ*, 36 (March 1919), 27.

Taylor, Frank J. "Meet the Girls Who Keep 'em Flying." *SEP*, 214 (May 30, 1942), 30-31.

Taylor, Toni. "I'm Proud of My Wife's War Job." *McCall's*, 70 (Sept. 1943), 41.

―――. "She Also Serves." *McCall's*, 70 (July 1943), 44.

Thompson, Dorothy. "For the Common Sense of Women." *LHJ*, 59 (Jan. 1942), 6.

―――. "If I Had a Daughter." *LHJ*, 56 (Sept. 1939), 4.

―――. "New Woman in the New America." *LHJ*, 62 (Jan. 1945), 6.

―――. "The Stake of Women in Full Postwar Employment." *LHJ*, 61 (April 1944), 6.

―――. "Women and Army Morale." *LHJ*, 58 (Sept. 1941), 6.

―――. "Women and the Coming World." *LHJ*, 60 (Oct. 1943), 6.

―――. "The World—and Women." *LHJ*, 55 (March 1938), 4.

Tigar, Jean. "Portrait of a Woman." *House Beautiful*, 86 (May 1944), 106-107.

U.S. Office of War Information. *War Jobs for Women*. Washington: OWI, Magazine Section, 1942.

U.S. War Manpower Commission. *Training Womanpower*. Washington: Bureau of Training, WMC, 1943.

U.S. Women's Bureau. *Effective Industrial Use of Women in the Defense Program*. Women's Bureau Special Bulletin no. 1. Washington: U.S. Government Printing Office, 1940.

―――. *Handbook on Women Workers*. Washington: U.S. Government Printing Office, 1942.

―――. *When You Hire Women*. Women's Bureau Special Bulletin no. 14. Washington: U.S. Government Printing Office, 1944.

"Veronica Lake." *Life*, 14 (March 8, 1943), 39-40.

Vilmos, William. *1943 War Job Guide for Women.* N.Y.: Kenmore Publishing Co., 1943.

Von Miklos, Josephine. *I Took a War Job.* N.Y.: Simon and Schuster, 1943.

Welshimer, Helen. "Does Miss Modern Surpass Her Sister of Long Ago?" *Independent Woman,* 13 (Jan. 1934), 6-7.

"When Women Wear the Overalls." *Nation's Business,* 30 (June 1942), 70-71.

Wiggam, Albert Edward. "New Styles in American Beauty: Brains and Pulchritude Now Go Together." *World's Work,* 56 (Oct. 1928), 648-658.

Wilder, Margaret Buell. *Since You Went Away . . . Letters to a Soldier from His Wife.* N.Y.: Whittlesey House, 1943.

Wilkinson, Virginia Snow. "From Housewife to Shipfitter." *Harper's,* 187 (Sept. 1943), 328-337.

Winn, Mary Day and Johnson, Charlotte. "We Learned About Women From Men." *LHJ,* 51 (May 1934), 16-17.

Winter, Alice Ames. "The Heritage of Womankind." *LHJ,* 43 (May 1926), 37.

———. "The Heritage of Womankind." *LHJ,* 43 (Aug. 1926), 27.

———. "The Heritage of Womankind." *LHJ,* 43 (Oct. 1926), 39.

———. "The Heritage of Womankind." *LHJ,* 43 (Nov. 1926), 35.

"Wisconsin, Where Women Are People." *Literary Digest,* 70 (July 30, 1921), 10.

Wolfson, Theresa. "Aprons and Overalls in War." *Annals of the American Academy of Political and Social Science,* 229 (Sept. 1943), 46-55.

"Woman's Place." *Business Week,* May 16, 1942, p. 20.

"Women and the War Effort." *Commonweal,* 36 (May 29, 1942), 125.

"Women and War." *Commonweal,* 35 (March 27, 1942), 549.

"Women at War." *Life,* 16 (June 5, 1944), 74-78.

"Women in War Work." *The* [Franklin] *Institute News,* 7 (Feb. 1943), 1.

"Women in War Work." *The* [Franklin] *Institute News,* 7 (March 1943), 1.

"Women in War Work." *New Republic,* 106 (May 4, 1942), 593.

Women in Wartime. Chicago: Institute for Psychoanalysis, 1943.

"Women, Now!" *Business Week,* Jan. 9, 1943, p. 72.

"Women Without Uniforms." *WHC,* 70 (Sept. 1943), 8.

Woodhouse, Chase Going. "The Status of Women." *American Journal of Sociology,* 35 (May 1930), 1091-96.

————. "Women." *American Journal of Sociology,* 38 (May 1933), 889-895.

Woodward, Helen. "Why I Would Like to Be a Man." *Pictorial Review,* 31 (June 1930), 18.

Woodward, W. E. "Why I Would Like to Be a Woman." *Pictorial Review,* 31 (June 1930), 19.

Woolf, S. J. "The Gibson Girl is Still With Us." *N.Y. Times Magazine,* Sept. 20, 1942, pp. 15-17.

Woolston, Florence Guy. "The Delicatessen Husband." *New Republic,* 34 (April 25, 1923), 235-238.

SECONDARY SOURCES

GENERAL

Boserup, Ester. *Woman's Role in Economic Development.* N.Y.: St. Martin's Press, 1970.

Braverman, Harry. *Labor and Monopoly Capital: The Degradation of Work in the Twentieth Century.* N.Y.: Monthly Review Press, 1974.

Brownlee, W. Elliot and Brownlee, Mary M. *Women in the American Economy: A Documentary History, 1675-1929.* New Haven: Yale University Press, 1976.

Garraty, John A. "The New Deal, National Socialism, and the Great Depression." *American Historical Review,* 78 (Oct. 1973), 907-944.

Gordon, Ann D.; Buhle, Mari Jo; and Dye, Nancy Schrom. "The Problem of Women's History." *Liberating Women's History*. Ed. Berenice A. Carroll. Urbana: University of Illinois Press, 1976.

Johanssen, Sheila Ryan. " 'Herstory' As History: A New Field or Another Fad?" *Liberating Women's History*. Ed. Berenice A. Carroll. Urbana: University of Illinois Press, 1976.

Klein, Viola. *The Feminine Character: History of an Ideology*. 1946; reprint ed. Urbana: University of Illinois Press, 1971.

Lerner, Gerda. "Placing Women in History: A 1975 Perspective." *Liberating Women's History*. Ed. Berenice A. Carroll. Urbana: University of Illinois Press, 1976.

Marwick, Arthur. *War and Social Change in the Twentieth Century: A Comparative Study of Britain, France, Germany, Russia and the United States*. N.Y.: St. Martin's Press, 1975.

Mead, Margaret. *Male and Female: A Study of the Sexes in a Changing World*. N.Y.: William Morrow, 1949, 1967.

Mitchell, Juliet. *Woman's Estate*. N.Y.: Pantheon Books, 1971.

Rhodes, Anthony. *Propaganda: The Art of Persuasion: World War II*. N.Y.: Chelsea House, 1976.

Rosaldo, Michelle Zimbalist and Lamphere, Louise. *Woman, Culture and Society*. Stanford: Stanford University Press, 1974.

Smith, Hilda. "Feminism and the Methodology of Women's History." *Liberating Women's History*. Ed. Berenice A. Carroll. Urbana: University of Illinois Press, 1976.

GERMAN

Abel, Theodor. *Why Hitler Came to Power: An Answer Based on the Original Life Stories of 600 of his Followers*. N.Y.: Prentice-Hall, 1938.

Adams, Mildred. "Women Under the Dictatorships." *Dictatorship in the Modern World*. Ed. Guy Stanton Ford. 2nd ed. Minneapolis: University of Minnesota Press, 1939.

Bachofen, J. J. *Myth, Religion, and Mother Right.* Trans. Ralph Manheim. Princeton: Princeton University Press, 1967.

Baird, Jay W. *The Mythical World of Nazi War Propaganda, 1939-1945.* Minneapolis: University of Minnesota Press, 1974.

Bäumer, Gertrud. *Der neue Weg der deutschen Frau.* Stuttgart: Deutsche Verlags-Anstalt, 1946.

Bleuel, Hans Peter. *Sex and Society in Nazi Germany.* Ed. Heinrich Fraenkel. Trans. J. Maxwell Brownjohn. N.Y.: Lippincott, 1973.

Boberach, Heinz. *Meldungen aus dem Reich: Auswahl aus den geheimen Lageberichten des Sicherheitsdienst der SS 1939-1944.* Neuweid and Berlin: Hermann Luchterhand Verlag, 1965.

Boelcke, Willi A. *The Secret Conferences of Dr. Goebbels: The Nazi Propaganda War 1939-43.* Trans. Ewald Osers. N.Y.: E. P. Dutton, 1970.

Bracher, Karl Dietrich. *The German Dictatorship.* Trans. Jean Steinberg. N.Y.: Praeger, 1970.

Brady, Robert A. *The Spirit and Structure of German Fascism.* N.Y.: Viking Press, 1937.

Bramsted, Ernest K. *Goebbels and National Socialist Propaganda, 1925-1945.* East Lansing: Michigan State University Press, 1965.

Bremme, Gabriele. *Die politische Rolle der Frau in Deutschland: Eine Untersuchung über den Einfluss der Frauen bei Wahlen und ihr Teilnahme in Partei und Parlament.* Göttingen: Vandenhoeck und Ruprecht, 1956.

Bridenthal, Renate. "Beyond *Kinder, Küche, Kirche*: Weimar Women at Work." *Central European History*, 6 (June 1973), 148-166.

——— and Koonz, Claudia. "Beyond *Kinder, Küche, Kirche:* Weimar Women in Politics and Work." *Liberating Women's History.* Ed. Berenice A. Carroll. Urbana: University of Illinois Press, 1976.

Briefe deutscher Mädel aus dem Dritten Reich. Strasbourg: Prometheus-Verlag, 1934.

Browning, Hilda. *Women Under Fascism and Communism.* London: Martin Lawrence, n.d. [1934].

Bry, Gerhard. *Wages in Germany, 1871-1945.* Princeton: Princeton University Press, 1960.

Bullock, Alan. *Hitler: A Study in Tyranny.* Rev. ed. N.Y.: Harper, 1962.

Carroll, Berenice A. *Design for Total War: Arms and Economics in the Third Reich.* The Hague: Mouton, 1968.

Commission Investigating Fascist Activities. *Women Under Hitler Fascism.* N.Y.: Committee to Aid Victims of German Fascism, 1934.

Coser, Lewis A. "The Case of the Soviet Family." *The Family: Its Structure and Functions.* Ed. Rose Laub Coser. N.Y.: St. Martin's Press, 1964.

Dahrendorf, Ralf. *Society and Democracy in Germany.* Garden City, N.Y.: Doubleday, 1967.

Deak, Theodore. *Women and Children Under the Swastika.* N.Y.: Universum Publishers, 1936.

De Witt, Thomas E. J. "The Nazi Party and Social Welfare, 1919-1939." Ph.D. diss., University of Virginia, 1972.

Dornemann, Louise. *German Women Under Hitler Fascism: A Brief Survey of the Position of German Women up to the Present Day.* London: Allies Inside Germany, 1943.

"The Effects of General Mobilisation on the Employment of Women in Germany." *International Labour Review,* 50 (Sept. 1944), 335-351.

"The Employment of Women in Germany Under the National Socialist Regime." *International Labour Review,* 44 (Dec. 1941), 617-659.

Engelmann, Peter. "Lady Führer Über Alles." *Reader's Digest,* 37 (Oct. 1940), 19-22.

Evans, Richard J. *The Feminist Movement in Germany 1894-1933.* Sage Studies in Twentieth Century History, vol. 6. London: Sage Publications, 1976.

————. "German Women and the Triumph of Hitler." *Journal of Modern History,* 48 (March 1976), on-demand supplement.

226

Fest, Joachim C. *The Face of the Third Reich: Portraits of the Nazi Leadership.* Trans. Michael Bullock. N.Y.: Ace Books, 1970.

——. *Hitler.* Trans. Richard and Clara Winston. N.Y.: Harcourt Brace Jovanovich, 1974.

Frauen gestern und heute. Wege in die neue Zeit, no. 3. Berlin: Union-Verlag, 1946.

Free German League of Culture in Great Britain. *Women Under the Swastika.* London: Free German League, 1942.

Gersdorff, Ursula von. *Frauen im Kriegsdienst 1914-1945.* Stuttgart: Deutsche Verlags-Anstalt, 1969.

Grunberger, Richard. *The 12-Year Reich: A Social History of Nazi Germany 1933-45.* N.Y.: Ballantine Books, 1971.

Grünfeld, Judith. "Mobilization of Women in Germany." *Social Research,* 9 (Nov. 1942), 476-494.

——. "Rationalisation and the Employment and Wages of Women in Germany." *International Labour Review,* 29 (May 1934), 605-632.

Guillebaud, C. W. *The Economic Recovery of Germany from 1933 to the Incorporation of Austria in March 1938.* London: Macmillan, 1939.

——. *The Social Policy of Nazi Germany.* 1941; reprint ed. N.Y.: H. Fertig, 1971.

Guirdham, A[rthur]. *Revolt Against Pity: An Indictment of the Nazi Martyrdom of Women.* London: J. Drowther, n.d. [1943?].

Hamburger, L[udwig]. *How Nazi Germany Has Mobilized and Controlled Labor.* Washington: The Brookings Institution, 1940.

Hamilton, Alice. "Woman's Place in Germany." *Survey Graphic,* 23 (Jan. 1934), 26-29.

Heiber, Helmut. *Goebbels.* Trans. John K. Dickinson. N.Y.: Hawthorn Books, 1972.

Heiden, Konrad. *Der Fuehrer: Hitler's Rise to Power.* Trans. Ralph Manheim. N.Y.: Lexington Press, 1944.

Hoegner, Wilhelm. *Die Frau im Dritten Reich.* Berlin: J.H.W. Dietz, 1931.

227

Homze, Edward L. *Foreign Labor in Nazi Germany.* Princeton: Princeton University Press, 1967.

Hull, David Stewart. *Film in the Third Reich: A Study of the German Cinema, 1933-1945.* Berkeley: University of California Press, 1969.

Jay, Martin. *The Dialectical Imagination: A History of the Frankfurt School and the Institute of Social Research 1923-1950.* Boston: Little, Brown, 1973.

Kinser, Bill and Kleinman, Neil. *The Dream That Was No More a Dream: A Search for Aesthetic Reality in Germany, 1890-1945.* N.Y.: Harper and Row, 1969.

Kirkpatrick, Clifford. *Nazi Germany: Its Women and Family Life.* N.Y.: Bobbs-Merrill, 1938.

Kirkpatrick, Doris. "The Role of Woman in Germany." *N.Y. Times,* Sept. 26, 1937.

Klein, Burton H. *Germany's Economic Preparations for War.* Cambridge: Harvard University Press, 1959.

Klein, Ernst. "Woman in National Socialism." *Fortnightly,* 157 (April 1942), 285-292.

Koonz, Claudia. "Mothers in the Fatherland: Women in Nazi Germany." *Becoming Visible: Women in European History.* Ed. Renate Bridenthal and Claudia Koonz. Boston: Houghton Mifflin, 1977.

―――. "Nazi Women Before 1933: Rebels Against Emancipation." *Social Science Quarterly,* 56 (March 1976), 553-563.

Kris, Ernst and Speier, Hans. *German Radio Propaganda: Report on Home Broadcasts during the War.* London: Oxford University Press, 1944.

Lane, Barbara Miller. *Architecture and Politics in Germany, 1918-1945.* Cambridge: Harvard University Press, 1968.

―――. "Nazi Ideology: Some Unfinished Business." *Central European History,* 7 (March 1974), 3-30.

Langer, Walter. *The Mind of Adolf Hitler: The Secret Wartime Report.* N.Y.: Basic Books, 1972.

Leiser, Erwin. *Nazi Cinema.* Trans. Gertrud Mander and David Wilson. N.Y.: Collier Books, 1974.

Long, Clarence D. *The Labor Force in War and Transition: Four Countries*. Occasional paper no. 36. National Bureau of Economic Research, 1952.

McIntyre, Jill. "Women and the Professions in Germany, 1930-40." *German Democracy and the Triumph of Hitler*. Ed. Anthony Nichols and Erich Matthias. N.Y.: St. Martin's Press, 1971.

Maschmann, Melita. *Account Rendered: A Dossier on my Former Self*. Trans. Geoffrey Strachan. London: Abelard-Schuman, 1964.

Maser, Werner. *Hitler: Legend, Myth and Reality*. Trans. Peter and Betty Ross. N.Y.: Harper and Row, 1973.

Mason, T. W. "Labour in the Third Reich 1933-39." *Past and Present*, 33 (1966), 112-141.

―――. "The Primacy of Politics—Politics and Economics in National Socialist Germany." *The Nature of Fascism*. Ed. S. J. Woolf. N.Y.: Vintage Books, 1968.

―――. "Women in Nazi Germany." *History Workshop: A Journal of Socialist Historians*, 1 (March 1976).

Merkl, Peter. *Political Violence Under the Swastika: 581 Early Nazis*. Princeton: Princeton University Press, 1975.

Meusel, Alfred. "National Socialism and the Family." *Sociological Review*, 28 (April, Oct. 1936), 166-186, 389-411.

Millett, Kate. *Sexual Politics*. Garden City, N.Y.: Doubleday, 1970.

Milward, Alan S. *The German Economy at War*. London: Athlone Press, 1965.

Mohl, Lieselotte. "Die Emanzipation gebar ihre Grossmütter." *Frankfurter Hefte*, 23 (1968), 324-330.

Mosse, George L. *Nazi Culture: Intellectual, Cultural and Social Life in the Third Reich*. Trans. by Salvator Attanasio. N.Y.: Grosset and Dunlap, 1966.

Neumann, Franz. *Behemoth*. N.Y.: Oxford University Press, 1943.

Orlow, Dietrich. *The History of the Nazi Party: 1919-1933*. Pittsburgh: University of Pittsburgh Press, 1969.

Orlow, Dietrich. *The History of the Nazi Party: 1933-1945.* Pittsburgh: University of Pittsburgh Press, 1973.

Peterson, Edward. *The Limits of Hitler's Power.* Princeton: Princeton University Press, 1969.

Petzina, Dietmar. "Die Mobilisierung deutscher Arbeitskräfte vor und während des zweiten Weltkrieges." *Vierteljahrshefte für Zeitgeschichte,* 18 (1970), 443-455.

Pross, Helge. "West Germany." *Women in the Modern World.* Ed. Ralph Patai. N.Y.: The Free Press, 1967.

Puckett, Hugh Wiley. *Germany's Women Go Forward.* N.Y.: Columbia University Press, 1930.

"Recent Aspects of the Employment of Women in Germany." *International Labour Review,* 45 (March 1942), 286-296.

Rupprecht, Nancy E. "Socialization of Girls in Nazi Germany: The League of German Girls 1933-39." Unpublished paper.

Schoenbaum, David. *Hitler's Social Revolution: Class and Status in Nazi Germany 1933-1939.* Garden City, N.Y.: Doubleday, 1966.

Schweitzer, Arthur. *Big Business in the Third Reich.* Bloomington: Indiana University Press, 1964.

Seward, Georgene H. and Williamson, Robert C. *Sex Roles in Changing Society.* N.Y.: Random House, 1970.

Singer, H. W. "The German War Economy in the Light of German Economic Periodicals." *Economic Journal,* 50 (1940), 534-546.

————. "The German War Economy in the Light of German Economic Periodicals." *Economic Journal,* 51 (1941), 192-215, 400-421.

————. "The German War Economy in the Light of German Economic Periodicals." *Economic Journal,* 52 (1942), 18-36, 186-205, 377-399.

————. "The German War Economy in the Light of German Economic Periodicals." *Economic Journal,* 53 (1943), 121-139, 243-259, 370-380.

————. "The German War Economy in the Light of German Economic Periodicals." *Economic Journal*, 54 (1944), 62-74, 206-216.

Slater, Philip E. "Social Change and the Democratic Family." *The Temporary Society*. Ed. Warren G. Bennis and Philip E. Slater. N.Y.: Harper and Row, 1968.

SPD. *Nationalsozialismus und Frauenfrage: Material zur Information und Bekämpfung*. Berlin: Werbeabteilung der SPD, 1932.

Speer, Albert. *Inside the Third Reich*. Trans. Richard and Clara Winston. N.Y.: Avon, 1970.

Stephenson, Jill. *Women in Nazi Society*. N.Y.: Barnes and Noble, 1975.

Strecker, Gabriele. *Hundert Jahre Frauenbewegung in Deutschland*. Wiesbaden: Büro für Frauenfragen in der Gesellschaft zur Gestaltung Öffentlichen Lebens, n.d. [1951].

Thomas, Katherine. *Women in Nazi Germany*. London: V. Gollancz, 1943.

Thönnessen, Werner. *The Emancipation of Women: The Rise and Decline of the Women's Movement in German Social Democracy*. Trans. Joris de Bres. London: Pluto, 1973.

U.S. Strategic Bombing Survey. *The Effects of Strategic Bombing on the German War Economy*. Overall Economic Effects Division, October 31, 1945.

Wendel, Else. *Hausfrau at War: A German Woman's Account of Life in Hitler's Reich*. London: Odhams Press, 1957.

Woodsmall, Ruth Frances. "Women in the New Germany." *Forum*, 93 (May 1935), 299-303.

Wright, Gordon. *The Ordeal of Total War, 1939-1945*. N.Y.: Harper and Row, 1968.

Wunderlich, Frieda. *Farm Labor in Germany, 1810-1945*. Princeton: Princeton University Press, 1961.

————. "Women's Work in Germany." *Social Research*, 2 (Aug. 1935), 310-336.

Zeman, Z. A. B. *Nazi Propaganda*. London: Oxford University Press, 1964.

AMERICAN

Anderson, Mary. *Woman at Work: The Autobiography of Mary Anderson as Told to Mary N. Winslow*. Minneapolis: University of Minnesota Press, 1951.

Arnow, Harriette. *The Dollmaker*. 1954; reprint ed. N.Y.: Avon, 1974.

Banner, Lois W. *Women in Modern America: A Brief History*. N.Y.: Harcourt Brace Jovanovich, 1974.

Beard, Mary R. *Woman as Force in History: A Study in Traditions and Realities*. N.Y.: Macmillan, 1946.

Black, Gregory and Koppes, Clayton. "OWI Goes to the Movies: The Bureau of Intelligence's Criticism of Hollywood, 1942-43." *Prologue*, 6 (Spring 1974), 44-59.

Blum, John M. "The G.I. in the Culture of the Second World War." *Ventures*, 8 (Spring 1968), 51-56.

————. *V Was for Victory: Politics and American Culture During World War II*. N.Y.: Harcourt Brace Jovanovich, 1976.

Breckinridge, Sophonisba. *Women in the Twentieth Century*. N.Y.: McGraw-Hill, 1933.

Buck, Pearl S. *Of Men and Women*. N.Y.: John Day, 1941.

Catton, Bruce. *War Lords of Washington*. N.Y.: Harcourt, Brace, 1948.

Chafe, William Henry. *The American Woman: Her Changing Social, Economic, and Political Role, 1920-1970*. N.Y.: Oxford University Press, 1972.

Dratch, Howard. "The Politics of Child Care in the 1940's." *Science and Society*, 38 (1974-75), 167-204.

Filene, Peter Gabriel. *Him/Her/Self: Sex Roles in Modern America*. N.Y.: Harcourt Brace Jovanovich, 1974.

Flexner, Eleanor. *Century of Struggle: The Woman's Rights Movement in the United States*. 1959; reprint ed. N.Y.: Atheneum, 1972.

Freedman, Estelle B. "The New Woman: Changing Views of Women in the 1920's." *Journal of American History*, 61 (Sept. 1974), 372-393.

Friedan, Betty. *The Feminine Mystique*. N.Y.: Dell, 1963.

Goodman, Jack. *While You Were Gone: A Report on Wartime Life in the United States*. N.Y.: Simon and Schuster, 1946.

Gregory, Chester W. *Women in Defense Work during World War II: An Analysis of the Labor Problem and Women's Rights*. Jericho, N.Y.: Exposition Press, 1974.

Groves, Ernest R. *The American Woman: The Feminine Side of a Masculine Civilization*. N.Y.: Greenberg, 1937.

Hartmann, Susan M. "Prescriptions for Penelope: Literature on Women's Obligations to Returning World War II Veterans." Forthcoming in *Women's Studies*.

――――. "Women in the Military Service." Unpublished paper presented at the National Archives 1976 Conference on Women's History, April 1976.

Haskell, Molly. *From Reverence to Rape: The Treatment of Women in the Movies*. N.Y.: Penguin, 1974.

Higham, John. *Strangers in the Land: Patterns of American Nativism 1860-1925*. N.Y.: Atheneum, 1963.

Hills, Thomas M. "The War Manpower Commission and Its Problem, April 18, 1942-February 1, 1943." MBA thesis, Wharton School, University of Pennsylvania, 1943.

Hofstadter, Richard. *The Age of Reform: From Bryan to FDR*. N.Y.: Vintage Books, 1955.

International Labour Office. *The War and Women's Employment: The Experience of the U.K. and the U.S.* Studies and Reports, NS vol. 1. Montreal: ILO, 1946.

Janeway, Eliot. *The Struggle for Survival: A Chronicle of Economic Mobilization in World War II*. New Haven: Yale University Press, 1951.

Kerr, Virginia. "One Step Forward—Two Steps Back: Child Care's Long American History." *Child Care—Who Cares?* Ed. Pamela Roby. N.Y.: Basic Books, 1973.

233

Kluckhohn, Florence R. "American Women and American Values." *Achievement in American Society*. Ed. Bernard C. Rosen, Harry J. Crockett, Jr., and Clyde Z. Nunn. Cambridge: Schenkman Publishing Co., 1969.

Koistinen, Paul A. C. "Mobilizing the World War II Economy: Labor and the Industrial-Military Alliance." *Pacific Historical Review*, 42 (Nov. 1973), 443-478.

Leary, William M., Jr. "Books, Soldiers and Censorship during the Second World War." *American Quarterly*, 20 (Summer 1968), 237-245.

Lemons, J. Stanley. *Woman Citizen: Social Feminism in the 1920's*. Urbana: University of Illinois Press, 1973.

Lifton, Robert Jay. *The Woman in America*. Boston: Houghton Mifflin, 1965.

Lingeman, Richard R. *Don't You Know There's a War On?* N.Y.: G. P. Putnam's Sons, 1970.

Link, Arthur. *American Epoch: A History of the United States since the 1890's*. 3 vols. N.Y.: Alfred Knopf, 1967.

Long, Clarence D. *The Labor Force in War and Transition: Four Countries*. Occasional paper no. 36. N.Y.: National Bureau of Economic Research, 1952.

————. *The Labor Force in Wartime America*. N.Y.: National Bureau of Economic Research, 1944.

McGovern, James R. "The American Woman's Pre-World War I Freedom in Manners and Morals." *Journal of American History*, 60 (Sept. 1968), 315-333.

"Magazine Reading Interests of Women By Economic Status and By Age Groups." *Business Week*, Oct. 28, 1939, p. 38.

Makosky, Donald R. "The Portrayal of Women in Wide-Circulation Magazine Short Stories, 1905-1955." Ph.D. diss., University of Pennsylvania, 1966.

Mead, Margaret. *Male and Female*. N.Y.: William Morrow, 1949, 1967.

National Manpower Council. *Womanpower*. N.Y.: Columbia University Press, 1957.

234

Nottingham, Elizabeth K. "Toward an Analysis of the Effects of Two World Wars on the Role and Status of Middle Class Women in the English Speaking World." *American Sociological Review,* 12 (Dec. 1947), 666-675.

Ondercin, David George. "The Compleat Woman: The Equal Rights Amendment and Perceptions of Womanhood, 1920-1972." Ph.D. diss., University of Minnesota, 1973.

O'Neill, William L. *Everyone Was Brave: The Rise and Fall of Feminism in America.* Chicago: Quadrangle Press, 1969.

Oppenheimer, Valerie Kincade. *The Female Labor Force in the United States: Demographic and Economic Factors Governing its Growth and Changing Composition.* Population Monograph Series, no. 5. Berkeley: Institute of International Studies, University of California, 1970.

Perrett, Geoffrey. *Days of Sadness, Years of Triumph: The American People 1939-1945.* Baltimore: Penguin, 1973.

Phillips, Cabell. *The 1940's: Decade of Triumph and Trouble.* The *New York Times* Chronicle of American Life. N.Y.: Macmillan, 1975.

Polenberg, Richard. *America at War: The Home Front, 1941-1945.* Englewood Cliffs, N.J.: Prentice-Hall, 1968.

————. *War and Society: The U.S., 1941-1945.* Philadelphia: Lippincott, 1972.

Quick, Paddy. "Rosie the Riveter: Myths and Realities." *Radical America,* 9 (July-Oct. 1975), 115-131.

Rosen, Marjorie. *Popcorn Venus.* N.Y.: Avon, 1973.

Ryan, Mary P. *Womanhood in America: From Colonial Times to the Present.* N.Y.: New Viewpoints, 1975.

Sanders, Marion K. *Dorothy Thompson: A Legend in Her Time.* N.Y.: Avon, 1973.

Sheean, Vincent. *Dorothy and Red.* Boston: Houghton Mifflin, 1963.

Shover, Michele J. "Roles and Images of Women in World

235

War I Propaganda." *Politics and Society*, 5 (1975), 469-486.

Smuts, Robert. *Women and Work in America*. N.Y.: Columbia University Press, 1959.

Sochen, June. *Movers and Shakers: American Women Thinkers and Activists 1900-1970*. N.Y.: Quadrangle/ The New York Times Book Co., 1973.

Steele, Richard W. "Preparing the Public for War: Efforts to Establish a National Propaganda Agency, 1940-41." *American Historical Review*, 75 (Oct. 1970), 1640-54.

Steinfels, Margaret O'Brien. *Who's Minding the Children? The History and Politics of Daycare in America*. N.Y.: Simon and Schuster, 1973.

Straub, Eleanor F. "Government Policy Toward Civilian Women During World War II." Ph.D. diss., Emory University, 1973.

―――. "United States Government Policy Toward Civilian Women During World War II." *Prologue*, 5 (Winter 1973), 240-254.

Tobias, Sheila and Anderson, Lisa. "New Views of Rosie the Riveter." Unpublished paper.

―――. "What Really Happened to Rosie the Riveter." MSS Modular Publications, Module 9 (1974).

Treadwell, Mattie E. *The Women's Army Corps*. United States Army in World War II. Ed. Kent Roberts Greenfield. Washington: Office of Chief of Military History, Department of the Army, 1954.

Trey, J. E. "Women in the War Economy—World War II." *Review of Radical Political Economics*, 4 (July 1972), 41-57.

U.S. Bureau of the Budget. *The United States at War*. Historical Reports on War Administration, no. 1. Washington: U.S. Government Printing Office, 1946.

Wald, Carol. *Myth America: Picturing Women 1865-1945*. Text by Judith Papachristou. N.Y.: Random House, 1975.

Weinberg, Sydney Stahl. "What to Tell America: The

Writers Quarrel in the Office of War Information." *Journal of American History*, 55 (June 1968), 73-89.

West, B. June. "Attitudes Toward American Women as Reflected in American Literature Between the Two World Wars." Ph.D. diss., University of Denver, 1954.

Winkler, Allan Michael. "Politics and Propaganda: The Office of War Information, 1942-1945." Ph.D. diss., Yale University, 1974.

Index

239

LIBRARY OF CONGRESS CATALOGING IN PUBLICATION DATA

Rupp, Leila J   1950-
  Mobilizing women for war.

  Bibliography: p.
  Includes index.
  1. World War, 1939-1945—Women.   2. World
War, 1939-1945—Propaganda.   3. Women—United
States—Social conditions.   4. Women—Germany—
Social conditions.   5. Propaganda, German.
6. Propaganda, American.   I. Title.
D810.W7R8   940.54'88   77-85562
ISBN 0-691-04649-2